AF360101

ISLAM IN SOUTH ASIA
ENCOUNTERING THE WEST :
BEFORE AND AFTER 1857

ISLAM IN SOUTH ASIA

VOLUME II

ENCOUNTERING THE WEST: BEFORE AND AFTER 1857

Edited by
MUSHIRUL HASAN

MANOHAR
2008

First published 2008
Reprinted 2008

© Individual contributors 2008

All right reserved. No part of this publication may be reproduced or transmitted, in any form or by any means, without prior permission of the editor and the publisher.

ISBN 81-7304-741-3 (Set)
ISBN 81-7304-743-X (Volume II)

Published by
Ajay Kumar Jain for
Manohar Publishers & Distributors
4753/23 Ansari road, Daryaganj
New Delhi 110 002

Typeset by
Ajay Art
'Delhi-110006

Printed by
Lordson Publishers Pvt. Ltd.
Delhi 110 007

Contents

Introduction

> The first really detailed descriptions of Eastern Europe by Muslim travellers did not come from any of the countries of the Middle East or North Africa but from further afield—from India. While the rulers of Turkey and Iran were fighting a desperate but on the whole successful rear guard action to preserve the Muslim heartlands of the Middle East from the advance of Europe—Russia from the north, the maritime powers from the south—the remoter lands of Islam had lost the struggle and fallen under foreign rule. The advance of the Russian and British empires in northern and southern Asia brought millions of Muslims under their control. For the first time, Muslims now met Europeans not just as neighbours or visitors but as masters. It was a chastening experience, but some of them set out to discover the homelands of these new and strange beings who had come to them out of the West.
>
> Bernard Lewis, *The Muslim Discovery of Europe*, p. 131

Contacts between different civilizations have often in the past proved to be landmarks in human progress. Greece learnt from Egypt, Rome from Greece, the Arabs from the Roman Empire, medieval Europe from the Arabs, and Renaissance Europe from the Byzantine. Persia, or Iran, after being no more than a mere name in the West, became in the eighteenth century progressively better known as contact became closer and more frequent. The conceptions of Persia formed by the Europeans differed widely, some regarding it merely as a country to trade with, others as a land to evangelize, while others again looked upon it as an ally against the Turks. No wonder, then, two small volumes entitled *Persia* were added, in the year 1835, to *Uncle Oliver's Travels* in the Library for the Young Series published by Messrs Charles Knight of Ludgate Street.

Again, as in India, European soldiers, diplomats, politicians, archaeologists, and missionaries visited Persia and wrote documented accounts of its flora and fauna, of religious practices, of the system of taxation and education, or the method of tying horses by the leg in the stables. As time went on, it came to be realized in Europe that Persia—a land in which civilization has flourished for nearly five thousand years of recorded history—meant something more than all this. The Persians themselves, like the *bhadralok* in Bengal and the Chitpavan Brahmans in nineteenth-century Maharashtra, retained great pride in their glorious past long after they were conquered, and guarded the traditions of the past so that they would not, and could not, give up such traditions by deliberately wiping out their memories. 'There is as much sense in Hafiz as in Horace, and as much knowledge in the world.' So Sherlock Holmes took leave of *A Case of Identity* and the sad romance of Mary Sutherland.[1]

Maxime Robinson, the historian, identifies three tendencies at work in the nineteenth century: a utilitarian and imperialistic sense of Western superiority, full of contempt for other civilizations; a romantic eroticism, with its delight in a magical east whose increasing poverty spiced its charm; and a specialized scholarship whose main concern lay with past ages. These three tendencies were more complementary than opposed. The unconscious eighteenth-century view, guided by the universalist ideology of the age, respected non-European peoples and cultures. This was replaced by the conscious, theoretical European self-centredness of the nineteenth century.[2]

Muslim perceptions of the West are no less deserving of study than Western perceptions of Islam.[3] Indeed, long before the attitude of disdain and lack of interest in the world of Islam started to change in the West, more and more Muslims were turning towards Europe with admiration, respect, or fear. Mirza Abu Talib Khan, the erudite Lucknow-born scholar, pioneered this trend in South Asia, even before his community's awareness of Europe became deepened and broadened by travel, schools, colleges, newspapers, and colonial institutions. It is true that Munshi Itesamuddin—'wanderer over the face of the earth'—produced his *Shigurf Nama-i Velayet* in 1765, based on his eighteen-month stay in Britain, and Dean Muhammad (b. 1759) published his *Travels* in 1793-4,[4] but it was Abu Talib's *Masir-i Talibi fi Bilad-i Afrang* which became 'a landmark of the first phase of interracial and intercultural contact'.[5] His range of scholarship was wider than the other two. Besides, Europe meant something more to him than it did to Itesamuddin or Lutfullah, who followed 'The Persian Prince' to London. It meant that it had a refined culture and literature of its own, its people had a fine taste for poetry, plays and operas, and a keen zest for philosophical speculation.

Charles Stewart, the translator, believed that this was the first time that 'the genuine opinions of an Asiatic, respecting the institutions of Europe' appeared in English. But how was the community going to react to his scholarly exertions? Although Abu Talib confidently posited the axiom that our knowledge of the world must be firmly rooted in experience, he apprehended that his work would scarcely merit attention owing to 'the indolent dispositions' of his countrymen and the 'many erroneous customs' prevalent among all ranks of Muslims. But Charles Stewart guaranteed that future scholars would, with the aid of his translation, access *Masir-i Talibi*.

A scholar and a soldier, Abu Talib's own modest claim was to describe 'the curiosities and wonders . . . [and] give some account of the manners and customs of the various nation [he] visited, all of which was little known to the Asiatics'. Therefore, he commenced a journal in which he daily inserted every event, and 'committed to writing such reflections as occurred to him at the moment'. Having revised and abridged his notes, he arranged them in the form of a book.

Writers describe Abu Talib as 'one of the most sensitive and critical social philosophers of his day'.[6] They rank him among the most discerning observers of the European scene,[7] admire his intelligent appreciation of the great efflorescence of European intellectual curiosity and scientific inquiry, and commend his weighty, objective and analytical travelogue. Some turn to him as the spokesman of the 'old patriotism' that resulted in a hybrid amalgam of Indian and political ethics;[8] others focus on his charm, energy and enthusiasm.[9]

Abu Talib's travelogue (based on his four and a half years from 7 February 1799 to 4 August 1803) also sheds light on national manners and customs, and, in this regard, corroborates the evidence marshalled by present-day social historians. What lends greater credence to his account is his vision which embraces the whole of mankind and his understanding of the cultural streams in the East and the West.

The fact is that Abu Talib's views have much contemporary resonance. At a time when there is talk of developing a wider and more truthful vision of the West,[10] *Masir-i Talibi* illustrates the representation of the West amongst the *non-Western*. At a time when the clash of civilization theory is frequently echoed, more so after

9/11, Abu Talib, who regarded history writing to be 'the most important of all means of conveying knowledge', offers an important corrective to such theories.

This being the case, it is useful to locate Abu Talib in the context of the most recent debates on dialogue among religions and civilizations. This is particularly so because of his awareness of humankind's values and an inclination to discover the common goal of all cultures and civilizations. All said and done, he does not convey the tension between Western and Eastern value systems that is currently everybody's hobby horse—from the much-maligned Samuel Huntington to the Islamists, and the votaries of Hindutva.

Some of the bare facts about the *Masir-i Talibi* are as follows: its first available manuscript, carrying the date 1806, was edited by his son Mirza Hasan Ali and Munshi Kudrat Ali in 1812, and printed at the Hindoostanee [Hindustani] Press in Calcutta as *Travels in Europe and Asia by Mirza Abu Taleb Khan*. In 1827, the School-Book Society's Press in Circular Road, Calcutta, published an abridged version as *The Travels by Mirza Aboo Talib Khan in the Persian Language*. David Macfarlane, put it together. Both these books are at Rampur's Raza Library.

The supplement to the *Calcutta Gazette* serialized the English translation of *Masir-i Talibi fi Bilad-i Afrang* from September 1807 to February 1808. In 1810, Charles Stewart, Professor of Oriental Languages at the East India Company's College at Haileybury, translated it into English and published it in 1810 with Boxbourne in London. The French translation (*Voyages du Prince Persian Mirza Abu Taleb Khan*) appeared in Paris in 1812, followed by a German translation a year later. In 1814, the English translation appeared in three volumes.

II

At this point it is worth recalling some of the insights offered by another traveller to the West, Lutfullah. He visited England in March 1844 in the company of Mir Jafar Ali Khan, son-in-law of the Nawab of Surat, and wrote his *Autobiography* in English, 'the genuine sentiments of a native of India on many matters connected with the Government of that country . . .'.[11] It appeared in London in the year of the great Indian revolt, and is acclaimed to be not only the first but also 'the best autobiography by an Indian in English'.[12]

What makes this recall useful is that Abu Talib and Lutfullah, even though the latter visited Britain nearly half a century after the former, tend to speak the same language, use the same methods of argument and reasoning, and adhere to identical or similar notions of what religion is all about.[13]

The second half of the eighteenth century saw the face of Britain transformed by immense economic and social changes. Although many sections of the agricultural and industrial classes were impoverished, the middle-class minority did well. Several factors contributed to the period of 'certitude and affluence'.[14] The progress of industry and the perfection of machines, which Abu Talib believed was the chief cause of wealth and power, was one. Thus, he describes the mills for grinding corn, the iron foundries 'driven by steam', and the machines for use in the kitchen to roast chicken, mince meat and chop onions. 'The men of this kingdom,' he observes, 'are extremely impatient and averse to trivial and time-consuming work. ...' He comments on the manufacture of cannon, flat metal sheets, needles, the hydraulic machines, especially the hydraulic pump used to supply London with water—'a stupendous work'—and the fire extinguishing machines. After a halt at one of the factories in England, he observes:

> The mind is at first bewildered by the number and variety of articles displayed therein; but, after recovering from this first impression, and having coolly surveyed all the objects around, every thing appears conducted with so much regularity and precision, that a person is induced to suppose one of the meanest capacity might superintend and direct the whole process.

While such descriptions abound in Lutfullah's *Autobiography* as well,[15] it was Abu Talib who uncovered the roots of Britain's maritime power and established the connection between the industrial revolution and economic prosperity. He was the first to attribute Britain's economic superiority over Napoleon's empire to industrial technology, and to 'the great perfection to which the English brought their navy is the chief cause of their prosperity, and the principal source of all their wealth'. By means of their navy, he added, the British 'can at all times send an army to invade their enemy's country. If they succeed, it is well; if not, they can return with little loss.' Similarly, Britain's conquest of Egypt and other colonies was because of 'the prowess of their own arms', to their being formidable on shore as at sea, and to 'the wisdom and skill manifested by the

English, in the construction and navigation of their vessels'. In this way, Abu Talib recognized the decisive role of sea power more than eighty years before Alfred Thayer Karl Mahan (1840-1914),[16] American naval officer and historian, published his lectures as *The Influence of Sea Power Upon History, 1160-1783* (1890), and *The Influence of Sea Power upon the French Revolution and Empire, 1793-1812* (2 vols. 1892).

III

> My Munshi, Lutfullah Khan, leaves me for three months to visit his family at Surat. In this world of accidents many circumstances may occur to prevent his return. I cannot, therefore, allow him to depart without recording my deep sense of the value of his services, and the high estimation in which I hold him as a friend and preceptor. I have had opportunities of narrowly observing his character at intervals during the last eleven years, and I can conscientiously affirm that, as a native of India, I have seldom met his equal, never his superior, in liberality of sentiment, in the feelings and manners of a gentleman, in an ardent desire of knowledge, and indefatigable industry in its pursuit. When the difference of the advantages of an Asiatic and European education is considered, he will bear a comparison with the best of my own countrymen. I can only add that I can never forget my obligations to him, and that, while his character remains the same, I shall always be proud to number him amongst my friends. That health, success, and prosperity may attend him wherever he goes is the sincere wish of his attached friend.
>
> W. J. Eastwick, Assistant Resident in Sindh
> Karachi, 19 December 1839

Lutfullah's book, a sequel to the one by Abu Talib,[17] is not a comprehensive exploration of the West. Yet both authors—influential intellectuals—reflect on the general processes in Europe and give expression to their particular contribution to the idea of the West. They are, therefore, intrinsically important as non-Western representations of the West in their own right, and possess a degree of autonomy from Orientalism. What is more they explore the West without celebrating it or defaming it.

'I made my first appearance in this world of wonders in the ancient city of Dharanagar, in Malwa,[18] on Thursday, the 7th of

Rajab, 1217 A.H., corresponding with the 4th of November, 1802, A.D.' These opening lines are from Munshi Lutfullah Khan's book *Autobiography of Lutfullah, A Mohamedan Gentleman; and His Transactions With His Fellow-Creatures*. Published by Smith, Alder, and Co. in London in the year of the 1857 revolt, this travelogue, 'a treasure as well as a rarity in literature', ran into two editions.

Lutfullah wrote in English, a language he spoke 'so well that some of my English friends often jestingly interrogated me whether both of my parents were natives in India, or one of them English, for my complexion and accent . . . were different from the natives'. On 24 November 1854, he had told Colonel W.H. Sykes,[19] to whom he had sent the manuscript of *Autobiography*, that, 'being self-tutored in your most difficult language, I stand far beyond the reach of critics, who will surely pardon me, when they are fully acquainted with my circumstances, by going through this book'. Indeed, Lutfullah expressed his thoughts simply, precisely and directly. Edward B. Eastwick (1814-83), who edited the *Autobiography*, approved of its style, presentation, and general accuracy.[20] He claimed to have introduced changes in the text, but we have no idea of what he amended, modified or altered.

Praise came from many quarters. 'We have read this book with wonder and delight', wrote *The Athenaeum*. 'Memoirs of a live Moslem gentleman are a novelty in our letters . . . Lutfullah's story will aid, in its degree, to some sort of understanding of the Indian insurrection.' *The Leader* remarked, 'Read fifty volumes of travel and a thousand imitations of the oriental novel, and you will not get the flavour of Eastern life and thought, or the zest of its romance so perfectly as in Lutfullah's book.'[21]

Some others regarded the *Autobiography* as a model. Mohammad Mujeeb, the historian, described it as 'not only the first but almost the best autobiography by an Indian in English';[22] its value enhanced by the many interesting and accurate observations about places, sites, people and their manners and customs. Notice, for example, Lutfullah's meeting with Mohammad Ali Pasha, Ottoman governor-general and virtual ruler of Egypt, and his remark that that an unlettered soldier had raised himself 'to the summit of sovereignty, like the European Cromwell and Bonaparte and our own Haider [Ali] and Ranjit [Singh]'.[23] Notice also, his reasoned rejection of the widely accepted view in Europe that Umar, the second Khalifa after Abu Bakr, had the famous Library at Alexandria burnt. Notice, moreover, his sensitivity to modern sciences and the inventions that had changed the face of Europe. There is, in his account, a marked approval and appreciation of the process of transformation taking place in that part of the world.

Yet, the *Autobiography*'s influence has not been far-reaching enough. Aziz Ahmad, the eminent historian of South Asian Islam, described Mirza Abu Taleb Khan's impressions of Western civilization in his book *Islamic Modernism in India and Pakistan* (1967), but chose to ignore Lutfullah. So has Gulfishan Khan, a recent historian. The omission is surprising, for even though time separated Abu Taleb and Lutfullah, they shared many ideas and feelings about the West. And because *Masir-i Talibi fi Bilad-i Afranji*, a model source of its kind, and the *Autobiography* shed light upon each other, they not only enrich our understanding but also add to what little we know about the histories of India's encounter with the West.

One writer has recently remarked that we are familiar with the West, and yet, the fact that we are familiar with it does not mean that we know much about it.[24] The principal reason why I have chosen to reprint Abu Taleb's *Masir-i Talibi fi Bilad-i Afranji* and now Lutfullah's *Autobiography* is to locate, in an historical perspective, some of the current debates on 'India and the West' and 'Islam and the West'. I leave the readers to judge whether or not they represent, as Homi Bhabha, Louis Gates, Edward Said, and other scholars have argued in the context of other Asian and African travelogues, their own experiences in their own terms as powerful modes of resistance to European cultural domination.

IV

Mohibbul Hasan's brief essay 'An Indian Prince and the French Revolution' brings to the fore the Muslim elite's favourable disposition to ideas on freedom, liberty and enlightenment. Here, as in the accounts of Abu Talib, Lutfullah and Itesamuddin, there is a marked acceptance rather than repudiation of the West. In fact, the article by Yusuf Ali, also included in this collection, describes this trend. He was one of the early writers to do so.

The next essay in this volume, the second in the series, analyses the early British administration. Thereafter, we have two vivid impressions of Calcutta and Lucknow. Finally, the last four 'documents' are on the 1857 revolt, an event of considerable significance in imperial history as well as in the histories of Indian nationalism. Each one of their authors was held in high esteem for his literary and creative skill, and each one wielded influence during and after his lifetime. Their views have to be taken into account in order to construct the contested histories of the 1857 revolt. This needs explanation.

The 1857 revolt was a bombshell. Here, wrote *The* (London) *Times* correspondent W.H. Russell, the British had not only a servile war and a sort of *jacquerie* combined, but a war of religion, a war of race, and a war of revenge, to shake off the yoke of foreign rule. The immediate cause was the so-called greased cartridge, used with an outer wrapping that had to be bitten off to expose the powder cap before firing. The soldiers were told that the cartridges were greased with the fat of cows and pigs, respectively taboo to Hindus and Muslims. This was the spark that set fire to all that was combustible in India.

In his first article on the revolt in June 1857, Karl Marx cited the famous greased cartridges and sepoy fears about religion as the reported cause of the trouble; he did so without comment or query. He was soon convinced of a conspiracy in the army on an immense scale, and also that anti-British feeling gripped the masses.

People in Meerut, on the left bank of the Jumuna, revolted on 10-11 May 1857. The rebel soldiers seized Delhi and set up Bahadur Shah as their leader. This was followed by risings at several places. The Jat ruler of Ballabhgarh, south-east of Delhi, pledged himself to its emperor in the name of the ancient loyalty of his house. The uprising in Lucknow began on 30 May in the 48th Native Infantry, and swept across Awadh in fifteen days. Canning, the governor-general, wrote on 19 June 1857, that in Rohilkhand and the Doab from Delhi to Kanpur and Allahabad the country was not only in rebellion against the British, but was utterly lawless. Marx wrote that there had been mutinies in the Indian army before, but the present revolt was different. For the first time sepoy regiments murdered their European officers. Hindus and Muslims, renouncing their mutual antipathies, placed Bahadur Shah on the throne of Delhi. The uprising, Marx observed, was not confined to a few localities but coincided with a general disturbance against British supremacy in Asia, the revolt of the Bengal army being connected with the Persian and Chinese wars.

Nobody knows why so violent an upheaval took place, and why

it petered out so quickly. Was it simply a sepoy mutiny, a people's resistance, a civil rebellion, the dying groans of an obsolete autocracy, or an attempt to turn back the clock of history to feudal isolation and tyranny? Little more than the spark that touched off a smouldering mass of combustible material? Was it the Indian War of Independence? The emotions that went into the making of Indian nationalism are visible in the expression of antagonism to the British in 1857, though the inchoate sense of nationality hadn't yet taken the conceptual form of the modern political nation. The revolt was led by feudal chiefs fighting to maintain their traditional privileges. Nationalism of the modern type was yet to come.

The clue to the meaning of the *war* is to be found in the legal relationships that existed between the Company and the Mughal emperors. The Company had accepted the role of vassal, but in 1843 the governor-general, by refusing to offer the customary present, severed the original bond that bound the Company to the emperor. What followed was not a revolt by the Company's soldiers, but their return to their king against the rebellious company.

Was the Great Rebellion, then, a Muslim conspiracy; the fruit of massive Muslim intrigue? No, declared Syed Ahmad Khan, who had rescued the entire British population in Bijnor district as *sadr amino*. In *An Account of the Loyal Mahomedans of India*, he tried to set at rest the widespread British belief that the insurrection had been organized and led by his co-religionists. In an earlier book, from which are produced some excerpts, he had listed the reasons why the 1857 revolt took place:

1. Ignorance of the government of the country and its people, with the result that the people were isolated; they had no champion to stand up for their rights and to see justice done to them, and they were constrained to weep in silence;
2. Overwhelming poverty of the people, particularly the Muslims;
3. Adoption of laws and regulations that jarred with the established customs and practice of Hindustan, and offended religious susceptibilities. There was no doubt that the people believed that the government intended to force Christianity and Western customs upon Hindus and Muslims alike;
4. Poor management of and disaffection in the army;
5. Resumption of revenue-free lands.

Syed Ahmad Khan was right, but he may not have known that the lineaments of revolt differed vastly from district to district, even village to village, and were determined by a complex counterpoint reflecting ecology, tenurial forms and the variable impact of the colonial state.[25] That is why it affected barely one-sixth of the country and less than one-fourth of its population. Both Punjab and Bengal remained loyal. The rapid disarming of the Bengal army sepoys in Lahore within twenty-four hours of the outbreak of violence in the Meerut cantonment was a momentous strategic success for the British. In Punjab, Muslims joined with Sikhs and the men of Kohat to form part of the reinforcements for British troops on the Ridge outside Delhi. In the northern provinces, they behaved better than expected. The princes in general stood firm, to be described by Canning as breakwaters in a storm. The Nizam of Hyderabad and the Nawabs of Rampur, Karnal, Moradabad and Dacca remained faithful. Not for nothing did Raja Hanwant Singh, one of the rebels, observe that the rebellion was suppressed principally because it occurred in Awadh and not throughout India.

'The Reigning Indian Crusade', as the men of 1857 viewed their own struggle, collapsed owing to disunity, lack of leadership, inferior generalship and poor military expertise. Ultimately, no coherent ideology or programme existed to channel the people's aspirations. Peasant millernarianism could not provide a common platform even to the extent that it did in the first stages of the contemporary Taiping Revolt in China. Too many representatives of the old order were red from the start.

Marx ascribed the defeat at Delhi to dissension between regiments, and between Hindu and Muslim, as well as between the soldiery and the traders whom they looted. Nana Sahib and the Rani of Jhansi were selfish, Sindhia was an 'English dog-man', together with the Maharaja of Patiala whom the German philosopher despised for collaborating with the British.

Yet the upsurge was not a movement of the disgruntled elements alone but a rising of the people, at any rate a considerable section of them, who felt, however dimly, the stirring of a common impulse. Its character and content points to a conflict which was larger in significance than that mutiny in the barracks. The legacy of a revolution is often laid up in the subconscious mind of the race. It is difficult to trace the causes that work silently to a certain end which is barely in sight. Indeed, despite the lack of a notion of national sovereignty, the rebels of 1857 were brought together by patriotic feelings grounded in older and more familiar notions of race, religion, and community.

Referring to the legacy, the historian S.B. Chaudhuri talks of the 'stirring of the common impulse';[26] Rajat K. Ray refers to the emotions that went into the making of Indian nationalism 'that were visible in the expression of antagonism to the British in 1857'; and R.C. Majumdar concedes that the memories of 1857 'inspired the genuine national movement for the freedom of India from British yoke'.[27] This is not all. The revolt produced many cult figures that have become part of the nationalist mythology: Mangal Pandey in Barrackpore, the largest garrison town in the area around Calcutta; Kunwar Singh in Bihar; Nana Sahib, son of the dispossessed ruler of Poona who held court at Bithur; Tantia Tope and the Rani of Jhansi in central India; and Ahmadullah Shah, the *maulvi* of Fyzabad. The *maulvi,* who toured the cities of Awadh preaching *jehad*, harassed Colin Campbell's forces during the hot season's campaign in 1858. Rani Beni Rao Madho, a folk hero, was exalted in rustic songs at carnival time. So were the Rani of Jhansi, an epic figure, and Kunwar Singh, the father of the Bhojpuris. The British wrote at length on Kunwar Singh's historic march. Two of the most popular folk songs on the Rani of Jhansi and Kunwar Singh are:

She fought well, that brave one, the Rani of Jhansi,
There were guns in the towers, and the magic shells were fired.
O the Rani of Jhansi, how well she fought that brave one.
Her soldiers were fed on sweetmeats but she took only coarse sugar and rice.
O Rani of Jhansi, how well she fought, that brave one.

Again,

O Babu Kunwar Singh,
We shall dye no more our garments in sacred saffron
Till your Raj comes again.
From hither came the Firingis to surround them.
And from thither
came the two Kunwar brothers.
As freely as the spray of colour in Holi
The guns of both spouted fire.
In the middle raged a grim battle.
O Babu Kunwar Singh,
We shall dye no more our garments in sacred saffron–
Till your Raj comes again.

This background serves to place Syed Ahmad Khan's *Asbab-i Baghawat-i Hind* and the other three documents in perspective. The first is by Allama Fazl-i Haq Khairabadi (1796-1861), a leading scholar from Khairabad who was deported to the Andaman Islands on charges of instigation to murder and high treason.[28] His pamphlet was translated by S. Moinul Haq and published in the *Journal of the Pakistan Historical Society* (vol. 5, 1, 1957). The *Dastanbuy* by the greatest Urdu poet, Mirza Asadullah Khan Ghalib, is reprinted in full. At the end there is a chapter from Abdul Halim Sharar on the eclipse of the last Nawab of Delhi and the British seizure of Awadh.

NOTES

1. L. Lockhart, 'Persia as seen by the West', A.J. Arberry (ed.), *The Legacy of Persia* (Oxford, 1953).
2. 'The Western Image and Western Studies of lslam', in Joseph Schacht and C.E. Bosworth (eds.), *The Legacy of Islam* (Oxford, 1979), p. 43. See also, Norman Daniel, *Islam and the West: The Making of an Image* (Oxford, 2000, rpt.).
3. Bernard Lewis, *The Muslim Discovery of Europe* (New York, 1982), p. 12.
4. Michael H. Fisher (ed.), *The Travels of Dean Mahomet: An Eighteenth-Century Journey through India* (California, 1997).
5. Aziz Ahmad, *Islamic Modernism in India and Pakistan, 1857-1964* (London, 1967), p. 6. For details, see Gulfishan Khan, *Indian Muslim Perceptions of the West during the Eighteenth Century* (Karachi, 1998), pp. 116-17.
6. Mohammad Mujeeb, *The Indian Muslims* (London, 1967), p. 496.
7. Humayun Kabir, *Mirza Abu Talib Khan* (Patna University: Patna, The Russell Lecture, 1961), p. 13.
8. C. A. Bayly, *Origins of Nationality in South Asia: Patriotism and Ethical Government in the Making of Modern India* (Delhi, 2nd impression, 2003), p. 58.
9. Rosie Llewellyn-Jones, *Engaging Scoundrels: The Tales of Old Lucknow* (Delhi, 2000), p. 95.
10. Alastair Bonnett, *The Idea of the West: Culture, Politics and History* (New York, 2004), p. 2.
11. E.B. Eastwick, (ed.), *Autobiography of Lutfullah: A Mohamedan Gentleman and his Transactions with his Fellow Creatures* (London, 1857), p. 404. Lutfullah belonged to a distinguished Sufi family of Malwa. But his fortunes dwindled to such an extent that his family had to starve for a day or so. Ultimately, Lutfullah travelled to Baroda, Ujjain, Gwalior, and Agra. He reached Delhi in early 1817. He found odd jobs in the course of his extensive travels, but, more importantly, he developed his

reputation as a teacher of Arabic, Persian and some Indian languages, notably Marathi.

12. Mujeeb, *Indian Muslims*, p. 497.
13. A study of Bengali travel narratives points out the underlying commonality that renders possible the clubbing together of the travellers. Simonti Sen, *Travels to Europe: Self and Other in Bengali Travel Narratives 1870-1910* (Delhi, 2005), pp. 27-8.
14. A.J. Toynbee, *Acquaintances* (London, 1967), p. 2.
15. For example, his description of the bridges in London: 'The first objects that engaged our attention were the enormous bridges in the city, especially the iron bridge, and the swinging bridge. It astonished us greatly to see large masses of cast iron regularly fixed and nicely cemented together in these useful fabrics. The country, we felt convinced, must have some inexhaustible mines of this metal, which is so necessary for man; for, besides these bridges, iron appears to be used profusely. No house seemed to be without iron railings, iron bars, and some houses are even roofed with iron, and some garden hedged with iron bars.' The following is what Abu Talib saw in Woolich: 'I there saw several large ships on the stocks; and such stores of timber, iron canvas etc. that had the war (Anglo-French) continued for ten years longer, they would not have required a fresh supply. I was particularly attracted by the mode of casting the cannon-balls and shells; also by the manner of boring and shaping the exterior surface of the guns at the same time, all done by the motion of a wheel turned by a steam-engine, which so facilitated the work, that an old woman or a child might have performed the rest of the operation.'
16. Kabir, *Mirza Abu Talib Khan*, p. 24.
17. *Westward Bound: Travels of Mirza Abu Taleb*. Edited, with an Introduction by Mushirul Hasan (New Delhi, 2005).
18. At the crossroads between northern India and the Deccan, and between the western provinces and the seaports of Gujarat. From 1780 until 1818, when the British established their supremacy, Malwa was one of the principal arenas in which Muslim, Maratha and European forces contended for empire.
19. William Henry Sykes (1790-1872) served in the Deccan, 1817-20, and commanded troops at the battles of Kirki and Poona. He would have met Lutfullah as the Director of the East India Company, of which he became Chairman in 1856.
20. Given his training in Oriental languages and his knowledge of Indian history, Eastwick should have known better. Besides editing the *Autobiography*, he translated Shaikh Sadi's *Gulistan*, Lutfullah's favourite book, and the *Bagh-o-Bahar*.
21. Quoted in Mujeeb, *Indian Muslims*, p. 501.
22. Mujeeb, *Indian Muslims*, p. 497. See Mujeeb Ashraf, *Muslim Attitudes*

towards British Rule and Western Culture in India (Delhi, 1982); S.A.I. Tirmizi, *Autobiography of Lutfullah: An Indian's Perceptions of the West* (Delhi: International Writers' Emporium, rpt., 1985).

23. For details, see, *Encyclopedia of Islam*, vol. 7, MIF-NAZ, pp. 423-31.
24. Alastair Bonnet, *The Idea of the West: Culture, Politics and History* (New York, 2004), p. 6.
25. Chris Bayly's concluding note in Eric Stokes, *The Peasant Armed: The Indian Rebellion of 1857* (Oxford, 1986), p. 226.
26. S.B. Chaudhuri, *Civil Rebellion in the Mutinies 1857-1859* (Calcutta, 1957).
27. R.C. Majumdar, *The Sepoy Mutiny and the Revolt of 1857* (Calcutta, 1957).
28. Jamal Malik, 'Letters, Prison Sketches and Autobiographical Literature: The Case of Fadl-e Haqq Khairabadi in the Andaman Penal Colony', *The Indian Economic and Social History Review*, 43, 1, 2006.

CHAPTER 1

The Travels of Mirza Abu Taleb Khan

MIRZA ABU TALEB

On 7 February 1799, Mirza Abu Taleb (1752-1805) sailed from Calcutta to Europe where he visited England, France, Turkey, and other countries, returning to India in August 1803. He reached London on 21 January 1800, the starting point of his trip to other parts of England. He set out on his return journey on 7 June 1802, travelling through France, Constantinople, Baghdad, Karbala, Najaf and Persian Gulf 'to describe the curiosities and wonders . . . (and) give some account of the manners and customs of the various nations (he) visited, all of which were little known to the Asiatics'.

Returning to Calcutta on 4 August 1803, Abu Taleb put together his notes and diaries to write a truly 'monumental assessment' of Anglo-Saxon civilization. *The Travels of Mirza Abu Taleb Khan* (hereafter *The Travels of Mirza Abu Taleb Khan*) was one of the first introductions to modern Western civilization. Translated by Charles Stewart, Professor of Oriental Languages in the East India Company's College at Hertford, the *Masir-i Talibi fi Bilad-i Afrangi* was published in 1810, in two volumes, by Boxbourne, London. A French translation appeared in Paris in 1812, the year of the publication of the Persian text by his son Mirza Husain Ali; its second version a year later. The same year a German translation appeared in Vienna.

Description of the courts of Law London—of English Juries—of the Judges and Lawyers, The Author prosecuted by tailor—his reflections

**The Travels of Mirza Abu Taleb Khan in Asia, Africa, and Europe during the Years 1799 to 1803.* Translated from the Persian language by Charles Stewart (London, 1814), pp. 156-85.

and determination thereon—Censures the establishment of English Courts of Judicature in India—Anecdote of a witness—Ambiguity of the English Law—Remedy proposed by the Author.

In London, there are several public courts of justice, each of which has its particular department, and separate judges. The court in which criminals are tried is called the Old Baily. As I had the happiness to be acquainted with several of the judges of this court, and was anxious to obtain some insight into English jurisprudence, I frequently attended their sittings.

The first circumstance that attracted my attention, and consequent applause of the English law, was the right which every British subject possesses, of being tried by a jury. These juries are composed of twelve respectable inhabitants of the city, who, being summoned to attend without having any previous information on the subject to be tried, or any opportunity of conversing with the parties, come into court perfectly disinterested and unbiased: they then take an oath to act impartially, and to decide according to the evidence. It is the duty of the jury to attend scrupulously to the whole of the proceedings, and particularly to the examination of the witnesses both by the counsellors and the judge: they are then to determine, whether the person accused is guilty, or not, of the crime laid to his charge. If they are unanimous in their opinions, the affair is immediately determined, and the judge pronounces the sentence of the law; but if they are of contrary opinions they are locked up in an adjoining apartment until they come to a decision on the case. Notwithstanding this is the boasted palladium of English liberty, it does not appear to me free from imperfections. The judge, being a person of great consequence and superior abilities, often impresses the jury with such awe, that, if he is inclined to pass an unjust sentence, he can, in his interpretation of the law, and his address to them, dictate what they are to do. I have frequently seen the judge reprehend the jury for their decisions, and send them back, once or twice, to reconsider their verdict. If, by the above means, the judge can bring a few of the jury over to his opinion, he can frighten the rest, by threatening to lock them up without food; while he and the lawyers retire from the court, and refresh themselves, for three or four hours. From the above circumstance, it appears to me that the decision in all cases depends more on the judge than on the jury.

The English judges are doubtless men of the strictest honour and probity, and, being independent both in their fortunes and situation, are above all temptation to act unjustly; but the laws being excessively voluminous, and in many instances either contradictory or obscure, the lawyers, whose only income arises from their practice (that is, the fees they receive from the plaintiff and defendant), endeavour to delay the decision of the business as much as possible, and frequently prevail on the judge to postpone the trial to another year: in this manner, civil cases are often carried on for twenty years, to the ruin of both parties. In other instances, the judges allow the lawyers to puzzle and intimidate the witnesses, in such a manner, that it is impossible for a person unaccustomed to their proceedings to give his evidence correctly; and it sometimes happens, that the judge yields his own better judgement to the interested arguments of a bribed counsellor, who, to serve his client will undertake to prove that black is white.

I was disgusted to observe, that, in these courts, law very often overruled equity, and that a well-meaning honest man was frequently made the dupe of an artful knave; nor could the most righteous judge alter the decision, without transgressing the law.

I myself had the misfortune to acquire a little experience in this way. Having purchased some cloth, I agreed with a tailor to make me a coat for ten shillings. Although there were two witnesses present, and I even had the agreement in his own hand-writing, he denied it, and sent me a bill for twenty shillings. I gave him the ten, but refused to pay him any more: he said it was well he should complain to the court of justice, and make me pay the remainder. He went immediately, and procured a summons for me to appear, but this he never delivered; and, after a certain time, produced a decree from one of the courts, ordering me immediately to pay the ten shillings, and a further fine of six shillings, for not having obeyed the summons. This I thought extreme injustice, and consulted one of my friends, who was an attorney, what I should do. He replied, 'Although the case is very hard, you must *immediately* pay the money: you may then sue him for having withheld the summons, and for having, by that means, obtained an unjust decision against you.' I was however perfectly satisfied with the experience I had already gained, and quietly paid the money. After that transaction, whenever any ***unjust claim*** was made on me, I endeavoured to compromise the matter, by offering to pay a third, or a half of the amount; and as my adversaries found it troublesome to go backward and forward in attendance on the court, they were, in general, reasonable, enough to comply with my wishes. This is the plan adopted by many sensible

Englishmen, who find it easier to settle with their opponents in this manner, than to contest the point in a court of law.

I cannot pass over this opportunity of freely expressing my sentiments with respect to the establishment of British courts of law in India; which, I contend, are converted to the very worst of purposes, and, unless an alteration takes place in the system, will some time or other produce the most sinister consequences.

In Calcutta, few months elapse that some respectable and wealthy man is not attacked by the harpies who swarm round the courts of judicature. Various are their modes of extorting money; and many of them have acquired such fortunes by these nefarious means, as to live in great splendour, and quite eclipse the ancient families.

Their general mode of proceeding is this: having by some means connected themselves with one of the attorneys of the court, they then, under a fictitious name, purchase a large quantity of goods on credit from some country trader; and when the time of payment arrives, they bring forward false witnesses, to prove that the merchandise was bought for half the price actually agreed on.

Another mode of acquiring money, is by frightening people with the terrors of the English law. They first make a demand on a person for a large sum of money, which they say is owing to them, either by himself or his father; to prove which they frequently forge bonds. If he is alarmed, and compromises the matter with them, it is well; but if he disputes their claim, they proceed to the court, and in the most hardened and villanous manner, make oath, or twenty oaths if requisite, that such a person owes them 50,000 rupees (£6,250), and is about to abscond to one of the foreign settlements within twenty miles of Calcutta. A summons is *instantly* issued: and the person accused, being seized and brought to the court, is told he must either give immediate security for a lac of rupees (£12,500), or go to jail: if he is fortunate enough to have opulent friends, who will immediately come to his assistance and give their security, he may escape the disgrace of being carried to prison, on condition of agreeing to attend on the day of trial: if, on that day, he should arrive in the court an hour too late, he is fined perhaps a hundred or two hundred pounds: but if he should, by any accident, neglect to attend, his securities are obliged to pay the whole of the lac of rupees. These circumstances are all very distressing to a native of India; unacquainted with the English laws and customs; and many of them, rather than have the trouble and run the risk, willingly pay a sum of money;

but [if] the person accused is a resolute man, who determines to go through the whole process, he is obliged to employ an attorney, who understands not a word of his language, and to intrust an important concern in the hands of a counsellor, whom he cannot understand but through the medium of an interpreter; and the attorney, not being paid by the year, month, or day, as is the custom of India, makes what charges he pleases, and postpones the trial till it suits his convenience. After a lapse of many months, or perhaps years, the case comes on, and if the defendant is fortunate enough to prove that the plaintiff and his witnesses have perjured themselves, he obtains a verdict in his favour, and the plaintiff is ordered to pay the *costs of suit.* It frequently happens, that the plaintiff, aware of the event, absconds on the day of trial: if he does not, he may be arrested for the amount of the costs, and carried to jail: he there pleads poverty, and the defendant, after such injuries, is obliged to pay him a weekly allowance; in failure of which the scoundrel is liberated, and again let loose on the world, to recommence his villanies.

Hitherto we have taken the favourable side of the question. But suppose the defendant [is] unable to give security for so large a sum of money; he is detained, the first day, in the court-house, under [the] charge of the constable; where, if he is a Hindoo, he cannot eat; and if a Mohammedan, he is precluded from performing the duties of his religion. The following day he is carried to the same prison in which the felons are confined; to the great disgrace of himself and family: there he is every night shut up in a dark and hot cell, where he lingers for months. Many are the respectable persons who die under such misfortunes, before the trial comes on. If the supposed debtor survives till the day of trial arrives, he is then conveyed, under a guard, to the court, where, probably, the plaintiff plays the same tricks as before described; and the only consolation the poor man receives is that the court are very sorry he should have suffered so much trouble.

The hardships and inconvenience which witnesses also suffer, when summoned to Calcutta, are so great, that no man in India will now give voluntary evidence in any case. The witnesses are sometimes brought down the country a month's journey; they are then detained five or six months in Calcutta: when brought into court, they are kept standing for two or three hours; and if puzzled by the various questions and cross-questioning of the lawyers and judges, they are then accused of being liars; and obliged to return home, at their own expense, without any renumeration [*sic*] for their loss of time and trouble.

An anecdote is related of a clever woman, who, having been summoned to give evidence before the court of judicature in Calcutta, deposed that such a circumstance occurred in her presence. The judge asked where it happened: she replied, in the verandah of such a house. 'Pray my good woman', said the judge, 'how many pillars are there in that verandah?' The woman, not perceiving the trap that was laid for her, said, without much consideration, that the verandah was supported by four pillars. The counsel for the opposite party immediately offered to prove that the verandah contained five pillars, and that, consequently, no credit could be given to her evidence. The woman perceiving her error, addressed the judge, and said, 'My lord, your lordship has for many years presided in this court, and every day that you come here ascend a flight of stairs: may I beg to know how many steps these stairs consist of?' The judge confessed he did not know: 'Then', replied she, 'if your lordship cannot tell the number of steps you ascend daily to the *seat of Justice,* it cannot be astonishing that I should forget the number of pillars in a balcony which I never entered above once or twice in my life.' The judge was much pleased with the woman's wit, and decided in favour of her party.

In short, the ambiguity of the English law is such, and the strategems of the lawyers so numerous, as to prove a source of misery to those who are unfortunate enough to have any concern with it or them.

As it may not appear fair or candid to censure any system so freely without an endeavour to point out some remedy to correct its defects, I shall here take the liberty of suggesting a few hints, which, I think, might be usefully applied.

For many years after the establishment of the Mohammedan religion, every person pleaded his own cause; and the cazies (*qazis*), being then men of great learning and sanctity, gave their decisions gratuitously.

As the English judges are at present paid from the public funds, and therefore cannot benefit themselves by prolonging suits, I recommend that the counsellors, attornies, etc., shall be placed on a similar footing, and that they shall not receive any fee or bribe from the litigating parties under a severe penalty. In order to defray the expence of this establishment, either let a small additional tax be laid on the nation at large, or a duty of so much per cent be levied on all litigated property. By this plan, I am convinced that the number and length of suits would be much curtailed, the time of the witnesses would be saved, the law would be purified from those imperfections which are now a reproach to it, and the courts purged of those pettifogging lawyers, who are [a] disgrace to their profession.

II

Of the Finances of England—Mode of assessing the Taxes—Government Loans—National Debt—Effects of the Heavy Taxes, on the Poor, the Rich and the Middling Classes of the People—Plan proposed by the Author for the liquidation of the National Debt.

In a work of this kind, it may be expected I should say some-thing of the Finances of England; but, as the system is tedious and complex, I shall confine myself to the principal points of it only.

The public revenue of England is not, as in India, merely raised from the land, or by duties levied on a few kinds of merchandise, but almost every article of consumption pays its portion. The taxes are levied by the authority and decrees of Parliament. They are, in general, so framed, as to bear lightly on the poor, and that every person should pay in proportion to his income. For this reason, bread, meat, and coals, being articles of indispensable use, are exempt from duties; but spirits, wines, etc., are taxed very high. The proprietors of land pay one fifth of their rents, besides the tenth of its produce to the clergy. The rich are taxed for every dog, horse, and man-servant, they keep: they are also obliged to pay for the liberty of throwing *flow* on their heads, and for having their *arms* (insignia of the antiquity and rank of their family) painted on their carriages, etc. Since the commencement of the present war, a new law has been framed, compelling every person to pay, annually, a *tenth* of his whole income. Most of these taxes are permanent, but some of them are changed at the pleasure of Parliament.

When the Chancellor of the Exchequer discovers that the revenue is not equal to the estimate of the expenses for the following year, he does not increase the taxes to supply the deficiency, but, by a refinement in finance, he borrows the amount, on Government security, and increases the duty upon some particular article of consumption, an eighth, or a tenth part, which suffices to pay the *interest* of the sum so borrowed. At first sight, it appears, that an additional duty, levied upon any particular article, would be an injury to the vender of it: the fact is, however, quite the contrary; for the vender, under pretence of realizing the duty, enhances the price of the commodity in a greater proportion than is requisite, and thus becomes a gainer by the circumstance, while the whole burden of the tax falls upon the consumers.

This system of Government loans commenced about a hundred years ago: and as the surplus revenue, during peace, has never been equal to the discharge of the debt contracted during a war, the national debt has been gradually increasing, and now amounts to the enormous sum of some hundreds of millions. As it seldom happens that any part of this debt is paid of, it appears extraordinary that people are willing to lend their money on such terms, particularly when the annual interest is not more than five or six per cent. But the state of the case, I conceive, is this. The moneyed capital in England far exceeds the amount required for carrying on the commerce of the nation: and as the legal interest of money is limited to five per cent by law, the bankers prefer lending it to Government on these terms, rather than to individuals upon indifferent security: and although they have no hopes of ever being repaid by the borrowers, yet has this ideal property received such sanction by time, and the regular payment of the interest every six months, that a number of persons are always ready to purchase the Government bonds from them, even at an advanced price. The amount of the debt is, however, become so enormous, that the payment of the interest, in addition to the current expences of the empire, is severely felt by every person in the nation. It is therefore impossible that this system can continue much longer. The poor, being exempt from most of the taxes, do not feel the severity of them, except in the price of provisions and clothes; and the rich have it in their power to avoid many of the taxes, by despensing with the use of some of the articles of luxury: but the middling classes of people, who have been accustomed to live in a certain degree of comfort and respectability, feel more severely than others the pressure of the times. They have already greatly curtailed their expences; and they cannot further reduce their establishments, without descending into a lower rank of life than they and their ancestors have been accustomed to move in.

This subject is well understood by some of their most intelligent politicians, who have calculated, that if the whole surface of both islands was covered with gold, it would not suffice to pay off the national debt. But as these gentlemen have not yet pointed out any remedy for this evil, I shall take the liberty of giving a few hints on the subject, the adoption of which may perhaps avert a calamity, that, I foresee, will one day overwhelm Great Britain, and lay her glories in oblivion.

Let the creditors of Government be assembled, in the presence of the Parliament; and let the Minister, clearly and dispassionately, explain to them, that the state of affairs is arrived at such a crisis, that is impossible the nation can continue longer to pay the amount of the enormous taxes which oppress them; that a revolution is to be apprehended; that the first act of the leaders of the revolution certainly will be to *cancel the national debt,* and that the rich may consider themselves fortunate if left in possession of their real wealth; that the national debt, being thus cancelled, they, the creditors, will lose *the whole* of their property invested in the funds; that therefore it will be much wiser to enter into an immediate compromise, and relinquish a part. For instance; those who have been receiving interest from the nation for a great number of years, shall give up half their claim; those who have received interest for a moderate number of years, shall yield a third of their demand; and those whose bonds are of a late date, shall relinquish a quarter of the amount. Now, as the creditors of Government are all rich persons, and, besides their property in the funds, possess great wealth, in gold, silver, merchandise, houses, and lands, there can be no doubt, if they were convinced of the danger of a revolution, by which they would risk much more fatal consequences, they would immediately comply with this requisition. By this plan the national debt would, in one day, be decreased at least one half. The Parliament should then curtail every unnecessary expence, and apply, each year, the surplus revenue to the payment of the remainder of the debt. By such means, in twenty or thirty years, the whole of the debt would be liquidated; some of the most oppressive taxes might be immediately abolished, and others gradually relinquished; provisions would, in consequence, become cheaper; and the people be rendered happy, and grateful to their Government.

III

The Author apologizes for the censure he is obliged to pass on the English character—He accuses the Common People of want of religion and honesty, and the Nation at large of a blind confidence in their good fortune, also of cupidity—A desire of ease, one of their prevailing defects—Picture of a London Gentleman—The English irritable, bad economists of their time, and luxurious—The advantage of simplicity, exemplified in the histories of the Arabs and Tartars—The English vain of their acquirements in learned or foreign languages—Governed by self-interest, licentious, extravagant—An instance of meanness and extravagance united—Bad consequences of these vices—The English too strongly prejudiced in favour of their own customs—The Author's mode of defending the Mohammedan customs—The English blind to their own imperfections.

It now becomes an unpleasant, and perhaps ungrateful, part of my duty, by complying with the positive desire of Lady Spenser and several other of my friends, to mention those defects and vices which appeared to me to pervade the English character, but which, perhaps, only existed in my own imagination. If the hints I shall give are not applicable, I hope they will be attributed to want of judgement, rather than to malice or ingratitude: but if my suggestions are acknowledged to be correct, I trust they (the English) will thank me for my candour, and endeavour to amend their errors.

VERSE

He is your friend, who, like a mirror, exhibits all
your defects:
Not he, who, like a comb, covers them over with
the hairs of flattery.

As my experience and knowledge of the common people were chiefly acquired in London, it may, and with great probability, be objected, that there are more vicious people to be found in the capital than in all the rest of the empire.

The first and greatest defect I observed in the English, is their want of faith in religion, and their great inclination to philosophy (atheism). The effects of these principles, or rather want of principle, is [*sic*] very conspicuous in the lower orders of people, who are totally devoid of honesty. They are, indeed, cautious how they transgress against the laws, from fear of punishment; but whenever an opportunity offers of purloining any thing without the risk of detection, they never pass it by. They are also ever on the watch to appropriate to themselves the property of the rich, who, on this account, are obliged constantly to keep their doors shut, and never to permit an unknown person to enter them. At present, owing to the vigilance of the magistrates, the severity of the laws, and the honour of the superior classes of people, no very bad consequences are to be apprehended; but if ever such nefarious practices should become prevalent, and should creep in among the higher classes, inevitable ruin must ensue.

The second defect, most conspicuous in the English character, is pride, or insolence. Puffed up with their power and good fortune for the last fifty years, they are not apprehensive of adversity, and take no pains to avert it. Thus, when the people of London, some time ago, assembled in mobs on account of the great increase of taxes and high price of provisions, and were nearly in a state of insurrection,—although the magistrates, by their vigilance in watching them, and by causing parties of soldiers to patrole [*sic*] the streets day and night, to disperse all persons whom they saw assembling together, succeeded in quieting the disturbance,—yet no pains were afterwards taken to eradicate the evil. Some of the men in power said, it had been merely a plan of the artificers to obtain higher wages (an attempt frequently made by the English tradesmen); others were of [the] opinion that no remedy could be applied; therefore no further notice was taken of the affair. All this, I say, betrays a blind confidence, which, instead of meeting the danger, and endeavouring to prevent it, waits till the misfortune arrives, and then attempts to remedy it. Such was the case with the late King of France, who took no step to oppose the Revolution, till it was too late. This self-confidence is to be found, more or less, in every Englishman: it however differs much from the pride of the Indians and Persians.

Their third defect is a passion for acquiring money, and their attachment to worldly affairs. Although these bad qualities are not so reprehensible, in them as in countries more subject to the vicissitudes of fortune (because, in England, property is so well protected by the laws, that every person reaps the fruits of his industry, and, in his old age, enjoys the earnings or economy of his youth), yet sordid and illiberal habits are generally found to accompany avarice and parsimony, and, consequently, render the possessor of them contemptible: on the contrary, generosity, if it does not launch into prodigality but is guided by the hand of prudence, will render a man respected and esteemed.

The fourth of their frailities is a desire of ease, and a dislike to exertion: this, however, prevails only in a moderate degree, and bears no proportion to the apathy and indolence of the smokers of opium of Hindoostan and Constantinople; it only prevents them from perfecting themselves in science, and exerting themselves in the service of their friends, upon what they *choose* to call trivial occasions. I must, however, remark, that friendship is much oftener cemented by acts of courtesy and good-nature, than by conferring permanent obligations; the opportunities of doing which can seldom occur, whereas the former happen daily. In London, I had sometimes occasion to trouble my friends to interpret for me, in the adjustment of my accounts with my landlord and others; but, in every instance, I found that, rather than be at the trouble of stopping for five minutes longer, and saying a few words in my defence, they would yield to an unjust demand, and offer to pay the items I objected to at their own expence: at the same time, an aversion to the employment of interpreter or mediator was so conspicuous in their countenance, that, latterly, I desisted from troubling them. In this respect I found the French much more courteous; for if, in Paris, the master of an hotel attempted to impose on me, the gentlemen present always interfered, and compelled him to do me justice.

Upon a cursory observation of the conduct of gentlemen in London, you would suppose they had a vast deal of business to attend to; whereas nine out of ten, of those I was acquainted with at the west end of the town, had scarcely any thing to do. An hour or two immediately after breakfast may be allotted to business, but the rest of the day is devoted to visiting and pleasure. If a person calls on any of these gentlemen, it is more than probable he is told by the servant, his master is *not at home;* but this is merely and idle excuse, to avoid the visits of people, whose business they are either ignorant of, or do not wish to be troubled with. If the suppliant calls in the morning; and is by chance admitted to the master of the house, before he can tell half his story, he is informed, that it is now the hour of business, and a particular engagement in the city requires the gentleman's immediate attendance. If he calls later in the day, the gentleman is just going out to pay a visit of consequence, and therefore cannot be detained: but if the petitioner, unabashed by such checks, continues to relate his narrative, he is set down as a brute, and never again permitted to enter the doors. In this instance, I again say that the French are greatly superior to the English; they are always courteous, and never betray those symptoms of impatience so conspicuous and reprehensible in the English character.

Their fifth defect is nearly allied to the former, and is termed irritability of temper. This passion often leads them to quarrel with their friends and acquaintances, without any substantial cause. Of the bad effects of this quality, strangers seldom have much reason to complain; but as society can only be supported by mutual forbearance, and sometimes shutting our eyes on the frailities or ignorance of our friends, it often causes animosities and disunion between the nearest relatives, and hurries the possessor into dilemmas whence he frequently finds it difficult to extricate himself.

The sixth defect of the English is their throwing away their time, in sleeping, eating, and dressing; for, besides the necessary ablutions, they every morning shave, and dress their hair; then, to accommodate themselves to the fashion, they put on twenty-five different articles of dress: all this, except shaving, is repeated before dinner, and the whole of these clothes are again to be taken off at night: so that not less than two complete hours can be allowed on this account. One hour is expended at breakfast; three hours at dinner; and; the three following hours are devoted to tea, and the company of the ladies. Nine hours are given up to sleep: so that there remain just six hours, out of the twenty-four, for visiting and business. If they are reproached with this waste of time, they reply, 'How is it to be avoided?' I answer them thus: 'Curtail the number of your garments; render your dress simple; wear your beards; and give up less of your time to eating, drinking, and sleeping.'

Their seventh defect is a luxurious manner of living, by which their wants are increased a hundred fold. Observe their kitchens, filled with various utensils; their rooms fitted up with costly furniture; their side-boards, covered with plate; their tables, loaded with expensive glass and china; their cellars, stocked with wines from every quarter of the world; their parks, abounding in game of various sorts; and their ponds, stored with fish. All these expences are incurred to pamper their appetites, which, from long indulgence, have gained such absolute sway over them, that a diminution of these luxuries would be considered, by many, as a serious misfortune. How unintelligible to them is the verse of one of their own Poets:

Man wants but little here below,
Nor wants that little long.

It is certain, that luxurious living generates many disorders, and is productive of various other bad consequences.

If the persons above alluded to will take the trouble of reading the history of the Arabians and Tartars, they will discover that both these nations acquired their extensive conquests, not by their numbers, nor by the superiority of their arms, which were merely bows and arrows, and swords: no, it was from the paucity of their wants: they were always prepared for action, and could subsist on the coarsest food. Their chiefs were content with the fare of their soldiers, and their personal expences [*sic*] were a mere trifle. Thus, when they took possession of an enemy's country they ever found the current revenue of it more than requisite for their simple but effective form of government; and, instead of raising the taxes on their new subjects, they frequently alleviated one half their burthen. The approach of their armies, therefore, instead of being dreaded, was wished for by the neighbouring people, and every facility given to their conquests. To this alone must be ascribed the rapidity with which they overran [a] great part of the globe, in so short a period.

An anecdote is related of the Commander of the Faithful. Aly (on whom be the grace of God!), which will corroborate what I have stated. The son-in-law of the Prophet, previous to setting out on an expedition, ordered a quantity of barley-bread to be baked at once, sufficient to last him for twenty days. This he carried on his own camel, and every day ate one of the cakes, moistened with water, which was his only food. His friends remonstrated with him on his abstemiousness, and requested he would order some other victuals to be dressed. He replied: 'My time is fully taken up with two things: first my duty towards God; and, secondly, my care of the army. I have therefore no time to throw away on the indulgence of appetite.'

The following anecdote of the Emperor Timour (Tamer lane) will also, I hope, be considered as applicable to the subject under discussion. When that great conqueror was returning to Samarcand after the conquest of Persia, he left a considerable army, under the command of some of his most experienced generals, in Azerbijan; but, previous to quitting that province, he summoned the generals to his presence, and, having given them much good advice respecting their conduct, and the government and security of the territories entrusted to their charge, concluded thus: 'By the blessing of God, and the prowess of our victorious arms, all our enemies have been extirpated from this part of the world, save Sultan Ahmed Jellair, and Kara Yusuf the Turkoman, both of whom have taken refuge in the territories of the Ottomans of Constantinople. The former of these is a king, and the son of a king; but as he has been bred up in Persian luxury, and habituated to ease and comfort, I have no apprehensions of him. But beware of Kara Yusuf; he is an experienced soldier, hardened in adversity, accustomed to privations, and capable of undergoing toil and labour: let all your views be directed towards him.' The penetration of the Emperor, and the justness of his remarks, were, in the sequel, fully proved; for, shortly after his death, both these princes invaded the province of Azerbijan. Sultan Ahmed was quickly defeated, and put to death; but Kara Yusuf, supported by the qualities ascribed to him by the Emperor, took advantage of the want of energy and the tyranny of the Tartars, and not only recovered his own province, but expelled them from [a] great part of Persia.

The eighth defect of the English is vanity, and arrogance, respecting their acquirements in science, and a knowledge of foreign languages, for, as soon as one of them acquires the smallest insight into the principles of any science, or the rudiments of any foreign language, he immediately sits down and composes a work on the subject, and, by means of the Press, circulates books which have no more intrinsic worth than the toys bestowed on children, which serve to amuse the ignorant, but are of no use to the learned. This is not merely my own opinion, but was confirmed to me both by Greeks and Frenchmen, whose languages are cultivated in England with more ardour than any others. Such, however, is the infatuation of the English, that they give the author implict credit for his profound knowledge, and purchase his books. Even those who are judges of the subject do not discountenance this measure, but contend, that a little knowledge is better than entire ignorance, and that perfection can only be acquired by degrees. This axiom I deny; for the portion of science and truth contained in many of their books is so small, that much time is thrown away in reading them: besides, erroneous opinions and bad habits are often contracted by the perusal of such works, which are more difficult to eradicate, than it is to implant correct ideas in a mind totally uncultivated.

Far be it from me to depreciate the transcendant abilities and angelic character of Sir William Jones; but his Persian Grammar, having been written when he was a young man, and previous to his having acquired any experience in Hindoostan, is, in many places, very defective; and it is much to be regretted that his public avocations, and other studies, did not permit him to revise it, after he had been some years in India. Whenever I was applied to by any person for instruction in the Persian language who had previously studied this grammar, I found it much more difficult to correct the bad pronunciation he had acquired, and the errors he had adopted, than it was to instruct a person who had never before seen the Persian alphabet. Such books are now so numerous in London, that, in a short time, it will be difficult to discriminate or separate them from works of real value.

A ninth failing prevalent among the English is selfishness. They frequently endeavour to benefit themselves, without attending to the injury it may do to others: and when they seek their own advantage, they are more humble and submissive than appears to me proper; for after they have obtained their object, they are either ashamed of their former conduct, or dislike the continuance of it so much, that they frequently break off the connection. Others, restrained by a sense of propriety, still keep up the intercourse, and endeavour to make the person they have injured, or whom they have deceived by promises, forget the circumstance, by their flattering and courteous behaviour. I had few opportunities of experiencing this myself in England; but the conduct in India of Colonel Hanny, Mr. Middleton, Mr. Johnson, and Dr. Blane, gave me convincing proofs of it; for, whenever they had any point to carry, they would accept of no excuse from me; and having, by persuation and promises, prevailed upon me to undertake their business, as soon as they had obtained their wishes they forgot their promises, and abandoned me to the malice of enemies. It might have been unnecessary to quote these instances; for this defect in the character of the English is so evident, that no doubts remain on the subject.

It is well known, that when Lord Hobart was Governor of Madras he wanted to interfere in the internal management of the revenues of the Carnatic, and for this purpose solicited the sanction of his superior, Sir J. Shore. In this, however, he was disappointed, for the Governor-general would not [as] 'It would be unjust, and an infraction of the treaty between the Nabob and the East-India

Company.' To this observation his lordship replied; that, 'if ever, in any former instance, the English had manifested this spirit of forbearance in aggrandizing themselves,' he should not have proposed the measure to his Excellency; but as it was evident to all the world that the contrary system had ever been pursued, he thought, 'to let the present opportunity pass by would be little less than an act of folly.'

The tenth vice of this nation is want of chastity; for under this head I not only include the reprehensible conduct of young women running away with their lovers, and others cohabiting with a man before marriage, but the great degree of licentiousness practised by numbers of both sexes in London; evinced by the multiplicity of public-houses and bagnios in every part of the town. I was credibly informed, that in the single parish of Mary-la-bonne, which is only a sixth part of London, there reside sixty thousand courtezans; besides which, there is scarcely a street in the metropolis where they are not to be found. The conduct of these women is rendered still more blameable, by their hiring lodgings in or frequenting streets which from their names ought only to be the abode of virtue and religion; for instance, 'Paradise Street', 'Modest Court', 'St. James's Street', 'St. Martin's Lane', and 'St. Paul's Churchyard'. The first of these is to be the residence of the righteous; the second implies virtue; and the others are named after the holy Apostles of the Blessed Messiah. Then there is Queen Anne Street, and Charlotte Street; the one named after the greatest, the other after the best, of Queens. I however think, that persons who let the lodgings are much more reprehensible than the unfortunate women themselves.

The eleventh vice of the English is extravagance, that is, living beyond their incomes by incurring useless expences, and keeping up unnecessary establishments. Some of these I have before alluded to, under the head of luxuries; but to those are now to be added the establishments of carriages, horses, and servants, two sets of which are frequently kept, one for the husband, the other for his wife. Much money is also lavished in London, on balls, masquerades, routs, etc. Sometimes the sum of £1000 is thus expended in one night's entertainment. I have known gentlemen in the receipt of six or seven thousand pounds a year, who were so straitened by such inconsiderate expences, that if asked by a friend for the loan of *ten pounds*, could not comply with this trifling request. This spirit of extravagance appears daily to increase; and being imitated by merchants and tradesmen, must have the worst of consequences; for if these people find the profits of their trade not sufficient to support their expences, they will attempt to supply the deficiency by dishonest means, and at length take to highway robbery. It also encourages dissipation and profligacy in the lower classes, which tend to the subversion of all order and good government.

During one of my excursions from London in a stage coach, I experienced the greatest extravagance and meanness, united in an Englishman, I had ever before seen. He was a genteel looking man, and, soon after we entered the coach, commenced a conversation with me. He asked a number of questions respecting India, particularly about the price of provisions, and was astonished at the cheapness of different articles: but after a short pause, he said, 'Probably the low price of provisions is owing to the scarcity of money, and the limited incomes of the inhabitants of that country?' I replied, he was much mistaken, that no country abounded more with wealth than Hindoostan, and that it was proverbial for making the fortunes of all adventurers. When we sat down to dinner, he called for the most expensive wines, and asked me to drink with him. As I had no inclination to do so, and was averse to the expense, I declined; but when the bill was brought in, he took it, and divided the amount equally to every person at table. I was surprized at his insolence; but as none of the other passengers chose to dispute the demand, although they all looked at him with astonishment, I was ashamed to appear more parsimonious than others, and for two days paid eight shillings for my dinner each day, being twice the amount usual for the passengers in a stage coach.

Should this spirit of extravagance ever pervade the Ministerial department, they will either commit frauds on the public treasury, or be open to bribery and corruption; than which nothing sooner brings a State to ruin.

It is said, that previous to the late revolution, the French Government expended immense sums on public buildings, gardens illuminations, etc., and were parsimonious in the expences of the navy and army; that the nobles lived in a superb style, whilst the lower classes were reduced to the most abject poverty; that the patience of the latter having been exhausted, they readily joined the leaders of faction, and drove their inconsiderate and domineering masters from among them.

If the English will take the trouble of reading ancient history, they will find that luxury and prodigality have caused the ruin of more Governments than was ever effected by an invading enemy: they generate envy, discord, and animosity, and render the people either effeminate, or desirous of a change. To these vices may be ascribed the subversion of the Roman empire in Europe, and the annihilation of the Moghul government in India.

Their twelfth defect is a contempt for the customs of other nations, and the preferences they give to their own; although theirs, in fact, may be much inferior. I had a striking instance of this prejudice in the conduct of my fellow-passengers on board ship. Some of these, who were otherwise respectable characters, ridiculed the idea of my wearing trowsers, and a night-dress, when I went to bed; and contended, that they slept much more at their ease by going to bed nearly naked. I replied, that I slept very comfortably; that mine was certainly the most decent mode; and that, in the event of any sudden accident happening, I could run on deck instantly, and, if requisite, jump into the boat in a minute; whilst they must either lose some time in dressing, or come out of their cabins in a very immodest manner. In answer to this, they said, such sudden accidents seldom occurred, but that if it did happen, they would not hesitate to come on deck in their shirts only. This I give merely as a specimen of their obstinacy, and prejudice in favour of their own customs.

In London, I was frequently attacked on the apparent unreasonableness and childishness of some of the Mohammedan customs; but as, from my knowledge of the English character, I was convinced it would be folly to argue the point philosophically with them, I contended myself with parrying the subject. Thus, when they attempted to turn into ridicule the ceremonies used by the pilgrims on their arrival at Mecca, I asked them, why they supposed the ceremony of baptism, by a clergyman, requisite for the salvation of a child, who could not possibly be sensible what he was about. When they reproached us for eating with our hands; I replied, 'There is by this mode no danger of cutting yourself or your neighbours; and it is an old and a true proverb, "The nearer the bone, the sweeter the, meat:" but, exclusive of these advantages, a man's own hands are surely cleaner than *the feet of a baker's boy;* for it is well known, that half the bread in London is kneaded by the feet.' By this mode of argument I, completely silenced all my adversaries, and frequently turned the laugh against them, when they expected to have refuted me and made me appear ridiculous.

Many of these vices, or defects, are not natural to the English; but have been ingrafted on them by prosperity and luxury; the bad consequences of which have not yet appeared; and, for two reasons, may not be conspicuous for some time. The first of these is the strength of constitution both of individuals and of the Government: for if a person of a strong constitution swallow a dose of poison, its deleterious effects are sometimes carried off by the power of the nerves; but if a weak person should take it, he would certainly fall a victim. The second reason is, that their neighbours are not exempt from these vices; nay, possess them in a greater proportion. Our poet Sady (Shaikh Sadi) has said,

To the inhabitants of Paradise, Purgatory
would seem a Hell:
But to Sinners in Hell, Purgatory
would be a Paradise.

Form what I saw and heard of the complaints and dissatisfaction of the common people in England, I am convinced, if the French had succeeded in establishing a happy and quiet government, whereby the taxes could have been abolished, and the price of provisions reduced, the English would, of themselves, have followed their example, and united with them: for, even during the height of the war, many of the English imitated the fashions, follies, and vices of the French, to an absurd degree.

Few of the English have good sense or candour enough to acknowledge the prevalence and growth of these vices, or defects, among them; but, like the smokers *of beng* (hempseed) in Turkey, when told of the virtues of their ancestors, and their own present degeneracy, make themselves ready for battle, and say, 'No nation was ever exempt from vices: the people and the governments you describe as possessing such angelic virtues were not a bit better than ourselves; and so long as we are not worse than our neighbours, no danger is to be apprehended.' This reasoning is, however, false; for fire still retains its inflammable nature, whether it is summer or winter; and the flame, though for a short time smothered by a heap of fuel thrown on it, breaks out in the sequel with the greatest violence. In like manner, vice will sooner or later, cause destruction to its possessor.

IV

The Author describes the Virtues of the English, under the following heads—Honourable—Respectful to their superiors—Obedient to the laws—Desirous of doing good—Followers of fashion—Sincere in their dispositions—Plain in their manners, and hospitable. Peculiar ideas of the English of the meaning of Perfection—The Author censures some of the customs of London—Fires—Description of the fire-engines—Hardship of the owner of the property burned, being obliged to pay for the use of the engines—The Author dislikes English beds—He censures the custom of retaining handsome footmen to wait on Ladies.

I fear, in the foregoing Chapter, I have fatigued my readers with a long detail of the vices, or defects of the English: I shall, therefore, now give some account of their virtues; but, lest I should be accused of flattery, will endeavour to avoid prolixity on this subject.

The first of the English virtues is a high sense of honour, especially among the better classes. This is the effect of a liberal education, and of the contempt with which those who do not possess it are regarded. This sense of honour is carried to such a degree, that men possessing every terrestrial enjoyment, as wealth, estates, wife, and children, will, on the smallest imputation, sacrifice their lives, and the welfare of their families, to recover their reputation, or to wipe off an ignominious slander.

Their second good quality is a reverence for every thing or person possessing superior excellence. This mode of thinking has this great advantage—it makes them emulous of acquiring the esteem of the world, and thus renders them better men. In other countries, this respect is not paid to superior merit: people will therefore not give themselves any trouble on the subject: wisdom, knowledge, and virtue, are consequently banished from among them.

The third of their perfections is a dread of offending against the rules of propriety, or the laws of the realm: they are therefore generally content with their own situations, and very seldom attempt to exalt themselves by base or nefarious practices. By these means the establishments of Church and State are supported, and the bonds of society strengthened; for when men are ambitious of raising themselves from inferior to exalted situations, they attempt to overcome all obstacles; and though a few gain their object, the greater part are disappointed, and become, ever after, unhappy and discontended.

The fourth of their virtues is a strong desire to improve the situations of the common people, and an aversion to do any thing which can injure them. It may be said, that in so doing they are not perfectly disinterested; for that the benefits of many of these institutions and inventions revert to themselves.

During my residence in England, and at a time when coals were extremely dear, one of their philosophers invented a kettle, with a small furnace below, which required so little fuel, that a piece of lighted paper, or a burning stick, thrown into the furnace, would cause the water to boil long enough to dress a joint of meat. By means of such machines, and the various conveniences adopted in the fitting up of a house, so much time and labour are saved, that two servants in England will do the work of fifteen in India.

Their fifth good quality is so nearly allied to weakness, that by some wordly people it has been called such: I mean, an adherence to the rules of fashion. By this arbitrary law, the rich are obliged not only to alter the shape of their clothes every year, but also to change all the furniture of their houses. It would be thought quite derogatory to a person of taste, to have his drawing room fitted up in the same manner for two successive years. The advantage of this profusion is the encouragement it gives to ingenuity and manufacturers of every kind; and it enables the middling and lower classes of people to supply their wants at a cheap rate, by purchasing the old fashioned articles.

Their sixth excellence is a passion for mechanism, and their numerous contrivances for facilitating labour and industry.

Their seventh perfection is plainness of manners; and sincerity of disposition; the former is evinced in the colours of their clothes, which are generally of a dark hue, and exempt from all tawdriness; and the latter, by their open and manly conduct.

Their other good qualities are good natural sense and soundness of judgement, which induce them to prefer things that are useful to those that are brilliant; to which may be added, their perseverance in the acquirement of science, and the attainment of wealth and honours.

Their hospitality is also very praiseworthy, and their attention to their guests can nowhere be exceeded. They have an aversion to sit down to table *alone*; and from their liberal conduct on this subject, one would suppose the following verse had been written by an Englishman:

'I May the food of the misanthrope be cast to the dogs!
May he who eats alone be shortly eaten by the worms!'

It is said, that all these virtues were formerly possessed in a greater degree by the English, and that the present race owe much of their fame and celebrity to their ancestors.

The English have very peculiar opinions on the subject of *perfection*. They insist, that it is merely and ideal quality, and depends entirely upon comparison; that mankind have risen, by degrees, from the state of savages to the exalted dignity of the great philosopher NOWTON: but that, so far from having yet attained *perfection*, it is possible that, in future ages, philosophers will look with as much contempt on the acquirements of Newton, as we now do on the rude state of the arts among savages. If this axiom of theirs be correct, man has yet much to learn, and all his boasted knowledge is but vanity.

Having thus given my opinion freely on the vices and virtues of the English, I shall now take the liberty to point out a few of the customs of the metropolis which appear to me reprehensible, and might easily be amended. The number of turnpikes in the vicinity of London are a great grievance: they not only oblige the traveller to stop, but compel him to take bad copper money in exchange for his silver, and, very often, abusive language into the bargain. This, however, is not quite so disgusting as when a stranger, wishing to visit the House of God, or the Tombs of the Kings (I mean the Cathedral of Saint Paul, and Westminster Abbey), is obliged every ten minutes to take out his purse, and pay another and another fee. The same vile practice exists at the Tower, and at most of the public buildings, and ought to be abrogated.

The number of fires which happen in London are a very serious evil, especially as most of them originate from the quantity of wood used in the construction of houses. It has been before mentioned, that the houses of this city are seldom lower than four stories, and join each other: all the floors, stairs, doors, and roof, are of wood; nay, many have great part of the walls supported by timbers, and some have the apartments lined with painted wainscot. In every room there is a fire-place; so that if, by the carelessness or malevolence of a servant, one of these houses is set on fire, it quickly communicates to the others, and before it can be extinguished burns down half a street.

I should be guilty of an act of injustice, were I not to give English credit for their invention and adroitness in extinguishing fires. They have machines which, being placed upon wheels and drawn by horses, can be conveyed to any part of the town in a very short time. These machines are worked by a mechanical power, and will throw up water fifty yards high; and as there are pipes of running water under every street, the situation of which is perfectly known to certain persons, a hole is in a few minutes dug in the pavement, and a plug being drawn from one of the pipes, the water rushes forth and supplies the engine, which may then be worked for twenty-four hours, or longer if necessary.

To each of these machines a number of people are attached, who are paid by the parish. These persons are called *firemen:* they are remarkable for their courage and their honesty: they have been known to enter a house all in flames, and bring thence many valuable articles, which they have delivered to the proprietor.

The only complaint I have against this system is, that a considerable sum of money must be paid to the first engine that arrives, a smaller to the second, and so on, thus, if fifty machines should come to extinguish a fire, and all their efforts prove inefectual, the sufferer, who is already ruined by the destruction of his property, is obliged to pay a large sum to the firemen, which doubles his loss, and adds to anguish of his mind. Notwithstanding the assistance of these machines, there is scarcely a day in which fires do not happen, and cause much mischief; but no pains are taken to make the people rebuild their houses on a better or more secure plan.

The beds, and mode of sleeping, in England, are by no means to my taste. They have, in general, two or three beds, laid one over other; and the upper one being composed of feathers, a person is immediately swallowed up in them, and finds the greatest difficulty in turning from one side to the other. In the very depth of winter, this is bearable; but as the weather becomes warmer, it causes pains in the back, and a general relaxation of the frame. Above them, they spread a sheet, two blankets, and a quilt; all of which are closely tucked under the bedding, on three sides; leaving an entrance for the person to creep in next the pillows; which always reminded me of a bear climbing into the hole of large tree. The bed being broad, and the clothes stretched out, they do not close about the neck, and, for a long time, do not afford any warmth; and if a person turns about incautiously the four coverings separate, and either fall off the bed, or cause so much trouble, that sleep is completely banished. All my other Indian customs I laid aside without difficulty, but sleeping in the English mode cost me much trouble. Our quilts, stuffed with cotton, and lined with muslin, are so light, and adhere so closely to the body, that they are infinitely more comfortable and warmer than blankets; and although it may be objected, that to sleep the whole season with the same quilt next the body is an uncleanly custom, I reply, that *we* always sleep in a night-dress, which prevents the quilt touching the skin; whereas the English go to bed nearly naked, and use the same sheets for a fortnight together. It also frequently happens, that a person, in travelling, is put into a bed with damp sheets, the moisture of which is quickly absorbed into the body, and infallibly brings on cold, surfeits, or a deadly fever.

Verse of Moulavy Roumy (Maulana Jalaluddin Rumi)

'These people wandered about in quest of shade, and
spread, blankets to cover them from the Sun:
They could not see the branching trees loaded with
fruit, because the thick viel of prejudice covered their eyes'

I cannot approve the custom of the nobility and gentry in London retaining a number of handsome footmen, and other male servants, to stand behind a lady's carriage, or to attend her when she walks out. These fellows, are, in generals well-looking, and when smartly dressed have an engaging appearance. It should be recollected that Cupid makes no discrimination between poor and rich, vulgar or noble, the beggar or the king; we are all his slaves, and the subjects of his power. Scandal and dishonour must sometimes be the consequence of such a system.

I think I have now fairly acquitted myself of my promise to describe minutely the character of the English, or at least such as it appeared to me. . . .

CHAPTER 2

Mirza Abu Talib Khan

HUMAYUN KABIR

Born in Faridpur, now in Bangladesh, Humayun Kabir (1906-69) studied at the Presidency College and the University College in Calcutta and at St. Exeter College, Oxford. Returning to India, he taught at the universities of Andhra (1932-3) and Calcutta (1933-45) before playing an active role in Bengal politics. He served on the Bengal Legislative Council (1937-45, 1946-48), and held a key position in Fazlul Haq's Proja Krishak Party. In the 1940s, the decade that brought him closer to Maulana Abul Kalam Azad, Humayun Kabir wrote extensively on various aspects of 'Muslim Polities', critiquing the 'two-nation' theory and advocating the cause of plural nationhood.

After Independence, Humayun Kabir held positions in the Ministry of Education, and also served as Chairman of the University Grants Commission (1955-6). He held ministerial positions until 1966, when he joined the Bangla Congress and returned to the Lok Sabha as its member in 1967.

Kabir was a prolific writer in Bangla and English. This lecture on Mirza Abu Talib, though published quite some time ago, is an indication of his wide-ranging scholarly interests. It is to date the only detailed summary of Abu Talib's fascinating book.

One of the most interesting personalities of eighteenth-century India is Mirza Abu Talib Khan, who may rightly claim to be one of the pioneers of modern historiography. A man of keen intellect and wide culture, he wrote on a variety of topics and tried his hand at poetry, criticism and travelogue, but it is as a historian that he made his most remarkable contributions to scholarship. He is one of the first

*'The Russell Lecture', Delivered on 16 April 1961 at Patna College, Patna.

historians in India or elsewhere to realise the importance of sea-power and held that Britain prevailed over revolutionary France mainly because of her naval supremacy. He traced the prosperity of Britain to the Industrial Revolution before most of his contemporaries, whether Indian or British, were aware that such a revolution had taken place. He has also a refreshing approach to the problems of Government and though by birth and upbringing an aristocrat, recognised clearly that without democratic principles, no country can attain durable prosperity. Perhaps more important still, he was one of the first, if not the first historian to realise vividly the importance of economic factors on the course of history and anticipated some of the findings of Marx by more than fifty years.

I

According to the prevailing custom of the day, Mirza Abu Talib Khan also opens many of his books with an account of his life and times. He was the son of Haji Muhammad Beg Khan, by descent a Turk but born at Abbasabad, Isfahan. Haji Muhammad left Persia while still a young man and came to India apparently to seek his fortune. He entered the service of Nawab Abul Mansur Khan Safdar Jang and was soon able to win his confidence. He became a great friend of Muhammad Quli Khan, nephew of the Nawab, and rose rapidly in the official hierarchy; but after the Nawab's death, this friendship became the cause of Haji Muhammad's downfall. The new Nawab, Shuja-ud-Daulah became jealous of his cousin Muhammad Quli Khan and contrived his death. He at first tried to win over Haji Muhammad, but soon became suspicious of him and decided to arrest him. Haji Muhammad had, however, received previous intimation of the Nawab's intentions and 'leaving all his goods and wealth on the spot, fled to Bengal' where he won the favour of Nawab Muzaffar Jang of Murshidabad. Haji Muhammad lived in Murshidabad 'beloved and respected' till his death in the year 1768.

When Haji Muhammad fled, he left behind in Lucknow his wife and young Abu Talib. 'The Nawab confiscated two lakhs of rupees in cash and property' belonging to the father and placed a guard over the child. After a short time, the Nawab removed the guard and provided money for the education of Abu Talib. This change in the Nawab's attitude must have been due to the fact that Haji Muhammad had married the daughter of Abul Hasan Beg Isfahani who was a close associate of Nawab Burhan-ul-Mulk Saadat Khan, the great grandfather of Nawab Shuja-ud-Daulah. Abu Talib observes in his *Masir-i-Talibi*, 'I was born at Lucknow in the year 1752 and although the Nawab Shuja-ud-Daulah was much displeased at my father's conduct, he nevertheless, recollecting the connection between our families supplied my mother with money for her expenses and gave her strict injunctions to let me have the very best education.' The impressive intellectual achievements of Abu Talib prove that the author had taken full advantage of the opportunity which was offered to him.

In 1766, Abu Talib left Lucknow with his mother to join his father at Murshidabad, but a year and a half after their arrival, the father died. Before his death, the father had betrothed Abu Talib to the daughter of a near relation of Nawab Muzaffar Jang. For several years, our author remained happy and contented in the service of that Prince, but his high spirits and love of adventure ruled out a peaceful and settled life for him. In 1775, after the accession of Nawab Asaf-ud-Daulah, to the throne of Oudh, Abu Talib received an invitation from his Prime Minister, Mukhtar-ud-Daulah to return to Lucknow. Abu Talib was appointed Amildar of Etawah and continued in that situation for about two years. He lived the greater part of this time in tents as his main duty was the collection of revenues which involved frequent excursions to the districts. This was his first introduction to village life and laid the foundation of his intimate knowledge of the economic conditions of the peasantry.

After the death of his patron, Mukhtar-ud-Daulah, Abu Talib was superseded and repaired to Lucknow, but in 1778, he was appointed to assist Col. Alexander Haney in the revenue administration of Gorakhpur. In that situation, writes Abu Talib, 'I continued for three years living the whole of the time either in tents or temporary houses composed of mats and bamboos.' It was thus that he gained a rare insight into the condition of the Oudh peasantry and the role which the small tenants played in the economic development of the State. Not only so, he also saw at first-hand how the dissensions between the representatives of the Nawab and those of the East India Company affected the finances of the State. Though the Collectors extorted larger sums from the tenants, the revenues annually decreased and 'the finances of the State were much deranged'.

Col. Haney was removed from office in 1781. Abu Talib also lost his job and remained unemployed at Lucknow for one year. The oppression of the Collectors increased so much that at last many of the landlords led by Raja Balbhadra Singh, a descendant of a former ruling dynasty of Oudh, rebelled. In the end Mr. Hastings, then Governor-General, felt it necessary to intervene and asked the British Resident, Middleton, to seek Abu Talib's aid to curb the rebels and restore order to the country. Abu Talib accomplished this task with signal success, but this brought him no recognition either from the Nawab or from the cabals that ruled the State. Abu Talib's strong criticism of the Government and the corrupt officials invited the displeasure of the Nawab's Court as well as the East India Company. When Mr. Middleton left Lucknow and Hastings went back to Europe, Abu Talib was left without any protection against the machinations of his enemies and finding it impossible to remain in Lucknow he returned to Calcutta in 1787.

The rest of Abu Talib's story can be briefly told. From 1787–92, he lived in Calcutta and devoted himself mainly to literary pursuits. In 1791, he brought out a scholarly edition of the *Diwan-i-Hafiz* which was followed in 1791–92 by *Khulasat-ul-Afkar*, a magnificent study of the work of about 500 ancient and modern poets based on material he had collected over a number of years. About the same time he composed two works of history, namely, a history of the kings of India and *Lubb-ut-Twarikh*, a compendious account of the kingdoms in Europe and America.

In 1792, Lord Cornwallis sent Abu Talib again to Lucknow with letters of recommendation to the British Resident and Nawab Asaf-ud-Daulah. He was graciously received by both, as was perhaps natural, but neither offered him an appointment. Soon after, Cornwallis left India and Abu Talib also returned to Calcutta for the third time in 1795. He was promised assistance by Sir John Shore, the Governor-General, but three years passed without any improvement in his material condition. All his dependents and supporters and even some of his children left him and Abu Talib was overcome with grief and despondency. It was at this juncture that his friend, Captain David Richardson, told Abu Talib that he meant to go to Europe 'to renovate his constitution and would return to India in three years'. Richardson invited Abu Talib to accompany him as he thought that the change of scene and the new experiences in Europe would disperse his mental gloom. In addition, Richardson undertook to teach him English during the voyage and to meet all his expenses.

Abu Talib accepted this generous offer and sailed for the British Isles in February 1799, and lived there till June 1802. Later he travelled in France, Italy, Turkey and Iraq and returned to India only in August 1803. He kept a record of his experiences which he later revised and compiled in the form of a book, *Masir-i-Talibi-fi-Bilad-i-Afrangi*, completed in 1804. The book even in manuscript became immediately popular and was translated into English in 1810. Charles Stewart, introducing this book to the English public, said in his Preface: 'We have several books of fictitious travels ascribed to natives of the East; but I believe this is the first time the genuine opinions of an Asiatic respecting the institutions of Europe have appeared in the English language.' It reveals Abu Talib not only as a shrewd observer of men and manners but also a keen student of natural phenomena in their many aspects.

In 1804, Abu Talib composed a metrical treatise on Astronomy with a prose commentary entitled *Mirj-al-Tauhid*. Writing, however, did not assure him a decent income and Abu Talib once again left Calcutta to seek his fortunes in Oudh. He was appointed an Amildar in one of the Districts of Bundelkhand but died in 1806 without getting in his lifetime the recognition which he so richly deserved.

II

Abu Talib published in 1791 his scholarly edition of *Diwan-i-Hafiz*. His magnificent survey of about 500 ancient and modern poets in *Khulasat-ul-Afkar* also indicates his love for poetry and his deep study of the poets. In the Preface to this work, Abu Talib says that from the earliest age to the present time (he was then about 40), he had read much and had been a great admirer of poetry. He had long conceived the project of composing a *Tadkira* of ancient and modern poets. In the year 1788, when he was engaged in the study of the late Ali Quli Khan's *Tadkira*, he chanced to meet Saiyid Mir Muhammad Husain. The Saiyid recommended that Abu Talib should make an abridgment of the work which 'in obedience to so esteemed a friend, I cheerfully undertook and augmented it with a *Khatimah* and memoirs of some of my contemporaries'. This abridgment, now unfortunately lost, was Abu Talib's first essay in writing a *Tadkira* and its successful completion encouraged him to undertake the more ambitious *Khulasat*.

In the *Khulasat* it is perhaps the *Khatimah* which constitutes the most interesting section as it gives a remarkable account of some of the leading Hindi poets of the age. Bland, who describes in detail the contents of the manuscript in his article, *The Earliest Persian*

Biography of Poets, says: 'At the conclusion of a memoir of an Indian poet, Rao Sunath Singh, the biographer takes occasion to mention that although a Persian writer, Sunath Singh was a Hindu and his proper language was *Bhakka*, the dialect of the people of Braja in which compositions existed in great number arranged in the old Indian metres differing widely from those of the Arabs.' Abu Talib then informs us that in that language a poet is called *Kabishwar* and *Kabishwaran* and that the number of such poets is so great that were he to make mention of all of them 'it would lead to prolixity. On the other hand, to pass them altogether in silence would fall far short of what is just, this language being sweet, sonorous and distinguished by all the properties essential to a polished and learned tongue.' Abu Talib concludes with an eulogium on the dialect and a sketch of some of its most distinguished poets, accompanied by 32 *kavitas* and 337 *dohrahs* (dohas) as specimens of their composition. There are about ten memoirs containing among others the names of Behari, Kesavadas and Sundar.

Abu Talib also wrote a *Diwan* which was edited by Swinton with an English translation under the title *Poems of Mirza Abu Talib Khan*, London, 1807. There is also a *Masnavi* available in Edinburgh University Library as well as his *Mirj-al-Tauhid*, a metrical treatise on astronomy with a prose commentary composed in 1804. Stewart has included in his translation of Abu Talib's travelogue English versions of the *Masnavi* as well as the poems *An Ode to London* and *An Elegy on Tufuzzul Husain Khan*. In addition, we find interspersed in the book many verses that Abu Talib composed or adapted on the spur of the moment. This surprised and delighted his British friends, particularly the women to whom many of these compositions were addressed. They were impressed the more as most of them were unaware that such impromptu composition or quotation was part of the training of an Indian gentleman of culture and refinement. Stewart also mentions a *Masnavi* which was a metric al version of Abu Talib's travels but nothing else is known about it.

III

Of all the works of Abu Talib, the account of his travels in Asia, Africa and Europe has proved most popular. He left India in 1799 at the request of his friend, Captain Richardson. It is evidence of his personal charm that the Captain not only requested Abu Talib to accompany him but also offered to pay for his expenses and in the bargain teach him English during the voyage. Both during the voyage and in Europe, his learning, ready wit and amiable manners made him a welcome guest wherever he went and he was lionised by English society in a way that has rarely been equalled. His intellectual quality can be judged from the fact that by the time he reached Britain he had acquired enough English not only to move about freely in the country, but also carry on intelligent conversation with the elite on various intellectual and cultural subjects.

Abu Talib was a keen observer of both nature and man and had the curiosity to learn and the desire to record whatever he saw. In his own words, 'It therefore occurred to him that if he were to write all the experiences of his journey through Europe, to describe the curiosities and the wonders which he saw and to give some account of the manners and customs of the various nations he visited, of which little is known to Asiatics, it would afford a gratifying banquet to his countrymen. He was also of the opinion that many of the customs, inventions, sciences and ordinances of Europe, the good effects of which are apparent in those countries, might with great advantage be imitated by Muhammadans.' In pursuance of these ideas, Abu Talib began a journal in which he recorded whatever impressed him and also put down his reflection on what he saw. After his return to Calcutta, he revised and abridged his notes and named the work *Masir-i-Talibi-fi-Bilad-i-Afrangi*, 'The Travels of Talib in the Regions of Europe'.

The first available manuscript bears the date 1806 and appears to have been published and edited by Mirza Hasan Ali and Mir Qudrat Ali in 1812. An English translation in two volumes by Charles Stewart had, however, appeared even earlier in 1810. A second English edition in three volumes appeared in 1814. A French translation from the English text was published in Paris in 1811 and a German translation from the French appeared in Vienna in 1813. The popularity of the book was such that a second version in French appeared in 1819. The response from his own countrymen was however poor. Abu Talib had apparently anticipated this, for in his preface he lamented, 'When I reflect on the want of energy and the indolent dispositions of my countrymen and the many erroneous customs which exist in all Muhammadan countries and among all ranks of Mussalmans, I am fearful that my exertions will be thrown away.' Perhaps to justify his worst fears, the first Urdu translation, and that also only of the first part of his book, appeared from Moradabad only in 1904.

We find evidence of Abu Talib's intellectual energy and alertness on almost every page of the book. The problem of refraction attracted his notice when he found that on approaching the Nicobar islands, he could see the land with naked eyes, but when he wished to look at it more minutely through a telescope, the land seemed to disappear. One of the naval officers explained to him that what Abu Talib had first seen was not actually the islands of Nicobar but their reflection in the atmosphere, and removed his doubts by a simple experiment in which a ring was first thrown into an empty bowl and then the bowl was filled with water. Abu Talib also watched with interest shoals of flying fish and observed that their motion was not that of leaping but of real flight. He also noticed how the pole star gradually sank in the horizon as the ship moved south, disappeared at the Equator and could not be seen again till the ship returned to the northern latitude after rounding the Cape.

During his travels abroad, Abu Talib was struck by the extensive use of coal as a fuel. He observed that the Irish use 'turf which is unfit for tillage but makes tolerable fuel; it is however not equal to the other kind of fuel used in these countries, called *coal* which is a species of black stone, dug out of mines, and affords a great heat.' He mentions that though coal is found in the Ramghur Hills in India—even today this is one of the richest coal belts of the country—it is not generally used. Abu Talib adds that even turf which is inferior to coal is much 'better than the composition of cow-dung used by the poor in India'.

Abu Talib admired many things in the West but he had an equally keen eyes for the defects he found. He compares Irish villages with those in India and remarks that the peasants in Ireland are even poorer than in India. Many of them could not afford shoes in spite of the cold climate and the stony country. Says Abu Talib, 'Notwithstanding the sharp stones over which they are obliged to travel and the excessive cold of the climate they never wear a shoe but during the whole year go about with bare legs and bare arms, in consequence of which these parts of them are as red as the feet of a Hindu woman who has been embellishing herself with Mendee.' As further evidence of their poverty he reports, 'I was informed that many of these people never taste meat during their lives but subsist entirely upon potatoes, and that in the farmhouses, the goats, pigs, dogs, men and women and children lie all together. Whilst on our journey the boys frequently ran for miles with the coach in the hope of obtaining a piece of bread.'

Abu Talib has many shrewd observations on the character of the Irish, the English and the Scotch. He saw their strong as well as their weak points and drew morals for his own country which have as much validity today as when Abu Talib wrote. He was struck by the quick wit of the Irish and their capacity to learn languages, but he also noted that the Irish sometimes carry their liberality to the point of extravagance. He also compared the British with the French and some of his remarks startle us by their accuracy and insight. He praised the British for their stress on education and their devotion to science, but at the same time he was not impervious to what he regarded as defects in British character. He has some uncharitable remarks about their defects, though he tries to soften the blow by stating that 'these defects and vices perhaps only exist in my own imagination. If the hints I shall give are not applicable, I hope they will be attributed to want of judgment rather than malice or ingratitude; but if my suggestions are acknowledged to be correct, I trust the English will thank me for my candour and endeavour to amend their errors.' After this apology, he draws out a long list of twelve vices of the English but hastens soon after to describe their virtues. Among the vices he mentions are want of faith in religion, pride, attachment to worldly goods, luxurious living, extravagance and contempt for the customs of other nations. Among the virtues, he was most struck by the British sense of honour and respect for authority, their law abidingness [*sic*], public spirit and devotion to science.

Abu Talib was an admirer of the British Government and held that it combined the advantages of monarchy, aristocracy and democracy. According to him, the English Constitution was 'a union of the monarchical, aristocratical and democratic governments, represented by the King, Lords and Commons; and in which the powers of each are so happily blended that it is impossible for human wisdom to produce any other system containing so many excellencies and so free from imperfections.' He was also impressed by the wide liberty which the common man enjoyed under the Constitution. 'Liberty', he says, 'may be considered as the idol or tutelary deity of the English; and I think the common people here enjoy more freedom and equality than in any other well-regulated government of the world.'

Abu Talib was thus a great admirer of the British Constitution and the British ideal of liberty but their defects did not escape his keen eye. He himself cites an instance of the King's absolute power when Pitt and his colleagues in the Ministry were dismissed even though their popularity was undiminished. He also recognised that the liberty of the subjects and their democratic equality were more apparent than real. Commercial magnates and proprietors of joint-stock firms enjoyed large extra-constitutional powers and Abu Talib frankly admits that 'in political importance, the East India Company ranks next to the House of Commons.' He saw vividly the wide disparity between the rich and the poor and observed that the fiscal policy of the government tended to accentuate the prevailing inequality. The industrialist and the merchant passed on the burden of taxes to the masses who also had to bear the increasing weight of the national debt, for the ruling classes made the debt a source of sure and comfortable income by advancing the loans. Even the equality guaranteed by law was often denied to the poor, for in Abu Talib's words, 'After all this equality is more in appearance than in reality, for the difference between the comforts of the rich and the poor is in England much greater than in India.'

Abu Talib's observations on English society and institutions reveal him as a keen analyst who could not be put off by facile explanations of historical phenomena. He always sought to penetrate behind appearances and discover the forces at work below the surface. This critical acumen is seen perhaps more clearly than anywhere else in his reflections on the influence of sea-power on English history. He refers to the skill and the wisdom of the English in the construction and navigation of their vessels and the discipline of their crew. He points out that it was naval power that enabled the British to defy the combined wrath of the kings of Russia, Prussia, Denmark and Sweden. He is in fact one of the first historians to recognise the importance of naval power in determining the course of events. He observes: 'The great perfection to which the English had brought their navy is doubtless the chief cause of their prosperity and the principal source of all their wealth. By means of their navy they can at all times send their army to invade their enemy's country. If they succeed it is well. If not they can return with little loss. Their neighbours, the French, on the contrary, although they possess an innumerable army of brave troops, cannot injure the English, who are constantly well protected by their floating batteries which suffer not a Frenchman to pass the sea.' Abu Talib did not develop the thesis but it is evidence of his historical genius that more than eighty years before the appearance of Mahan's classical work on the subject, Abu Talib had recognised the influence of sea-power on history. His achievement is the more remarkable as India had rarely paid due attention to the role of the navy.

Abu Talib also noted how the British had utilised science for the purposes of industry and commerce. He saw that it was the introduction of machinery that had led to larger production and the consequent reduction in prices of British goods. He points out that the British used machines for grinding corn, running iron foundries and working on copper and lead. The manufacture of needles astonished Abu Talib but he was even more surprised by the spinning engine. Says Abu Talib, 'By the turning of one large wheel, a hundred others were put in motion which spun at the same time some thousand threads of sufficient fineness to make very good muslin.' He was also impressed by the hydraulic machine for supplying London with water. In addition, the English have 'engines for pressing oil from seeds and others for thrashing and winnowing corn. In short, the English carry their passion for mechanics to such an extent that machineries were introduced into their kitchens and a very complete engine is used even to roast a chicken.' He pointed out, 'Whatever requires strength or numbers is effected by engines. If clearness of sight is wanted, magnifying glasses are at hand. If deep reflection is necessary to combine all the parts whereby to ensure united action, so many aids are derived from the numerous artists employed in the different parts of the work that the union of the whole seems not to require any great exertion of genius.' Abu Talib observed: 'In England, labour is much facilitated by the aid of mechanism, and by its assistance the price of commodities is much reduced. If in their great manufactories they made use of horses, bullocks or men, as in other countries, the prices of their goods would be enormous.' He concluded that this was the reason why 'the English excel the other nations of Europe.' In most of the industries the articles produced by them 'are carried to all parts of the world and sold to great advantage.'

Abu Talib was also impressed by the general level of education and culture among the shopkeepers and tradesmen of London. He observed that they did not differ in dress and manners from noblemen or gentlemen. They are 'so courteous and polite that should the purchasers be ever so troublesome or litigious, they never give a rude or angry answer.' This, according to Abu Talib, was a general feature of English social life. He refers with admiration to the behaviour of a lady whose servant broke a valuable piece of crockery in his presence. The lady did not interrupt her conversation with Abu Talib even once in order to admonish the servant. He also quotes an amusing incident in a shop which made a deep impression on his mind. A customer went into a shop and after spending a whole hour in inspecting various types of cloth finally ordered one shilling worth of a quality which was selling at twenty-five shillings a yard. The shopkeeper instead of expressing annoyance or anger coolly cut out a piece of the size of a shilling and presented it to the gentleman. Abu Talib remarks, 'They then parted, bowing respectfully to each other.'

Abu Talib also comments on the status of women in England and Asia. He held that women in England work harder than in Asia, but according to him this was due to the fact that 'the English legislators and philosophers have wisely determined that the best mode of keeping women out of the way of temptation and their minds from wandering after improper desires is by giving them sufficient employment. Therefore whatever business can be effected without any great exertion of mental abilities or corporal strength is assigned to the women.' After detailing the many restraints and restrictions placed upon women in England, Abu Talib concluded that in spite of the apparent freedom of women in Europe, Asian women enjoyed superior advantages. Nor were French women, in his opinion, better off. After expressing his disapproval of the manner and dress of peasant women in France, Abu Talib remarked that 'the attire of the village girls in India, in comparison with these, is infinitely superior.' In the end, he wrote a special appendix to his travelogue to vindicate the liberties of Asian women. He mentions eight heads under which Asian women, both by law and custom, have greater rights than women in Europe. His account is curious reading today but it is doubtful if Indian women will accept either his analysis or his conclusions.

Abu Talib was greatly impressed by the way in which the British organised charity. He had an abhorrence for the beggars in India and refers with appreciation to the way in which the British maintained poorhouses, hospitals and museums. He admired the public libraries and hospitals in Britain and remarked that 'in these countries, it is common for persons when dying to bequeath an estate or large sums of money to endow hospitals and for other charitable purposes. This custom is truly praiseworthy'.[1]

One could go an adding to the list of his acute observations. We may therefore conclude this section by briefly discussing Abu Talib's analysis of British legal practice. He was impressed by the right which every British subject possessed of being tried by a jury and held that this was a great protection of individual liberty. He however shrewdly observed that 'the judge being a person of great consequence and superior abilities, often impressed the jury with such awe that if he is inclined to pass an unjust sentence, he can in his interpretation of the law and his address to them dictate what they are to do. I have frequently seen the judge reprehend the jury for their decisions and send them back once or twice to reconsider their verdict. If by the above mear^r the judge can bring a few of the jury over to his opinion, he can frighten the rest by threatening to lock them up without food while he and the lawyers retire from the court and refresh themselves for three or four hours. From the above circumstances, it appears to me that the decision in all cases depends more on the judge than on the jury.'

Abu Talib admired English judges as 'men of the strictest honour and probity' and generally 'above all temptations to act unjustly', but says Abu Talib, 'the laws being excessively voluminous and in many instances, either contradictory or obscure, the lawyers whose only income arises from their practice (i.e. the fees they receive from the plaintiff and the defendant) endeavour to delay the decision of the business as much as possible and frequently prevail on the judge to postpone the trial to another year. In this manner, civil cases are often carried on for twenty years to the ruin of both the parties.' Abu Talib also observed with regret that 'in these courts, law very often overruled equity and that a well meaning honest man was frequently made the dupe of an artful knave. Nor could the most righteous judge alter the decision without transgressing the law.' Abu Talib contrasts with this the practice in early Muslim law where 'every man pleaded his own cause: and the *cazis*, being then men of great learning and sanctity, gave their decisions gratuitously.' He recognised that in course of time this system revealed grave defects and he freely admitted that the British practice under which the judges were paid from public funds was a great improvement. Nevertheless, he held that the introduction of the British legal system with all its complexity and ambiguity had led to many serious abuses in India. This he wrote 160 years ago, but his observations about the voluminousness and obscurity of the law and the length of time taken in settling even the simplest of suits holds good to this day.

Abu Talib has also something to say about the way in which the public reacted to procedures in the court. He found in England that many sensible Englishmen so dreaded the thought of appearing in a court of law whether as plaintiff or defendant that they were willing to compromise even unjust claims and preferred to settle cases with their opponents in this manner than to contest them in a court of law. In India, the position was even worse. Says Abu Talib, 'The hardships and inconveniences which witnesses also suffer when summoned to Calcutta are so great that no man in India will now give voluntary evidence in any case. The witnesses are sometimes brought down from the country by a month's journey. They are then detained five or six months in Calcutta. When brought into court, they are kept standing for two or three hours and if puzzled by the various questions and cross-questions of the lawyers and judges, they are then accused of being liars; and obliged to return home at their own expense without any remuneration for their loss of time and trouble.'

Abu Talib was not however a merely destructive critic and suggested a remedy for this state of affairs. He held that so long as judges had been paid by the parties, they had tended to prolong suits and sell justice. When this was changed and judges were paid from public funds, they not only gained in dignity and status but lost the incentive for prolonging suits. Abu Talib recommended 'that the councillors, attorneys, etc., shall be placed on a similar footing and that they shall not receive any fee or bribe from the litigating parties under a severe penalty. In order to defray the expenses of this establishment, either let a small additional tax be levied on the nation at large or a duty of so much per cent be levied on all litigated property. By this plan I am convinced that the number and the length of suits would be much curtailed; the time of the witnesses would be saved, the law would be purified from these imperfections which are now a reproach to it and the courts purged of those petty fogging lawyers who are a disgrace to their professions.'

IV

Masir-i-Talibi is thus not only an interesting but in many ways a most illuminating work. It reveals the author's intellectual acumen and his acute powers of observation, and can be studied with profit by both Asians and Europeans even after a hundred and fifty years. Abu Talib will, however, be remembered primarily for his historical work. I have already mentioned his *History of the Kings of India*. The manuscript is unfortunately lost, but perhaps the substance is retained in the supplementary section of Jonathan Scott's *History of the Deccan*. Scott says that his account of the Golconda kings was based exclusively on *Lubb-ut-Twarikh*. He does not mention the name of the author, but it seems that there is no other work of this name dealing with the subject. It is therefore possible that Scott used Abu Talib's *History of the Indian Kings,* which in all probability formed a section of his more comprehensive *Lubb-ut-Twarikh,* or Essence of History, Abridgment of the Geography and the History of Europe. No manuscript bearing this title has been found, but the author has referred to it in his *Masir-i-Talibi*.

Lubb-ut-Twarikh is most probably an earlier composition than *Lubb-us-Siyar*, but it already indicates the historical approach which was later developed in *Lubb-us-Siyar*. Abu Talib's book was largely based on *A History of Europe* by Scott and though the original work of Scott is lost, there are many references to it in a number of subsequent writings.

Abu Talib's new approach to history is fully seen in his book, *Lubb-us-Siyar wa Jahan Numa*, or the Essence of Biographies and the World Reflecting Mirror, to give the book its full title. True to its name, it seeks to present in a concise form the entire vista of human history. The author tells us that he had consulted many works of history and travels but found among them none that contained a history of the world from his own point of view. He was not able to complete his ambitious project and in fact could not begin even a preliminary sketch for a long time. He was, however, able to compile an abstract giving a synopsis of the fuller work he had in view and bring it out in 1793. In the preface to this synopsis, the author claims that he has abstracted information from thousands of books and tried to make up for the deficiency of the well-known general histories which give no account of Europe and America. He also claims to have utilised European sources for his compilation. He added that if he lived long enough, he intended to enlarge the work, but if he failed to do so, he expressed the hope that someone else would undertake this useful labour.

The synopsis has unfortunately not been translated, but a brief account of its contents helps us to realise the broad canvas on which Abu Talib wished to paint. It is divided into four sections as follows:

Preface

Bab I	Prophets.
Bab II	Early Caliphs, Imams, Umayyads, Abbasids, Ismailis, Prominent Saiyids, Sharifs of Mecca.
Bab III	Sages of Greece and Europe (Galileo & Copernicus and their knowledge of Geography and Astronomy). Sages of Iran and Hindus. Companions of the Prophet and their followers. Muslim Saints, Ulema and poets.
Bab IV	Geography of the World (including a map). Chronology of the Rulers of Iran, Arabia, Byzantium, Egypt, Syria, Spain and Turkistan. Rulers of Europe. Rulers of India.

Lubb-us-Siyar is one of the first works written in India in which there are references to Copernicus and Galileo, to the discovery of America and to the geography as well as the history of Europe. The chronology includes an enumeration of the kings of different countries in Europe and though we may doubt if the book came up to the author's claims, we may agree with Bland who says, 'It is of considerable length and the author seems to have bestowed great pains and attention to its composition. It is particularly interesting as comprising in its general outline a concise description of the countries of Europe and of America and even a sketch of their history. The portion relating to Great Britain is of more extent than that devoted to other European nations. The reigns of each king are separately noted and the origin of the East India Company and its dominion is reviewed in the proper place. The whole is highly curious and though too remote from literary interest in connection with poetry, it is well worthy of at least a partial translation to exhibit the amount of knowledge possessed by its accomplished author on so varied and extensive a field as that of general history and geography and especially on many subjects usually beyond the limits of Asiatic enquiry and means of research.'

V

The genius of Abu Talib as a historian is, however, best seen in the small History of Oudh which he wrote at the request of his friend,

Captain David Richardson. *Tafzihul Ghafilin,* which is a contemporary record of events connected with the administration of Asaf-ud-Daulah, is based on the first-hand knowledge of affairs that the author acquired through his official connection with the Nawab Wazir and the East India Company's agents in Oudh. The original manuscript of the work has been lost, but it survives in an excellent English translation published by Dr. W. Hoey in 1885. In the words of the translator, 'The chief value of this record is that it is a contemporaneous history, and the author was intimately acquainted with all the affairs about which he wrote and was indeed a principal actor in most of them. He is fearless in his disclosures and if he is scathing in the denunciation of the Nawab Wazir and his ministers, he is certainly warm in the defence of his patrons when he considers them unjustly attacked.'

The appeal of Abu Talib's study lies principally in the fact that he is refreshingly free from the obsession with military events, palace intrigues and court cabals which is the besetting sin of eighteenth-century Indo-Muslim historiography. Abu Talib was not unaware of their influence on the course of events, but he recognised that they were themselves often due to deeper economic and political causes. He therefore discusses personalities and their role in history only in the context of the social, economic and political conditions of the country.

Dealing with events up to June 1797, *Tafzihul Ghafilin* is perhaps Abu Talib's last historical work. His earlier essays in *Lubb-ut-Twarikh* and *Lubb-us-Siyar* had helped him to develop his historical methods and we find in this last work evidence of a mature and precise style. He did not live to write his *magnum opus* on the history of the world or a systematic treatise explaining his view of history, but *Tafzihul Ghafilin* makes it abundantly clear that his main concern was with the forces that govern the health of society. In this intimate study of Oudh under the rule of the Wazirs, he discovered with an unerring insight the malaise which was slowly eating into the vitals of the State. He was not misled by the empty pomp of the Lucknow court or the vulgar extravagance of the nobles, courtiers and the public officials. He saw that the luxury of the rich was invariably based on the neglect of ordinary men. The result was discontent among the people at large and dishonesty and corruption among the ruling classes. The oppression of the rich provoked lawlessness among the peasantry and Abu Talib saw clearly the retribution that was awaiting the thoughtless evil-doers.

In speaking of the extravagance of the Wazir and his chief deputy Haider Beg Khan, Abu Talib says: 'The expenditure on the Wazir's pigeon-house, cockpits, sheep-folds, deer park, monkey, snake, scorpion and spider houses is so great that if they were carefully managed, the money would suffice for the maintenance of all the children of the late Nawab and of his women; for three hundred thousand pigeons and fighting cocks are kept, and there are some snakes a pair of which eat a maund of flesh. All things are fondly cared for by the Wazir save men, especially his relatives and old dependents. . . . The prodigality of Haider Beg Khan may be guessed when, after his death, Tikait Rai set down his table expenses at 50 lakhs, and this foolish expenditure was not confined to the Wazir, and Haider Beg or to Mirza Hasan Riza Khan and Tikait Rai, but every one who had anything to do with Government or revenue collection. And this was the case with all their agents and dependents, so that this waste was not confined to them only, but was the general rule in matters of food and clothing, buildings, amusements, and all expenses of both males and females. . . . If they spend lavishly, they must have money. Hence under the pressure of necessity they have resorted to swindling and whole families have been ruined.'

Again, Abu Talib complains: 'The expenditure of the Wazir in buildings alone is 10 lakhs per annum and has continued regularly from the beginning of his rule up to the present day. Each new building that is completed is occupied for two or three days and is left empty ever afterwards. A lamp even is not lighted in it by night, nor is it swept by day. And the wrongs which God's people suffer by this building-mania are many. First, whenever he lays out a building, the residents of the place who for years lived there are ordered by him to leave at once without either money compensation or another house. Second, the Wazir's work-men, on every possible pretext, utilise the houses of the people to furnish bricks, timber and other buildings materials. They ruin the whole family for the sake of fifteen or twenty thousand bricks and pull down the house. Third, the dearness of building materials caused by the hurry and want of method on the part of the officials imposed further hardships on the taxpayer.'

Again, 'In this year Wazir Ali Khan's marriage with the daughter of Ashraf Ali Khan, son of Bunde Ali Khan, took place. The amount of fireworks, illuminations and other vanities displayed was so vast that the details would swell this book. More than 20 lakhs of rupees were squandered.'

It is not surprising that with such extravagance and luxury of the rich, there should be dishonesty and lawlessness at every level of society. Mirza Abu Talib refers to the lack of ordinary sense of justice even in the capital city of the State. In his own words, 'Notwithstanding the immense population and the magnificence of Lucknow, there was not and there is not any recognised jurisdiction of courts of criminal or civil law. All transactions of money-lending are stopped and every one who has the power oppresses someone else. The only punishment meted out to an oppressor is when the sufferer takes his life in his hands and seeks to revenge himself or when some influential man in the city takes him under his wings:

Justice is pushed aside, complaint is vain
Mid all this wrong, alas! what can we gain?

Abu Talib refers to the utter disregard for the feelings and property of the poor in the following terms: 'Another oppression is that which the Wazir's subjects suffer in his two regular tours; for his camp-followers have permission to take grass, *bhusa*, firewood, earthen pots and other such things, and the subjects are so accustomed to oppression that they reckon this tyranny nothing; but these men, on pretence of taking these things, levy as much grain and money as they go along from the fields and houses of the peasantry as keeps them for two or three months on tour and forms a fund for two or three months at Lucknow. Add to this, they burn at night for illuminations the houses of the peasants, which are vacated because of the nearness of the camp; and the consumption of firewood and other supplies already mentioned is so great in the camp that they pull out the pillars of the people's houses and throw down the thatch to get wood for cooking their half seer of flour.'

Abu Talib had no sympathy with the ideas of false charity which looked upon the poor as a means for the gratification of the benevolent propensities of the rich. We have seen that in his travelogue, he referred with appreciation to the British custom of organising public charity. In the present work, he ridicules the astrologers who said that giving of gifts to the poor would avert evil. Says Abu Talib, 'Haider Beg Khan was from the commencement of his career given to distributing money in such ways that the hands, feet and heads of the poor were broken, for he had a thorough belief in the sayings of astrologers. These men used sometimes to weigh him in a balance and got the equal of his weight in silver, copper and clothes, and sometimes they ordered him to distribute coppers to the poor. Sometimes also, when he was himself in fear for any reason, he used to do the same. To this day, one result of Haider Beg's folly is seen in Lucknow surviving as a memento. A number of professional beggars who post themselves at particular places have taken to demand false charity such as he used to give. Hundreds of persons in every street of the city pull the hands and clothes of respectable passers-by so that it is difficult to go along the road. If anything be given, they drag the donor from his vehicle or horse and the strong among them kick and thump the weak and take their share. If nothing is given, they indulge in every abuse that comes to their tongues. Anyone who has been in Lucknow and felt the hands or tongues of these rascals knows that there can be no greater evil than alms-giving of this kind.'

Abu Talib was deeply concerned by the social and political malaise of Oudh and held that its causes were to be found in the top-heaviness of the administration, the economic wastage resulting from ill-conceived, badly planned and badly executed public measures and above all, in the glaring economic disparity between the rulers and the ruled. The activities of the ruling classes showed a chronic apathy to public weal and everything they did accentuated further the distress of the people. With a callous disregard for the common man, 'building materials and carpenters and masons are frequently interdicted to the public. When this happens, the people are so hampered in their urgent requirements that they cannot get bricks to repair their houses for the rains. The servants of the Wazir, nay even all moneyed men . . . follow the example of the Wazir and engage in building mansions and oppressing the poor.' Abu Talib concludes with regret, 'There is no knowing how God's people will obtain release from the wrath of the oppressors.'

The condition of the common man was rendered even more desperate by the system of artificial inflation in which the Government often indulged. These measures were not 'confined to building materials alone but to most commodities such as sugar, firewood, rice and so on.' Even articles of everyday use were subjected to sudden rise in prices several times in the year 'to suit the caprices of the ruling classes'. There seemed to be a perverse pleasure in perpetuating the sufferings of the poor. Mirza Abu Talib comments, 'Although the ice manufacturers have frequently represented to the Nawab that if he would allow them to sell ice they would manufacture an even greater stock for him than they were doing and their expenses would be less, he had refused to allow them. Although he possesses hundreds of gardens in Lucknow and Fyzabad and in the suburbs of both cities and they yield such quantities of fruit and flowers that hundreds of low caste men among his orderlies gather them, and there is still to spare, yet fruits and flowers decay, fall and are thrown away. In the mango season, he attaches all the groves of the residents of Lucknow and Fyzabad and in this way many houses of the poor are plundered by the *piadas* who are appointed to confiscate the produce of the groves. The restriction in the sale of *keora* and roses, and all perfumes is so strict that people import essence of *keora* from Bengal, and the better classes at the marriages of their children make garlands of flowers gathered from the jungles and put them round the necks of their guests, for the sale of flowers is forbidden in the city. Rare fruits are interdicted but such fruits as ground melons, mangoes and so on are barred only during the first fifteen days of their respective seasons.'

Abu Talib pointed out that the rulers of the day were so shortsighted that they did not recognise even their own interests and failed to see that a rich and prosperous country would yield greater revenues. In their anxiety to grind the poor, they thus denied themselves the opportunity of greater wealth. Not only was the sale of fine clothing to the ordinary man banned but nobody could introduce easily a new invention. Says Abu Talib '. . . someone introduced a new invention into Lucknow for calico printing. The Wazir ordered that he should deliver all his outturn to him. One day the Wazir happened to see a specimen of this chintz on some one, and he put the masterprinter on a donkey and had him paraded through the city, although he was a respectable man and the employer of four or five hundred apprentices.' It was in fact difficult for an ordinary citizen to ply his normal trade without continual official interference. To fill his cup of misery, the tax collectors subjected him to constant harassment. Abu Talib says, 'He who is weak cannot get leisure from the annoyance of the Collector to scratch his head. Whatever he can in any way raise the Collector takes from him. Nay more, the Collector has his eyes open to sell his bullocks and agricultural implements.'

Such oppression inevitably led to the impoverishment of the producing classes. There was a fall in production and consequently in public revenue. This led to further exactions which in turn meant further impoverishment. In Abu Talib's own words, 'The cause of the great falling off in the revenue was the thriftlessness of the Rajas who were bent on sensual pleasure. . . Tenants were forced to rely on grazing for their maintenance and abandoned agriculture. Thus a village which a hundred years ago paid a revenue of Rs. 2,000 per year now paid only Rs. 100 and that too when there are 500 tenants' houses in the village.'

There have been some critics of Abu Talib who say that his criticism was reserved only for the Nawab of Oudh. This however is not wholly correct for he has critical things to say of the way in which the British were administering Bengal at the time. He had however no sympathy with those who used the plea of ancestry, nationality or religion to defend the misdeeds of the ruling classes. He says sarcastically, 'Notwithstanding such treatment of his relatives, old acquaintances and of respectable men of every rank, nobles, military men and private citizens and that wasteful expenditure and enormous waste, of which a little has been mentioned in these pages, the Wazir expects that people will yield him allegiance on account of the claims and names of his ancestors, will submit to the tyrannies with perfect complacence, will wink at his evil practices which are harder than death to endure and will not open their lips to complain. If anyone is foolish enough to reproach the Wazir for these action and shun him, he and the place-seekers charge him with sedition, disloyalty and enmity to Musalmans.'

Abu Talib was also disgusted with the Indian attitude which condemns evil but will not oppose it. He complains that even men who recognised the existing evil would not take any action, for they felt 'if one individual attempts to rectify these abuses, what can he effect?' Others said that the native tyrants were bad enough but if the British came, things would be even worse, for 'the English as soon as they get a footing will make the condition of the people here like that of those in Bengal.'

Abu Talib held that the rapid deterioration in the condition of the country was due to the enormous economic cleavage which separated the rulers from the ruled. He regretted that there was no open rebellion against the system but observed that this was due to the 'habitual reconciliation of the people to the customs of India and the support given by the English to the Wazir.' Appeal to religion and class allegiance dulled the sense of grievance and foreign power supplied the prop which averted an immediate collapse of the tottering State. Abu Talib was however convinced that these palliatives could have only a temporary effect. He saw the writing on the wall and his fear that soon the State of Oudh would cease to be was realised within fifty years of his death.

If the lessons which Abu Talib drew from his study of Oudh history were gloomy, the conclusions he drew and the remedies he suggested were revolutionary. He feared that catastrophe could not be avoided unless things changed radically and there was a complete transformation of the social structure. He began on a comparatively modest scale and suggested that first of all the ministers should be properly disciplined and their expenses limited. He was a great admirer of British discipline and recommended that English officers should be appointed to superintend the troops and see that the men were paid regularly every month. He also advised that 'every one—soldier, official or subject—who breaks the new regulations or resists be at once expelled from the country, so that those who remain may pursue their occupations in security, and every evil-doer vanish.'

Abu Talib had become so critical of all existing officials that he recommended their wholesale dismissal. In his own words, 'All the old collectors and subordinates and nearly all the old military officers should be got rid of, for they are puffed up with pride and are given to prodigality and will not discriminate as between benefactors and mischief-makers. It is impossible to correct them.' In fact, he had become so disgusted with the rule of the Wazir that he was at one stage prepared even to tolerate the intervention of the British. He reflected that 'though the prosperity of some persons who are now in the ascendant and rob thousands of others would wane, the prosperity of those thousands would result.' Here, as also in his reflections on the French Revolution, one finds that in spite of all his intellectual acumen and foresight, Abu Talib could not always transcend the aristocratic attitudes that he had imbibed through heritage and training.

In the end he however realised that the impending crisis could be averted only by eliminating the functionless ruling class and giving the common man his rightful place in the body politic. He held that 'the interest of the tenantry lies in security for the poor and reducing the strong'. In order to ensure that the new order was served honestly and faithfully, 'the middle classes and the poor must be brought forward and appointed to offices. They will act according to orders and disinterestedly in the hope of gaining position and increased credit.' Again, Abu Talib says: 'Honest collectors should be selected from the middle and poorer classes and should have no power to change the revenue assessment.'

VI

More than fifty years before Marx, Mirza Abu Talib asserted that economic disparity between the ruling classes and the masses not only militates against material development but also impedes cultural progress. The idle rich were too self-complacent to feel the urge for any extension of their intellectual horizon. The common people were too absorbed in the bare struggle for existence to have the energy or time for the pursuit of knowledge. He was drawn towards this conclusion by his study of conditions in Oudh, but it was only after his travels in Europe that he was confirmed in his belief. Perhaps the clearest statement of his view is found in the *Masir-i-Talibi* when he says, 'The great and the rich intoxicated with pride and luxury and puffed up with the vanity of their possession[s] consider universal science as already comprehended in the circle of their own scanty acquirements and limited knowledge, while the poor and the common people from their want of leisure and overpowered by the difficulty of procuring a livelihood, have no time to attend to their personal concerns, much less to form desires for the acquirement of information on new discoveries and inventions, although such a passion has been implanted by nature in every human breast as an honour and an ornament to the species.'

Although Abu Talib was aware of the role of economic factors in the development of history, he was no dogmatic believer in the economic interpretation of history. In view of the vicissitudes of his life, he did not have the opportunity to arrange his ideas in a systematic way and develop a definite philosophy of man. It is also likely that his wide experience of life made him feel that rigid laws could not be formulated in matters that concern human affairs. He was essentially a pragmatist, but he has scattered among his writings shrewd observations on men and affairs. It would be going too far to claim that he aimed at the formulation of a systematic social philosophy, but his observations, particularly on the decay of societies and institutions, show his keen awareness of the importance of economic factors. Thus, in describing the causes of the downfall of the *ancien regime* in France, he remarks: 'Previous to the late

Revolution, the French Government spent immense sums on public buildings, gardens and illuminations. The nobles lived in a superb style, while the lower classes were reduced to the most abject poverty. Their patience was finally exhausted and they readily joined the leaders of faction and drove their inconsiderate domineering masters out.'

As a result of his tours in Europe, he also drew the following general conclusion: 'Luxury and prodigality have caused the ruin of more governments than was ever effected by an invading enemy. They generate envy, discord and animosity and render the people desirous of a change. To these vices may be ascribed the subversion of the Roman Empire in Europe and the annihilation of the Mughal government in India.'

Preoccupation with these ideas led Abu Talib to attempt an economic interpretation of the phenomenal success of the nomadic races in their conflict with sedentary civilisations. Referring to the Arabs and the Tartars, he says: 'These nations acquired their extensive conquests, not by superiority of their arms which were merely bows and arrows and swords; no, it was from the paucity of their wants. Their chiefs were content with the fare of their soldiers and their personal expenses were a mere trifle. Thus, when they took possession of an enemy's country, they ever found the current revenue of it more than requisite for their simple but effective form of government, and instead of raising the taxes on their new subjects, they frequently alleviated one half of their burden. The approach of their armies, therefore, instead of being dreaded, was wished for by the neighbouring people, and every facility given to their conquests. To this alone must be ascribed the rapidity with which they overran a great part of the globe in so short a period.'

It is thus not unfair to claim that Abu Talib anticipated by almost half a century some of the theories of Marx without however claiming for them the rigidity and infallibility which have converted Marxism into a dogma rather than a scientific approach. Similarly, Abu Talib foresaw almost a century before Mahan the importance of sea-power on the course of human history. With his intellectual background and his singular freedom from many of the prejudices of his class and times, it was not surprising that he should feel dissatisfied with all existing books on history and plan to write a history of the world based on his own original approach. Though he did prepare an abstract giving a synopsis of the work he had in view, it will always be a matter of regret that he was not able to complete his task and present us with the first history of the world based on economic and sociological analysis.

NOTE

1. The author proceed to discuss Abu Talib's analysis of British legal practice see Humayun Kabir, 'Mirza Abu Talib Khan', The Russell Lecture, 1961, pp. 47-80.

CHAPTER 3

Autobiography of Lutfullah

LUTFULLAH

Lutfullah belonged to a distinguished Sufi family of Malwa. But his family's fortunes dwindled to such an extent that 'we sold all we had, and sometimes starved for a day or two, after which we obtained some food through our own hard labour'. The family travelled to Baroda, Ujjain, Gwalior, and Agra until it reached Delhi in early 1817. Soon thereafter, Lutfullah found odd jobs during his travels. He developed his reputation as a teacher of Arabic, Persian, and some Indian languages, notably Marathi. In March 1844, he accompanied Mir Jafar Ali Khan, son-in-law of the nawab of Surat, to England. His *Autobiography*, acclaimed in England, appeared in 1854 and is dedicated to Colonel W.H. Sykes. It was later edited by Edward B. Eastwick and published in London, in 1857. The following excerpts are from his *Autobiography*.

Land at Southampton.—London.—Kind friends.—Mr. Latham.—Mr. Pulsford.—The sights of London.—The Opera.—Mr. Baring.—Lord Ripon.—Return to India.

On the morning of the 14th of May, at seven o'clock, we landed near the Custom House, whence our baggage passed without the difficulty and loss of time customary in India, and we put up in a very nice inn, called the Union Hotel, which commanded a view of both the sea and the town. Our party, it appears, was looked upon by the curious natives as one of the seven wonders of the world. Luckily for myself, I had purchased a Turkish dress at Cairo, and thereby found myself safe from being stared at. As for my companions, they, except Mir Jafir, were impatient to go to the bazar; and,

**Autobiography of Lutfullah, Mohamedan Gentleman; and His Transactions with his Fellow-Creatures,* edited by Edward B. Eastwick, London, 1857, pp. 403-35.

immediately after breakfast, they proceeded to the market places in their simple Indian dresses, where they were not only gazed at by all with curiosity but followed by a crowd. Being annoyed at this, they returned home without being able to buy anything, and with a mob at their heels. Before they entered the door of the hotel, they turned right about face, to see their unwelcome audience, and a shout of 'Hurrah!' resounded from all directions. 'Over-curious white devils,' exclaimed our doctor, Badru'd-din, very angrily to me; 'they have no respect for caste or age: I have a great mind to pelt stones at them.' —'Don't you do so, Hakim Sahib,' said I to the old doctor, 'or you will bring evil on yourself and the hotel: these people don't fear any one. It is true, they are over curious, but, after all, they have done you no harm: let, therefore, well alone.'

On the morning of the 15th, we proceeded by rail to London. Seating ourselves in these fairy vans, we proceeded on most comfortably in this unfatiguing journey. Beautiful, but momentary were the views of the country, green and watered with silvery brooks; and magnificent were the sights of the villages, towns, and parishes that presented themselves to our eyes during our progress. The objects appeared and disappeared successively in most delightful forms, until we reached our destination. The doors of the carriage then being opened, we alighted in a very spacious yard, all paved with black stones.

In a few minutes, two nice carriages, drawn by horses of gigantic make and power, being brought near, we got up into them and drove into the far-famed City of London. Street after street and square after square that we passed through for about three quarters of an hour, were all paved, clean and regular, thronged with the busy inhabitants of both sexes, almost all the females good looking, and the males well made and active. Palaces of nobles and dukes are distinguished by their large porticos and superior construction. In one of them I saw two well-dressed men with ashes sprinkled over their heads, and thereby concluding that some death might have occurred in the house, I told Mr. Scott, who sat by me, that a mournful event might have been the cause of the dust on their heads; but the young man laughed at my beard, and said it was the old custom still preserved by some of powdering their hair. Upon the whole, one might imagine that this vast city, whose population is no less than twenty lakhs of inhabitants, contained the riches of the whole world. Surrounded by such wonders and curiosities, we travelled on to a quarter termed Brook Street, and alighted at a magnificent house, called Mivart's Hotel.

Supplied with all kinds of luxuries suitable to princes, we lived in this inn for three days, and then our chief, being frightened at the enormous charges of about two hundred rupees per diem, engaged a private lodging, No. 7, Sloane Street.

Here we settled after our long voyage from the middle of the globe to the end of the world, where the sun appears, far to the south, as weak as the moon, and the polar star nearly vertical; where the country all over is fertile, and the people ingenious, civil, and active; where the language, customs, and manners are entirely different from our own; where, in fine, the destiny of our sweet native land lies in the hand of some twenty-five great men. It cannot be, I am sure, without the will of that one Supreme Being that this small island, which seems on the globe like a mole on the body of a man, should command the greater part of the world, and keep the rest in awe.

On the 16th I had the pleasure of seeing my old friend and patron, Captain Eastwick, after three years and a half, and he took me along with him to his own house.

We passed a week in quietude at home, I mean my chief and his other attendants; as for myself, I had no rest, even when at home, having the onerous task of acting as secretary and interpreter to all. None of them knowing the language of the country, I was required to be the medium of their business, barters and negociations [*sic*], with the natives. During this time I had the pleasure of gaining the acquaintance of two gentlemen of high station in life, namely, Alfred Latham and R. Pulsford, Esquires, the first a great merchant, and the second a member of Parliament; and, through the kindness of these two good gentlemen, I had the satisfaction of obtaining much information, and seeing many places free of charge.

On the 24th we were taken by our kind friends to see some of the famous places in the town. The first object that engaged our attention were the enormous bridges in the city, especially the iron bridge, and the swinging bridge. It astonished us greatly to see large masses of cast iron regularly fixed and nicely cemented together in these useful fabrics. The country, we felt convinced, must have some inexhaustible mines of this metal, which is so necessary for man; for, besides these bridges, iron appears to be used very profusely. No house seemed to be without iron railings, iron bars, and some houses are even roofed with iron, and some gardens hedged with iron bars. After about half an hour's drive here and there, we were conducted to St. Paul's Cathedral, an edifice that, in my opinion, has not its equal in the world.

What I dislike most was the multitude of statues and images, all of them scientifically sculptured it is true. I know they are not worshipped, according to the Protestant tenet: but a temple dedicated to sacred purposes, whether humble or majestic, ought to be plain, so as not to withdraw the attention of the congregation from the sermons and preachings. After seeing this grand cathedral, we proceeded on to a subterraneous passage called the Thames Tunnel.

On the 25th our kind friends, Mr. and Mrs. Latham, invited us to the Italian opera. In the evening, at about eight o'clock, we repaired to this house of entertainment, and found it to be a large palace of substantial construction, erected upon rows of pillars of cast iron. The interior is built up in rich and splendid style. Five tiers of small rooms, called the boxes, for the spectators to sit in, wide enough to hold four or five persons in each, are built up one above another, running in semicircular lines, one end of which begins from one corner of the stage hall, and ends at the other. The boxes and the chairs therein are lined and cushioned with rich demask. The seats of Her Majesty and the royal family are to the right side of the stage. Our seat was just opposite to the stage, in the same line with the royal seats. We sat comfortably for about half an hour, looking at the grandeur of the place, and remarking upon the convenience of the gas lights, which brightened or dimmed at pleasure. Hundreds of lamps at one time were reduced to the dimness of night, nearly depriving the vision of its free exercise, and at another they were made at once to shine as bright as daylight. At half-past eight the curtain was pulled up, and two very handsome ladies, very indecently dressed, and an old man, representing their father, appeared on the stage. They sang, I fancy, some historical ballad, in conjunction with the instrumental music, and danced very expertly. Whilst the females whirled round in their dancing, their short gowns flew up to the forbidden height. Tantalizing the assembly it appears was their principal aim by such a violation of decorum. We enjoyed the music well, but could not understand a word of what was said.

Having gained acquaintance with a number of respectable inhabitants and great men here, we were almost every evening invited to partake of their hospitable entertainments, and passed our evening hours delightfully in the enjoyment of their good society. As for myself alone, when I had no invitation to accompany my chief, I proceeded to the theatres, generally to the Haymarket Theatre and the Lyceum, sometimes alone, and sometimes in company with my friend and pupil, Captain T. Postans, whom chance had brought here with his amiable and learned wife.

On the 27th I dined and passed a happy evening with Captain and Mrs. Eastwick, who had invited a party of their friends and relatives to meet us. On the 28th, having had an invitation to the fancy ball house, we proceeded thither in the evening, and were highly gratified by seeing persons dressed in various costumes of different countries. One gentleman in Persian dress actually deceived us, as he passed by; not only his dress, but his manners, too, appearing to us those of a Mughal. My chief's brother-in-law accosted him, and after formal salutation in Persian, asked him how he did, and how long since he had left Shiraz? But the man, instead of answering him in that language, smiled and spoke in English, which betrayed him to be an Englishman wearing a false beard, better than a true one in every respect.

On the 30th I accompanied my chief to the East India House in Leadenhall Street. They call it a house, but it is a palace, containing a great number of apartments and halls, all well furnished. It is the place where the destiny of my sweet native land lies in the hands of twenty-four men, called the Honorable Directors of the Honorable East India Company, who are the principal movers of the string of the machine of Government in India. On our arrival, we were conducted by two state ushers to a room in the middle of the palace, where we found the chairman, with his deputy next to him, sitting on their chairs. The chairman's name was Captain John Shepherd, and that of his deputy, Sir Henry Willock. Both of them appeared to be grave and intelligent persons; the latter spoke Persian well. By these gentlemen we were received politely. The conversation first began in Persian with Sir Henry Willock, who, finding it somewhat irksome to explain our meaning every now and then to the chairman, let down the burden of interpreting on me; so I went on partly explaining the ideas of my young chief and partly coining some out of my own head, whatever I thought expedient to serve the interest of my client. The result of the conference gathered from the remarks of these two great men was, that my chief's coming to this country to obtain justice was an imprudent act, as he might have obtained it in his own country by simply writing to them, without undergoing the hardships of a long voyage and incurring heavy expenses. Little did they know that a despotic stroke of the pen of Lord Ellenborough, their own Governor General in India, deprived my chief of his rights, and so compelled him to proceed to England to seek for justice.

After about half an hour's conversation we took our leave of these great men, who are the fountainhead of all the affairs of India. We were then, by a kind friend, taken up stairs, where we saw the Honorable Company's museum, which is a great collection of rarities from all parts of the world, and had the honor of being introduced to three men of learning, viz., John Shakespear, the author of the Hindustani Dictionary, Professor Wilson, the first-rate oriental scholar, and Colonel W.H. Sykes. Knowing the first named gentleman to be the author of a book in our language, I addressed to him a very complimentary long sentence in my own language. But, alas! I found that he could not understand me, nor could he utter a word in that language in which he had composed several very useful books. There is no doubt but the second gentleman, the professor, was a learned man, as his conversation with us demonstrated his high acquirements at once. The third gentleman, we were informed, was one of the directors, as well as a member of the Royal Asiatic society. He was a tall, thin, and handsome looking man, in appearance more like a noble Arab than an Englishman. His previous long residence in India, it appears, had made him quite conversant with our manners, languages, and feelings. So this accidental interview with him produced a genial delight in our hearts, and his civility, complaisance, and kindness, attracted our minds at once to seek for his friendship. During my stay in London, I had often the honor of seeing him, and conversing with him; and he was always particularly kind towards me. I found him to be a man of sublime mind, endowed with high attainments, considerable ability, and acute understanding.

This evening, Mr. Latham kindly took me to the Royal Institution. On my arrival, I was introduced to three or four noblemen, whose names I have quite forgotten; but they treated me like their own brother, made me sit near, and explained to me what I could not understand. The fact is, that in England you will find those that are highest in rank are the politest in society. The lecture was ably delivered on anatomy—which has been a favourite study of mine for many years past—by professor Faraday; and I declare, what I learnt in hearing this one lecture I could not have acquired in one years' hard labor with my books. Mr. Latham further was so good as to obtain permission for me to be admitted whenever I liked, free of charge. Besides, he kindly promised to speak to the Superintendents of the St. George's Hospital, and the College of Surgeons, who would kindly send for me whenever a dissection might take place in those institutions, most beneficial to mankind.

On the 1st June, we were introduced to a nobleman, by name Colonel T. Wood, and met with a kind reception at his house, from himself, his wife—a lady of high rank—and his two daughters, exquisite in beauty, and adorned with the accomplishments obtained from high education. After this, we paid another visit to the East India House; and were taken thence by Mr. Pulsford to the British Museum and the Zoological Gardens, with which we were highly delighted.

On the 2nd, it being Sunday, the whole city appeared to be in a very dreary and dull state. No shop was open, and no carriages, cabs, or omnibuses were to be seen running to and fro as usual. But all the inhabitants were richly and neatly dressed within doors. Our English servants, too, having already performed last night what was required of them to-day, dressed themselves very smartly, and went away to the place of their worship. Sunday is called the Sabbath, and it is scrupulously held sacred just the same as Friday with us, and Saturday with the Jews; though the word Sabbath, both in Hebrew and Arabic signifies Saturday, and not Sunday. This being not a day of business, we took a long drive to the two places called Highgate and Hampstead, and being gratified with the fresh air and scenery of the town and the country, returned home in the evening.

On the morning of the 3rd we paid our visit to a learned man, by name Dr. Bowring, and derived much benefit concerning our business by conversing with this able man. In the afternoon we visited the House of Lords, and the Parliament, and heard the question of the duty on sugar most ably discussed.

On the 4th I received an invitation to visit the St. George's Hospital, through the recommendation of Mr. Latham, where I was received with great attention and kindness by Dr. Culter and Mr. Prescott Hewett, and was kindly taken by the latter along with himself on going round to see all the patients in the hospital, and then was allowed to participate in the fresh dissection of a subject expired only two days before. Here I became convinced that a great part of what I had studied in 'Galen's Anatomy' in Persian and Arabic was founded upon fancy and conjecture, and that it was impossible for anybody to acquire a thorough knowledge of this most useful study for mankind, without the practical course of dissection.

On the morning of the 5th, we proceeded to see the Ascot races, a few miles from town. We beheld a great concourse of people assembled to see what horse would win, and what horse would lose. Almost all the spectators, I am informed, lay wagers among themselves; and these races are to be the cause of gain and loss of large sums of money amongst the inhabitants. The English racers are the best animals I have ever seen. We cared but little for the amusement, but gained a grand object by taking the trouble of coming to this place; that is, we were blessed with a near sight of our gracious Sovereign, and her husband the Prince, to whom we made our profound bows, which were very politely returned by her Majesty and her illustrious Consort. It appears that our dresses, our faces, and our obeisance, without taking off the turbans, attracted the attention of the Royal pair, and of the nobility in their cavalcade; but it was all without the vulgar curiosity of common people. Those who are crowned with greatness by the grace of the almighty, their minds are also endowed with greatness.

On the 7th we paid a visit to the Institution-house of the Civil Engineers, and had the pleasure of an interview with Mr. Walker, the President, and Mr. C. Manby, the Secretary of the Institution, both men of great ability.

In the evening of the 8th, having been invited, we proceeded to the Asiatic Society, and had the pleasure of hearing a very able lecture on geology, delivered by Dr. Falconer. After which, Lord Auckland, our former Governor-General, made a speech which we could not understand, as his lordship used a language too high for a foreigner to follow him; so this speech, acting as a narcotic dose upon our brain, we conversed with other lords and nobles that happened to be near us.

On the 9th, it being Sunday, we took another drive to the village of Richmond, about seven miles from the town, with an English friend.

On the 10th, we attended the meeting held at the Society for the Encouragement of Arts, Manufactures, and Commerce. The assembly was presided over by Prince Albert himself. We had the honor of getting seats next to the Duke of Sutherland, and His Grace conversed with me in a very polite and friendly manner, whenever his attention was not required to the meeting. On the arrival of the noble President, all present rose up to pay him their respects; and we also made obeisances in our own Asiatic manner; and the Prince, returning his compliments to all, very gracefully took his seat on the high chair placed in the middle. The artificers and manufacturers then, one by one, presented their patent articles to the Prince, and described them minutely. The things presented met with the approbation of the President and members, and the makers received their applause, and subsequently, perhaps, some reward in money too. After this, we went down stairs to inspect a large collection of the specimens of various kinds of articles, formerly patented; and, in going our round again, we had the honor to meet the Prince, to whom we made our profound bows; and His Royal Highness very gracefully addressed my chief, asking him the usual first question of every Englishman, 'How do you like this country?' The answer given through me was, that we liked it much. The next question was, 'What did we admire most in England?' I boldly, but respectfully, answered, on the part of my chief, that the civility of the people of high rank and station was the thing most admirable to us; which answer, producing a slight smile on the Royal face, His Highness walked on. Thus ended our accidental interview with a Prince whom fortune has aided to ascend the summit of the highest authority in the world.

In the afternoon we saw the Chinese Exhibition; and, at night, proceeded to another fancy ball, which we found superior to the former.

Not being fully satisfied with our former visit to the British Museum, on the 11th we repaired to that place again, and had the satisfaction of seeing what remained unseen in our previous visit. We then proceeded to see Westminster Abbey, and found it to be a lofty edifice of great beauty and splendor, finished in the ancient Gothic style. It is said to have been built by Henry III, one of the former Kings of England, in 1221 AC. The pavement of the choir of this sacred place attracted our attention first, being a rich mosaic of innumerable pieces of jasper, porphyry, alabaster, lapis lazuli, and serpentine marbles, all varying in size, and skilfully arranged. The portico, termed Solomon's gate, leading into the northern cross, presents a magnificent view to the observer. This sacred place, too, is not destitute of the images of the great men of England, but they are not so numerous as at St. Paul's. The abbot, a very polite young man, of great ability and talent, took us to the west door, whence we had a most beautiful view of the inner body of the convent, which impressed us with awe, caused by the loftiness of the roof and the range of columns by which the whole edifice is supported. The double ranges of the colored glass windows of the two upper galleries, based upon the arcade of the aforesaid pillars, freely admitted beams of light to the whole Abbey without glare. After going through all the convent, the abbot took us to a large hall, where coronations of the Kings of this land take place. The great chair upon which they are seated, seems to be a very old-fashioned one; and we could not leave the hall without touching this high chair, the seat of empire. We then were taken by the good abbot to his own residence, near the Abbey, and each of us was treated with the best of beverages, a glass of water. After this, having conversed with our host for a while on the subject of his cross, and our crescent of the ancient time, my chief went home and I was taken by Captain Postans, to visit a great man, the Honorable W.B. Baring, Secretary to the Board of Control.

On going to the house, we were kindly received by the Secretary, a young man of about thirty. He put several questions to me regarding the Government in India, and I answered them according to my humble opinion, of course in favor of my own country, which answers seemed not to agree with the spirit of our host. My friend, Captain Postans, talked with him for a while, and we took our leave.

On the 14th, we went to an evening party at Lord Ashley's. His lordship and his beautiful lady received us with great courtesy. Here we had the pleasure of being introduced to Viscount Jocelyn and his wife, the loveliest of English beauties. After a little while I had the honor of playing at chess with this nymph of Paradise. I played two games with her, and allowed myself to be beaten both times to please her.

On the 19th I attended the Court of Proprietors, assembled in the India House, and had the satisfaction of hearing an able speech from Mr. Sullivan, tending to the welfare of both the rulers and the ruled of India.

On the 25th, we had the honor of paying our visit to Lord Ripon, President of the Board of Control. This Minister received us with the courtesy natural to the nobility of England; but, feeling his pulse with regard to our business, we found his lordship to be a very stiff and different man altogether.

On the 27th, we went to an evening party at Major Jervis's house in the company of several beauties and great men, amongst whom I found Colonel Miles, the same Arabic scholar whom I had the pleasure of seeing at Vira, twenty-four years before. I told him there was a great difference between the two places of our meeting; and he remarked, that the difference was not only in places, but in time. I paid him another visit at his own house, which he never returned, thinking, perhaps, that he was still in India, and not in the land of freedom where all are equal.

On the 28th we proceeded to Regent's Park to see a wonderful place called the Diorama. On our arrival at this place of incantation, we were conducted by the keeper into a room as dark as an infidel's heart, and were kindly seated upon chairs. I say kindly, for having placed ourselves at his disposal, he might have maltreated us in this dungeon with impunity if he liked. In the meantime our sense of hearing was gratified with distant music, and then a beautiful scene of a frosty morning gradually presented itself to our deceived vision, in which we saw a rough clownish vegetable vendor at the river side, having landed his large parcels of cargo in a tremendous heap, himself shrivelled with the weather, sitting half asleep in his boat, and his wife and a child sleeping on the bundles. The motion of the water of the river was nature itself, and by the side of the stream there appeared a magnificent palace, whose inmates were engaged in various employments. In the meantime the sun shone brilliantly, and extended his rays all over: and then the evening came on, the scene changed, so much so, that the vegetable seller was metamorphosed into a pretty woman, the stars became visible, and the moon rose, casting her serene light over the scene. The palace, too, appeared illuminated with lamps and chandeliers. And the scene then gradually vanished, and the first darkness again prevailed, in which the distant music once more allured our attention. After a little while, the light of morning again began to appear, and in about one minute the interior of a grand church presented itself to our view, first vacant, but in another minute filled with the congregation. The morning then turned to day, and the day, in a few minutes, into evening, and then night came on, and then to our great delight we were helped out by the keeper from this house of false magic. The secret of this place was that the house was partly blocked up and partly orificed with windows, turning on a pivot, and the windowed part coming in contact with perspective paintings, placed behind large magnifying glasses, formed this optical deception. But how the water moved, how the sun, the moon, and the stars appeared and disappeared, how the objects were transformed and the times changed, was still beyond my comprehension. Thus, half satisfied and half puzzled, we returned home. Some of my companions would have the house to be under the power of evil spirits.

On the 29th I received permission to visit the College of Surgeons in Lincoln's Inn Fields, and met with a kind reception from the superintendant [*sic*], Professor Owen, who gave instructions to his assistants to show me all that I should like to see, and describe everything in full. I walked round the several stories of the house, and inspected human bodies, both whole and in parts, arranged in regular order for the benefit of the students, who, by this help can easily, in a short time, ascend the summit of the science of anatomy in both theory and practice.

On the 1st of July we paid a visit to the National Gallery. From this place we proceeded to a theatre where Herr Dobler, a juggler, exhibited his arts. We admired very highly his performances, in making an automaton shoot at the mark with its gun, in producing pigeons from dry fish, destroying watches, burning handkerchiefs and then producing them safe, and similar tricks. But, after all, our Indian jugglers are superior to these Europeans. In the first place, the latter are furnished with all suitable materials for their performance, with the advantage of the stage-house, which can be darkened or lightened at pleasure; whereas the poor Indian juggler stands in an open plain before the public, and performs such tricks as giving his snake to his mongoose, who devours it before all, the animal's mouth being seen stained with blood, and then the man pulls out the reptile, all alive, from the tail of the mongoose. An Indian juggler stabs his own child and cuts the throat of his wife before your eyes; you see the blood issuing from the wounds, and then you find that all is sleight of hand. I myself once contracted a friendship with a Brahman juggler, by name Lalbhatt, who pretended to have had a divine inspiration from his goddess, performed such tricks as in former ages would have surely been taken for miracles. Once I took my two European friends, Dr. J. Patch and Dr. W. Leggett, to the place where this wonderful man sojourned, at Surat. The two doctors were greatly astonished to see the man clapping his hands, and producing a quantity of cardamom and betel nuts; asking one of my native friends to hold fast his own emerald ring in his hand, which in two or three minutes vanished from his hand, and was found upon the lower dress of Dr. Leggett; and similar wonders.

The first week of July passed pleasantly in comparative idleness. In the afternoons I took a walk to Kensington Gardens, not far from our quarters, where I sat peacefully for an hour or two, looking at the beauties of nature.

On the 10th I accompanied my chief to the Polytechnic Institution, Regent Street. Among other things the diving bell amused us much. I undertook to descend into the water by this extraordinary vessel, while my chief and companions would not only not venture to descend, but dissuaded me very strongly from undertaking the trial, telling me that it was an act of great imprudence to endanger life in such useless sport. Turning a deaf ear to such remonstrances, I hastened to the brink of the water, and pronouncing my Bismillah (in the name of the most merciful name of Allah) I got into the bell with four Englishmen. Upon our entering, we found a commodious seat, and then the bell being let down into the deep, we felt a queer compressing sensation in our ears, but that was all the inconvenience we experienced. We saw a patch of the water on one side, where the bell was left open near our feet; but the vacuum of the vessel being filled up with the air, with which we were constantly supplied by means of a communicating tube between the inner part of the bell and the outward atmosphere, prevented the water from rushing in. On reaching the bottom we saw the pebbles and gravel, and then were pulled out again from the dangerous deep to the open air of the world.

On the 11th, we proceeded to the Court of Justice of this city; and, on our arrival, were received with kindness by the Lord Chancellor, and were requested to take our seat near the high chair of his lordship, on the right side of the court. His lordship, perhaps being hard of hearing, gave me, as interpreter, a chair at his elbow, and my chief sat at a little distance. The case before his lordship at the time was that of an Indo-European, Colonel Dyce Sombre, an unlucky man, who had lost his large fortune by falling in love and entering into a marriage contract with an English lady of rank. After a little conversation, not wishing to take up his lordship's valuable time, we took our leave of the Court, and proceeded to return a visit to another nobleman. Then, in company with our shipmate and very obliging friend, Colonel Stratton, of the Madras army, we waited on prince Soltikoff, a young man of very high talent and great ability. He showed us a portfolio containing beautiful drawings of cities, castles, and vegetable productions of various countries in Asia, worked by himself, which showed great knowledge of drawing. Upon the whole, he was an amiable, fine-looking man, not in the least elated with the pride of birth.

The next day I was ordered by my chief to wait again upon the Russian Prince, and invite him, on his part, to Astley's Theatre, where he had engaged a box. I proceeded forthwith to execute my orders, and delivered over the message to the Prince, who accepted the invitation for the night. There was a tall, well made, and very handsome young Englishman in the room at this time, who seemed to take interest in my conversation with His Highness; and the Prince, observing this, introduced me to him, pronouncing my name to him and his name—Lord John Elphinstone, the late Governor of Madras—to me. I was glad to make acquaintance with this nobleman, as my little conversations with him clearly showed that his cultivated mind corresponded with his outward appearance.

In the evening, the Prince having arrived in time, we proceeded to Astley's Theatre, and the performances that we saw there were most admirable. The horses of this theatre understood man's language and music, for they turned and returned, ran and stopped, at the words of command and notes of the music. Upon one horse, whilst cantering, a very pretty young damsel, with a smiling countenance, jumped from the ground and stood upon the saddle, urging the animal to speed. In the meantime, one of the performers threw an ivory ball at her, which she caught with alacrity, and playfully tossed it up and caught it repeatedly, as if the atmosphere was under her command and placed it in her hand quite safe whenever she threw it up. This was not all; but, in every turn, she caught an additional ball from the performer, and went on tossing it up, until she had received seven; and all she tossed up and caught invariably in both hands with wonderful dexterity. Every one of the seven balls appeared continually to be in motion at the miraculous touch of her hand; and the horse ran its rounds as fast as possible, whilst the fairy stood upon it, with her smiling lovely countenance, unshaken. After this, the warfare and the political affairs of China were acted upon the stage; and all ended in a laughable farce.

On the 17th, having heard of a wonderful dwarf's arrival from the country, we went to see him at his lodging, and found him to be but 16lbs. in weight, and 28 inches in stature, aged thirteen years. He was free from all the dwarfish deformities, such as a curve in the calf bones or vertebrae, or a lump upon the back, etc. He was called the General Tom Thumb; and, by receiving rational answers to our questions from him, we found his reason to be quite sound. He was dressed in a military uniform, with a cocked hat upon his head and a small sword buckled to his side, which gave him a most ludicrous appearance and excited the laughter of his visitors, especially when he sang love songs and danced with a girl, somewhat bigger than himself, in a very lively manner.

On the 24th, being invited to spend the day with Mr. A. Latham at his country house in the suburbs of Windsor, we proceeded thither by the first train early in the morning, and reached the famous Windsor, 22 miles west of London, in something less than an hour. The town is well populated, and situated on a pleasant site by the River Thames. Our good host having obtained permission, we entered the magnificent castle, and had the satisfaction of seeing the palace inside, and the ancient church. We then proceeded to Mr. Latham's house, and passed a very happy day under his hospitable roof.

On the 31st we were invited by our friend, R. Pulsford, Esq., to take a whitebait dinner with him at Greenwich, so we proceeded thither at noon in his company on board one of the small steamers running to and fro on the River Thames, and arrived in about half an hour. We put up in a nice inn at the river side, and partook of our friend's hospitality. The town of Greenwich is situated at the bank of the river, five miles east of London, and is very populous. It is noted for its magnificent hospital for decayed seamen, its beautiful park, and for its astronomical observatory on the summit of a hill, whence all the English seamen reckon their first meridian of longitude.

The beginning of the month of August passed in business until the 14th, when, whilst walking in the bazar, I was informed of the arrival of some Americans in the Egyptian Hall. I went in, and, having paid a piece of silver as a fee to the owner, I saw my fellow creatures, nine in number, in their uncivilized rude state, dressed in skins, feathers and straws, made up and interwoven by themselves. Their complexion was copper-colored, their appearance wild, their body proportionate, excepting the arms, which were too slender.

They spoke a jargon, in sound resembling Marathi, and a young Englishman interpreted their ideas, which were simple and chaste in their nature. They painted their foreheads and bodies somewhat like the Hindus. This day I received a handsome present of a valuable telescope from R. Pulsford, Esq., as a token of friendship, which I very reluctantly accepted. I prize the keepsake, however, very highly, it being from a gentleman who took much interest in the welfare of my native land and myself.

On the 26th the news of the birth of a prince to our gracious Sovereign at Windsor having been telegraphed, I was, according to our Asiatic customs, ordered by my chief to carry a letter of congratulation to the Castle. So again I proceeded to Windsor, delivered my letter to the secretary, and, receiving his reply, returned home in the afternoon.

On the 27th, having obtained a letter of introduction to Lord Bloomfield, commanding at Woolwich, we proceeded thither early in the morning, accompanied by Captain T. Postans. We sent the letter to the great man, and were informed that we would be received in the afternoon at his lordship's residence. In the meantime, an officer was deputed to remain in attendance upon us, and to show us over the different departments. So, by the kindness of this officer, we had the satisfaction of seeing the instruments of the British wealth; and the use of them was explained most minutely to us. It was Sir Charles Forbes who procured us this attention at Woolwich; and, from the time of our arrival, we were helped through difficulties in a most friendly manner by this good baronet, who was one of the staunch patrons of India.

Now, my chief having received answers to his petitions from the Court of Directors, and, in the beginning of September, having obtained assurance from the Chairman that his business would be satisfactorily settled in India, we had nothing to detain us in England, except the gratification of the pleasures of my young chief; upon whom, with much difficulty, I prevailed to leave this city of enchantments as soon as possible, and our passage was taken in the mail steamer that was to leave the shores of England, on the third proximo. So we had one whole month, free from the burthen of business, to bid farewell to our friends, and to see something more that remained unseen. Amongst our new friends in London we had also the pleasure of having a true believer in Saiyid Aminu'd-din Al Ali, commonly called Ali Effendi, the ambassador on the part of the

Sultan of Constantinople to the Court of England. We had the honor of several interviews with this noble minister of the Sovereign of Islam. My chief made him a present of a very valuable Indian sword in token of his most sincere regard and profound respect. On the 12th of September, we paid our parting visit to him, and his Grace would not allow us to leave him without a mark of his friendship. He gave my chief a very valuable volume of a Turkish book, and a similar one to myself, endorsed by himself. And then, after a long conversation about the Indian Government, we took our leave of him, assuring him that our services at all times were at the disposal of the Islam Government whenever they were required.

I may now sum up the character of the English, by saying they are entirely submissive to the law and obedient to the commands of their superiors. Their sense of patriotism is greater than that of any nation in the world. Their obedience, trust, and submission to the female sex are far beyond the limit of moderation. In fact, the freedom granted to womankind in this country is great, and the mischief arising from this unreasonable toleration is most deplorable.

I must now leap over the course of ten years, from 1844 to 1854, during which time I experienced many vicissitudes; to enter into the particulars, I require another volume, which I intend to fill when I am master of my own time, retired from the service of Mir Jafir, and peacefully sitting at my own desk at home.

In short, on the 3rd of October we left England, and on the 12th of November, we reached Bombay, thanks to the Almighty Allah, all safe, where we stayed for a fortnight, during which time we got over the official business, in paying visits to the Honorable Governor, delivering the letters to him, both from his friends and from his superiors, and seeing other friends at Bombay. My chief then proceeded to Surat by sea and I by land, and I reached sweet home once more on the 5th December, 1844, AC. My dear wife, may God bless her soul! was delighted to see me after this long journey, and I was twice as much delighted to see my only sincere friend in the world and my beloved partner in pleasure and adversity.

It is quite evident that the pecuniary circumstances of my chief and myself were improved by having proceeded to England, in proportion to our individual capacities. But a severe misfortune at the same time lurked behind the invisible curtain of destiny to inflict a deep and unhealable wound upon our hearts. His dear wife, the source of his aggrandisement and wealth, departed this life on the

9th of January, 1845, of consumption; and then, on the 15th of January, 1847, my dearest wife too, having had an attack of the cholera, left this world for the next. My grief for this severe and irreparable loss was so great that I thought of renouncing the world at once. But my friends and companions, especially my chief, blindfolded me again and led me into the worldly delusions by degrees, and again I gave in my neck to be yoked to the wagon of worldly cares.

On Monday, the 12th of July, 1847, again I entered into the marriage contract with Wilayati Khanum, the adopted daughter of Najibu'nnissa-begam, eldest daughter of her late Nuwab of Surat; and by this lady I am blessed with four children, three girls and one boy. May God bless them all! My domestic cares are now aggravated, my years advanced, and my income inadequate to cover the expenses of a large family. But I resign myself to the will of that Omniscient Being, whose omnipotent power first creates the food and then his creatures destined to live upon it. Amen!

CHAPTER 4

An Indian Prince and the French Revolution

MOHIBBUL HASAN

Mohibbul Hasan received his education in Lucknow and London. He taught in the universities of Calcutta (1943-56), Aligarh (1956-63), Jamia Millia Islamia, New Delhi, and Kashmir. He presided over the Medieval Section of the Indian History Congress in 1957, and also over the Medieval Section of the Punjab History Congress in 1967. He published *History of Tipu Sultan, Kashmir under the Sultans, Babur,* and edited *Waqai-i Manazil-i Rum* (1969) and *Historians of Medieval India* (1968).

This paper describes the adventures of Mirza Ahmad Khan of Broach, a town in Gujarat, situated on the right bank of the Narbada, about 30 miles from the mouth. Since his father's state had been forcibly annexed by the governor of Bombay, he, with his three brothers, decided to proceed to England in order to appeal to the Court of Directors. On the way he visited Masqat, Basra, Baghdad and Constantinople, and thence sailed for Marseilles. From here he went to Lyons and then to Paris. The revolutionary government of France was generous to him and gave him financial help for his stay in Paris and for going to London.

Mirza Ahmad has not left any diary, but the brief account of his travels and his life in France is obtained from the letters he wrote to the French Commissaire of external Affairs, the reports of Ruffin, the French government's interpreter of Oriental languages, and the Extracts from the Register of the Committee of Public Safety, which bear signatures of Robespierre, Carriot, d'Herbert and other members of the Committee. As regards his visit to London and his return

**Iran Society Silver Jubilee Spl.* (*1944-1969*), Calcutta, 1970, pp. 137-40.

to India, references are found in Dispatches to Bombay and Letters received from Bombay, India Office Library.

Mirza Ahmad Khan was descended from 'Abdu'llah Beg, the Mughal governor of Broach, appointed in the time of Sarbuland Khan, who had replaced the Nizamu'l-Mulk as Viceroy of Gujarat in 1724. When Abhay Singh of Marwar succeeded Sarbuland Khan, 'Abdu'llah Beg, owing to reasons not clear, did not wish to serve under him. Since Broach still continued to be the *Jagir* of the Nizamu'l-Mulk, although he was now viceroy of the Deccan, 'Abdu'llah Beg requested him to be allowed to hold it as his deputy. His request was granted and he was given the title of Nek 'Alam Khan in 1734. On his death in 1739, he was succeeded by his second son, Mirza Beg, who assumed the title of Nek 'Alam Khan II and acted as governor of Broach.[1] But, shortly after, taking advantage of the disintegration of the Mughal Empire, he declared his independence.[2] However, after death in 1754, power was usurped by his brother, Khairtalab Khan, while his son, Hamid Beg Khan, had to take refuge in Surat. Khairtalab, who was a profligate, died within a few months and was succeeded by 'Abdu'llah Beg's minor son, Hasan 'Ali Beg, under the regency of his ('Abdu'llah Beg's) mistress, Bibi Bulan. Meanwhile Hamid Beg returned from Surat and claimed the throne. This led to a conflict from which, however, he came out victorious and became the ruler, securing a royal *sanad* and the title of Nek Nam Khan. He was succeeded by his son, Imtiyazu'd-Daulah Dilir Jung Mu'azzaz Khan in 1769.[3]

By this time the Mughal Empire had virtually ceased to exist and the English star was in the ascendant. Since the town of Broach was an important trading and manufacturing centre and the Nawwab would not allow the English to establish a factory there,[4] the governor of Bombay decided to seize it. Under the pretext that the Nawwab had violated the treaty with the East India Company and insulted Morley, its representative, Broach was attacked and stormed on November 18, 1772, and the state was annexed.[5] However, as soon as the Company's authorities in London came to know of this, they instructed the governor of Bombay to restore the state to the Nawwab. But the governor ignored this.[6] Shortly after, the Nawwab died. Thereupon, four of his sons decided to proceed to England and petition the Court of Directors for the redress of the injustice done to their family. The governor of Bombay, having come to know of this, ordered their movements to be watched and later detained them. In spite of this, after five months, they managed to escape and boarded a ship which took them to Masqat. From here they went to Basra and, following the overland route *via* Baghdad, they arrived in Constantinople, where two of the brothers, namely, Mirza Anwar 'Ali Khan and Mirza Wahidu'd-Din Khan, decided to settle and gave up the idea of going to England. The other two, Mirza Nawazish Khan, the eldest, and Mirza Ahmad Khan, made up their minds to continue the journey. Accordingly, they left Constantinople for Marseilles. On arriving in Marseilles, the town authorities provided them with a carriage which took them to Lyons. Here Mirza Nawazish Khan fell ill and after an year's illness passed away. By this time Mirza Ahmad's money had run out and he, therefore, appealed to the town authorities for help. He was given money for his journey to Paris and, since he did not know French, he was given a companion named Francoise who could converse a little in Persian.[7]

On arriving in Paris in May 1794, Mirza Ahmad appealed to the Committee of Public Safety for financial help and for news of his two brothers who were living in Constantinople, either at the Khanqah of Nu'man Beg or with Darwish 'Abdu'llah Hindi. Since the Committee was anxious 'to fulfil towards this foreigner the duty of hospitality', because the 'French nation honours the unfortunate', it instructed the French ambassador in Contantinople to obtain information about Mirza Ahmad's brothers and to convey to them news of their eldest brother's death.[8] It also authorised the Minister for External Affairs to give Mirza Ahmad 1200 livres, so that he might be able to continue his journey to England. Furthermore, the Committee ordered that Francoise who, out of goodness of heart, had accompanied Mirza Ahmad to Paris, should be sent back to his home in Lyons at the expense of the government.[9]

Later, the Committee issued instructions to the Commissaire of External Affairs that, since the date of Mirza Ahmad's departure was uncertain, his stay in Paris must be made agreeable, and since he did not know French, Ruffin, Government Interpreter of Oriental Languages, should be asked to keep him in his house at Versailles as a paying guest and teach him French, which he was so anxious to learn. This would make him useful to the Republic.[10] Ruffin was greatly impressed by Mirza Ahmad's intelligence, good education, frankness and honesty,[11] and it was due to his suggestion that Mirza Ahmad's allowance was fixed at 360 livres per month, excluding the expenses for board and lodging.[12]

Mirza Ahmad learnt French in three months, and in gratitude for what the Republic had done for him, he paid his homage to it by translating the Declaration of the *Rights of Man* into Persian. He then presented it to the Committee of Public Safety, which sent it to be deposited in the Bibliotheque Nationale.[13] It was felt that the learning and use of French language by a Musalman was a victory of French culture.[14] This translation of the Declaration of the *Rights of Man* was the first to have been made in any Oriental language.

Although the Revolutionary government of France was opposed to kings, princes and nobles, it adopted an extremely generous attitude towards Mirza Ahmad. This was due partly to the ill-treatment he had received from their enemies and partly to the ideals of the French revolution—to help the underdog, the oppressed, and the wronged.

Meanwhile, before Mirza Ahmad was able to leave Paris, Mirza Wahidu'd-Din Khan, one of his brothers whom he had left behind in Constantinople, arrived in London in January, 1794, and claimed certain rights from the Company on behalf of himself and his brothers. All his claims were not granted, but each brother was granted a stipend of Rs. 200/- monthly.[15]

After this Mirza Ahmad visited London and secured funds from the Company for carrying the body of his brother, who had died at Lyons, to India overland for burial beside his father's tomb. He was already suspected by the British authorities to be pro-French. The British charge d'Affairs in Constantinople was firmly convinced that he was not only French in his sympathies, but was actively working as an agent on behalf of France. When, therefore, he reached Basra, the English Resident was suspicious and persuaded him to embark on a ship for Bombay. On arrival at Bombay, Mirza Ahmad was handed over to the police 'as a spy inimical to the British interests, and in collusion with our enemies.' In 1798 he petitioned the Company which ordered the Bombay government to 'examine his allegations and report thereon.'[16]

NOTES

1. Commissariat, *History of Gujarat* (*1573-1758*), vol. II, p. 443.
2. Ibid.

3. Ibid., pp. 520-22, see also *Selections from the Letters, Despatches, and other State papers Preserved in the Bombay Secretariat,* Home Series, vol. 1, pp. 389-90, ed. G.W. Forrest, Bombay, 1887. Cited hereafter as *Selections from State Papers in Bombay Secretariat.*
4. *Selections from State Papers in Bombay Secretariat,* I, p. 390.
5. Ibid., II, pp. 173-4.
6. *Archives des Affairs Etrangères,* vol. 20, p. 102a.
7. Ibid.
8. *Archives des Affairs Etrangères*, f. 132a.
9. Ibid., ff. 104a-b.
10. Ibid., ff. 110a-b.
11. Ibid., f. 103a.
12. Ibid., f. 111b.
13. Ibid., ff. 136a-b. It is not traceable in the Oriental Section of the Bibliotheque Nationale.
14. Ibid., f. 134b.
15. Despatch to Bombay (Public Department) 30 May 1794; Despatch to Bombay (Public Department) 17 February 1797 (paras. 28 and 29); Despatch to Bombay (Political Department) 20 March 1799 (para. 7); Despatch to Bombay (Public department) 29 May 1799 (para. 30) ; Letter received from Bombay (Public Department) 19 January 1796 (paras. 173a to 183); Letters received from Bombay 22 August, 1796 Public Cousultations; Letters received from Bombay (Political Department) 18 December 1796 (para. 27).
16. Ibid.

CHAPTER 5

An Eighteenth-Century Indian Historian on Early British Administration

QEYAMUDDIN AHMAD

A historian based at the University of Patna, Professor Qeyamuddin Ahmad was a leading scholar of medieval India. His best known work is on the Wahhabi movement.

A distinctive feature of Ghulam Husain Khan Tabatabai's well-known work, *Siyarul Muta'akhkhirin*,[1] is the awareness displayed in it of the growing political power of the East India Company and the transitions heralded by it. Written in 1781, it presents a general history of India from 1707 to 1781,[2] with particular reference to the rise of the British power in the eastern provinces of Bihar and Bengal. The period covered by it was one of transition, when important political, socio-economic and administrative changes were taking shape.

Several other writers-Ghulam Husain Salim, Karam Ali and Kelyan Singh, to mention only a few-have dealt with part of this period and area but none shows any deep awareness of the rise, much less the impact, of the British power in India. Ghulam Husain, on the other hand, gives considerable attention to this major political development and its wide-ranging effects and gives a perceptive account of early British administration (1765-83). He also refers, briefly, to such topics as the English political institutions at home, some national traits of Englishman, the composition and functions of the Company's Councils and Committees, the Anglo-Dutch political rivalry, the founding of the English colonies in North

**Journal of Indian History: Golden Jubilee Volume*, ed. T.K. Ravindran, Department of History, University of Kerala, 1973, pp. 893-907.

America, the War of American Independence, etc. Such a candid discussion of Englishmen and English rule in India is very rare, if not altogether unique, in contemporary Persian historical accounts. It was this quality of the work which caught the attention of F. Raymond,[3] the translator of the *Siyaru'l Muta'akhkhirin* in English, when he came across a decayed copy of a part of the work. He was surprised to find a book whose author 'talked with encomiums of the British Parliament in Europe, and with some asperity of the English Government in Bengal', and exclaimed, 'A Persian discourse upon English politics. Strange indeed!'

Ghulam Husain does not seem to be conscious of the basic economic and military factors responsible for the rise of the British power in India, although in a brief reference to the circumstances leading tot he first Anglo-Maratha war he makes a shrewd reference[4] to the English tactics of exploiting dynastic and succession disputes among the Indian rulers for extending their political influence. But more often than not he seems to look upon the advent of the English as some sort of a Divine Punishment[5] for the sins of the Indian ruling circles. He seems convinced that the English rule had come to stay but feels that the new rules were hampered by the ignorance of the previous administrative system and local customs. They were 'quite alien to this country, both in customs and manners, and quite strangers to the methods of raising tributes as well as to maxims of estimating the revenues, or of comprehending the wage of tax-gathering'.[6] Whatever the English knew about these things was from such petty officials and sycophants who did not know 'why such a custom has been instituted and what might be its cause or ground, these are matters which they never discover themselves nor ever ask of others; or if they comprehend anything in them they willingly counterfeit ignorance, and I do not comprehend the benefit of this deliberate ignorance.'[7] It was this ignorance, genuine or self-imposed, of the previous administrative system and local customs, compounded by the misinformation by interested Indians[8] which according to Ghulam Husain, was responsible for the failures and the oppressiveness of the Company's rule. Believing that 'ruling and government need the assent and satisfaction of the governed, and that it was far from finding its account in the injury and the ruin of the subject',[9] Ghulam Husain took up himself the task of explaining to the new rulers, 'with the candour of a faithful witness', the origins and true intent of some of the administrative institutions of the land, so that they may work them in the original spirit and give relief and satisfaction to the people.[10] He enumerates twelve 'causes' for the prevailing state of affairs and suggests some remedial actions.[11] The 'causes' have been discussed in a rather disjointed, repetitive manner, but for the present discussion they have been grouped as administrative, social and economic.[12]

Administrative Causes

Ghulam Husain gives a brief account of some of the institutes and maxims of this land and point out 'what end was intended in each of them by our ancient Lawgivers'. He shows how the original aims and objectives underlying the constitution of certain offices, such as those of the *Sadr*, the *Qazi* and the *Muhtasib*, had either been lost sight of or were being abused, and describes such 'parts of the English Government as differ totally from, or even clash essentially with, the customs and usages by which these countries have once flourished.' To him it was this 'contrariety' between the two systems which was responsible for the constant failure of the Company's administration.[13] To begin with, he notes the difference between the benevolent despotism of the Mughal rulers and the collective, impersonal, rule of the 'Council'. The Muslim rulers, after the initial period of conflict, had settled in the country and 'lived amongst their people and amongst their nobles as kind condescending parents amongst their children', and in course of time the sense of attachment had become reciprocal. However, 'since the conquest made by the English of these three provinces this country seems to have had no master at all, and this because-there is no apparent owner whose children and offspring might be interested in inheriting his estate.'[14] Even if it was to be supposed that the 'English nation at large are the owners of this land', the fact remained that the (East India) 'Company is not one individual. It is a numerous body; nor are the members of it permanent.' There were no 'supreme rulers' to whom 'everyone' was accountable; the head of the administration had neither security of tenure nor full powers, he must consult and manage with four or five members of the Committee who were 'perpetually at variance with each other'. The Company's dominion was like 'a house that has no owner' nor 'likely to be tenanted'; it was bound to totter for 'want of repairs'.[15] The Company's administrators had no sense of belonging to the country, they functioned like a stranger, 'eager to draw his own profit', caring little what 'ruins shall remain after him'. There were a few exceptions, such as Governor Hushtin (Warren Hastings, to whom Ghulam Husain was much attached), but his achievements were largely due to 'his own genius'.[16]

Ghulam Husain then moves on to a discussion of the actual functioning of the different branches of administration, and specifically enumerates the composition and the function of the 'Council' as one of the 'causes'. The Council was 'an assembly of Gentlemen intent on a particular business, where if there be a diversity of opinion, that opinion gets the better, and is approved of, that has most members on its side whereas if the votes be equal then as the Governor, in consequence of his superior station and dignity, is counted for two men, his side prevails. . .'.[17] This method, based on 'consultation' was extremely advantageous, but it had some defects too. Although good for 'occasions of extreme importance', it was not useful in attending to 'every minutae that may occur'. Matters were not attended to as they occurred, or when a petition was submitted. They were 'kept in store for the day of assembling the Council', and even after the Council met there were delays and stalemates either due to 'opposition of votes' [either a tie or when opinions were more or less equally divided] or because the members owing to 'friendship to anyone or out of disgust to the petitioners' expressed divergent opinions.[18] Ghulam Husain contrasts this with the quick, even if arbitrary, functioning of the officers in the earlier period. Even during the period immediately after the grant of *Diwani* (1765) the work proceeded briskly, favouritism and other anomalies notwithstanding. Moreover, it was easier to 'make up matters' with one man than to 'find one's way to the favor of fifteen or twenty persons, or even more, that compose a Council, or to guard against their resentment'.[19] Formerly, when Raja Shitab Rai[20] was the *Naib Diwan* of the province of Bihar, the Indians had to present *Nazars* (presents) only to him on ceremonial occasions, but after his dismissal and the constitution of the 'Council' they had to present *Nazars* to all the five members of the Council. Even though Vansittart, realising that 'whoever hitherto had been clear with presenting one *mohur*, or one rupee only, would now be obliged to provide five,' ordered that in future *Nazars* should be paid only to the Chief of the 'Council, 'some professed flatterers who wished no good to any money that might remain in a Hindostani's pocket' continued to pay *Nazars* to each member of the Council, while those who could not do so remained 'moping in their corners'.[21]

Over-centralisation, too much emphasis on the principle of seniority, and quick transfers are also mentioned as impediments to speedy and efficient administration. Much time was wasted, on the one hand, in seeking orders from above and, on the other, in calling for information from below. Both the central and provincial Councils, apart from their heavy load of normal work were frequently occupied in attacking or defending a particular policy. As it was, the Governor and the Council had their attention constantly divided 'betwixt that infinity of public transactions and businesses that concern their dominions and conquests; and that other infinity of matters that concerns their own state of personal warfare; what betwixt watching over their dominions in these provinces, and answering very long letters from Europe; guarding against their national enemies abroad, both in Europe and Hindostan, and providing against personal enemies at home; betwixt examining accounts of crores of rupees and providing for the company's mercantile purchases; betwixt receiving as Sovereigns the revenue of so many dominions in their old and new conquests . . . and an infinity of other avocations, public or private'.[22]

Ghulam Husain criticises the fact that each of the 'six districts into which the English had divided this country' was governed by 'five or six persons all disagreeing among themselves' and having no superior with full powers over all of them. Even when there was such a superior, he did not have 'any hopes of his remaining long in his post' and had his 'ears eternally pricked up against every report of change and confirmation.'[23] Ghulam Husain stresses that 'talent and abilities,' not 'seniority of service or recommendation' should be the criterion in appointing local officers. A European officer put in charge of a district should be allowed to remain there for some time, and he should be made 'independent of the revolutions of the Council'.[24] He should be assisted by an experienced Indian *Diwan*.[25]

The former rulers had apportioned their time for different kinds of works and strictly followed that routine. Collection of revenue and administration of justice were two important functions of the government and for each of them two days in a week had been reserved. For administering justice, the king or the officers 'appeared publicly in all their pomp and grandeur and glory'; anyone could 'speak face to face' and seek redress. Matters were now different; the

'English Gentlemen hate appearing in public audiences' and when they did so, they exhibited 'uneasiness, impatience and anger on seeing themselves surrounded by crowds and on hearing their complaints and clamours'.[26] Owing to this reluctance to meet the common people directly the English were 'in the dark with respect to the real state of the country'. Ghulam Husain feels that a renewal of the old practice, although it would involve some inconvenience and expense, would be beneficial.

The working of the Supreme Court of Judicature at Calcutta has been criticised strongly and at some length. Ghulam Husain gives a graphic description of the harassments and fleecings which a common man had to undergo if he got involved in a case coming under the purview of the Supreme Court.[27] To quote, 'On the first complaint lodged by anyone, be it ascertained or not, the defendant is obliged to find security to double the amount of demand, and if he cannot afford such a security, the poor man must go to prison; and if he cannot find bail, and the complaint is not withdrawn or hushed down, he must remain in prison ten or twelve years, whether he be guilty or not guilty. Add to these miseries, that to translate a petition in the English language, the translator extracts as many *eshreffies* (or double guineas) as there are lines translated; and over and above all those miseries heaped over the heads of poor Hindostanies, it is to be lamented that, on the first summons of the Court to answer to a complaint, whether proved or not, whether real or frivolous, and even to give evidence on so small a matter as having once heard of the affair in question, . . . a poor man must directly forsake his family and children, leave them in misery, want and distress, and run down for a whole month's journey to a spot where both air and water are bad (Calcutta); and if before his arrival the term of the Court be over, or its Chief be gone out to some other country for a change of air, then the poor man must, without reason, and without subsistence endure whole months at Calcutta. . . . There are other troubles and other miseries to be undergone at that tribunal . . . the least of which is, that the English law and statutes are so enormously voluminous, that were a man to spend his whole life on them, still the attaining of a full knowledge would be impossible. After all these miseries, how painful it must be to a man, to be in the dark about the event, and all the while in a cruel suspense about his fate; constantly bereft of his family and beloved children; and without being able to guess at what is to become of himself at last?'[28]

It may be remarked here that although the introduction of the modern judicial system, based on the rule of law, was undoubtedly an improvement upon the previous paternalistic, and often capricious, system, it is evident from this contemporary account that it entailed much hardship and harassments to the common man. At the same time, it should be noted that observations relate to the period immediately following the introduction of the new system, when its long-term benefits had not come to be felt.

Social Causes

More harmful and productive of misunderstanding and resentment was the general attitude of superiority and social exclusiveness adopted by the English. Ghulam Husain refers to it frequently, and complains that the English 'undervalued' the Hindostanies and took no notice of 'natives from the highest to the lowest; and they carry their contempt so far, as to employ none but their own selves in every department and in every article of business, esteeming themselves better than all put together'.[29] He again observes that 'such is the aversion which the English openly shew for the company of the natives, and such is the disdain which they betray for them, that no love and no coalition . . . can take root between the conquerors and the conquered'.[30] Even if they ever condescended to 'taking notice of a Moghul or a native, or in courting an acquaintance with him' it was only to 'pick up anything relative to the laws or business of this land'.[31] Ghulam Husain shrewdly adds that the Englishmen would immediately set it (information acquired) down in writing, and lay it up in store for the use of another Englishman'.[32]

The barrier of language was another factor. 'The tongue, is the key to the treasures of the heart and mind, and which serves as a medium to strengthen the bands of society . . . happens to be deprived of its office between the Hindostanies and the English. Most of the English Gentlemen do not understand the language of their subjects, and none of the last understand a word of English'. While this was a mutual handicap, to some extent, Ghulam Husain shrewdly remarks that the Indians suffered more due to it as the Hindians [*sic*] are always the petitioners, they always prove the greatest loss from that inconvenience, being always at a loss what to do next.[33]

A more deterring, but avoidable, barrier was that created by the household staff of the English officers. Almost all of them employed a set of Indian Staff, consisting of a *Munshi* (Persian Secretary), a *Diwan* (a sort of a Private Secretary) and a *Harcara* (servant-cum-spy). The last-named was particularly a terror to all Indian gentlemen trying to meet the English either on business or otherwise. Usually recruited from the 'lowest clan' and of a 'vile nature', he took delight in humiliating and insulting[34] the Indian visitors. He often acted in league with the other two, and influenced the decisions on the petitions of Indian gentlemen, while they were left in the 'anti-chamber, ranged against the wall like so many statues, . . . so many by-standers of no account'.[35] As a result of all this the English were living in a state of splendid but dangerous isolation.

Economic Causes

Among the economic 'causes', Ghulam Husain mentions the resumption of rent-free land holdings, the wrong pro-*zamindar*, attitude of the Company's administrators, monopolies of trade and neglect of local handicrafts. The different categories of land grants and rent remissions conferred by the Mughal rulers served to propitiate and keep contended not only their own relatives and followers but also the 'most considerable men of the land itself.'[36] The East India Company changed this policy, and started a sweeping resumption of all kinds of *jagir* lands, thereby affecting the means of livelihood of a large number of common people and also antagonising different categories of landholders.

As regards the position of the *zamindars*, 'in contradiction to ancient maxims, and to rules of old standing . . . the English rulers have thought proper to compare the *zamindars* of this country to the *zamindars* and landholders of their own'. The latter were generally educated and cultured persons and held small estates. On the other hand, the Indian *zamindars* were 'a refractory, short-sighted, faithless set of people . . . an incorrigible race,'[37] whose conduct could not be trusted and who were governed with a strict hand by the previous rulers. It was not that the Company's government could not be equally strict with them; in fact, the *zamindars* were overawed 'by the heavy blows they have received from the hands of the English'. It was the wrong, favourable attitude of the new government towards the *zamindars* which enabled them to continue their petty tyrannies. 'The English rulers' either did not notice their oppressions or overlooked them because they had 'within their breasts some scheme' which was a 'profound secret' to 'ignorant men' like the authors.[38]

More ruinous was the policy of monopolies. Once again, Ghulam Husain compares and contrasts the policy of the new rulers with the previous ones. The latter 'left open to the subjects various ways of revenue and livelihood amounting to many crors [*sic*] a year, as a provision to the bulk of the inhabitants . . . from merchandising and from the exercise of arts and trade, all these were left open for all the world and although they (old rulers) were made to see various branches of revenue in those articles they never turned their eyes that way'.[39] As against this, 'of the various branches of trade, heretofore open to all, none is left free. They are all engrossed by the Company themselves or by the English in general; as these, whether they enjoy the Company's service, and of course have power and influence, or chance to be otherwise circumstanced very seldom are without concerns in trade'.[40] Under the circumstances, how could the 'poor subject pretend to derive a subsistence from merchandise? Would they dare it?'[41]

A connected problem was the decay of various crafts and cottage industries. Many skilled artisans became unemployed because their 'arts and callings' were of no use to the English, and 'as these rulers have all their necessaries from their own country, it follows that the handicraftsmen and artificers of this land suffer constantly, live in distress, and find it difficult to procure a livelihood'.[42] Only certain types of workers found employment with the English, such as carpenters, silver-smiths and iron-smiths; in fact their wages and working conditions had improved, but 'numerous artificers of other denominations' had nothing to fall back upon except 'begging or thieving'. Nor could the 'nobility of the land' render them any help, as it did before, because of the financial distress to which it was reduced.

Significantly, Ghulam Husain notes that formerly the English 'imported every year gold and silver into this land' and this together with the local stock of bullion produced 'an abundant circulation, and promoted everyone's good'.[43] Contrary to it, they now held it to be 'of Divine obligation' to amass as much money in this country as they cán, and to carry it 'in immense sums to the kingdom of England'. It was 'not surprising' that the practice should be ever undermining and ruining the country.[44]

These observations of Ghulam Husain have been briefly noticed by a few previous writers. Dowson, while noticing with satisfaction the 'testimony which Ghulam Husain bears to the merits of the English', explains away his adverse remarks by saying that 'Persian writings and books are not committed to the press and disseminated by publication as in Europe. This author's MSS., for many years, were handed about privately among natives. He could therefore have no fear of giving offence to the English by what he brought forward.'[45] However, this would be a misreading of the author's intention, clearly stated in the book itself.[46] In fact, the point about Ghulam Husain's intended audience, which adds to the distinctive value of his work, has not received due attention.

Another anonymous, writer[47] drew attention to these observations of Ghulam Husain as a contemporary verdict on British rule. He also tried to draw a balance sheet of his favourable and unfavourable comments to underline his objectivity and impartiality. But in doing this he seems to have missed the point that Ghulam Husain was essentially for the old order.

Recently, an American scholar has examined Ghulam Husain's history in a fresh manner.[48] Seeking literary evidence of the Indian response to the advent of the West in the eighteenth century he selects Bihar as a case study, and examines the works of some Bihar intellectuals belonging to different sections of the society. This is a more meaningful way of looking at this portion of the *Siyarul Muta'akhkhirin*. Ghulam Husain's observations may well be taken as indicating one facet of the Indian response to the changing political and social conditions.

Before assessing these observations, it may be pointed out that Ghulam Husain was very advantageously placed to write his account and to record his impressions. A contemporary, trained along traditional lines and with wide experience of administrative and diplomatic work, related to the Nawab and other high officers and also acquainted with some of the leading Englishmen, Ghulam Husain occupied a number of vantage points. He has rightly been described in the title page of the published English translation as one 'who wrote both as Actor and Spectator'. One may add that he was a spectator with a very keen understanding and unusual objectivity. However, Ghulam Husain, though fond of the old order, seems convinced that the British rule had come to stay. He could not envisage its removal: he only wanted to make it a little less oppressive.

It is evident that Ghulam Husain judges the Company's rule largely in administrative terms and attributes its lapses and failures to the same cause. It is also evident that he considers the benevolent despotism of the Mughals as eminently suited to the country and as widely accepted by the people. He shared the widely prevalent view that sovereignty resided in and was personified by the monarch, and that monarchy was something like a personal property, inheritable and alienable. All this is rather surprising, for at another place Ghulam Husain expresses his admiration for the constitutional monarchy of England based on the principle of 'consultation' and representation. His actual description of this system is worth quoting for it shows his remarkable understanding of its operation. He writes, 'the Sovereigns of that nation (English), whom these people call King, although absolute in his commands, cannot give them any order without the advice and consent of his Council and that of his nation; and if he should venture so far, the order would not pass the seals and would remain unexecuted. . . . The Council of the nation is composed of a number of persons, which the principal inhabitants of every city and town of that land have chosen amongst themselves, some one and some two, and whose attachment and knowledge they have approved. So that these chosen men are entrusted with the concern of the whole and hence the advocates and attorneys of those by whom they are sent. All these assemble in the capital . . . whatever is proposed by the Sovereign and his Council as objects likely in their opinions to become beneficial to themselves, to their senders and the people in general, they weigh and examine it carefully amongst themselves and when it has been approved by them it is from that moment willingly admitted and obeyed as law by all the inhabitants of the land. . . . As an admirable institution this is extremely useful and beneficial . . . it is so capable, so productive of order.'[49] However, Ghulam Husain's complaint is that the English used this beneficial system 'only amongst themselves' and not for governing their dominion in India. In another context, while referring to an instance of indirectly taking bribes, Ghulam Husain makes an astute remark that 'there never comes out of the hands of an Englishman any such transaction or matter as may reflect an ill-renown on their own countrymen directly. It is the Indians that are made use of for such purposes. . . .'[50]

It may also be pointed out that the frequent comparisons he makes with the old administrative system are not well the one immediately preceding the Company's rule, but the one which operated during the 16th and 17th centuries. That the immediately preceding set-up (of early and mid-18th century) was very corrupt and oppressive is repeatedly admitted by Ghulam Husain.

The observations on the social and economic aspects of the Company's rule are also very significant. With a remarkable insight and precision, Ghulam Husain picks up the two main defects of the early period of the Company's rule—the attitude of superiority and social exclusiveness by the English and the monopolies of trade in their favour. Both in regard to the administrative defects[51] and economic exploitation,[52] Ghulam Husain's criticism is borne out by some contemporary Englishmen as well as later writers.

Also notable is the sarcasm of the style and the adroitness with which pungent remarks are often made in the garb of apparently innocuous and traditional phrases of humility.[53] These remarks gain additional significance in view of the partly justified charge of a pro-English bias in Ghulam Husain's account.

Ghulam Husain's observations anticipate some of the criticisms of early British rule expressed later in academic and nationalist circles. For instance, his criticism of the *zamindars* as a class, apart from its relevance in the context of the controversy raised at the time of the promulgation of the Permanent Settlement of Land Revenue (1793), found expression in many of the subsequent writings on the subject. Similarly, in referring to the large inflow of buillion into the country during the earlier period and the reversal of the situation subsequently ('carrying of immense sums to the kingdom of England'), Ghulam Hussain seems to be giving expression to the idea that came later to be labelled as 'the drain' theory.

NOTES

1. For a brief description of the work and biographical particulars of the author see, Elliot & Dowson, *History of India as Told by its Own Historians*, Allahabad, 1964, vol. VIII, pp. 195-8; and an article entitled 'Historian Ghulam Husain Khan Tabatabai' by M.A. Rahim, *Journal of Asiatic Society*, Pakistan, vol. VIII, no. 3, 1963, pp. 117-30. A Ph.D.

thesis, entitled 'Life and Works of Ghulam Husain' has recently been submitted by M.A. Muzaffar in the Patna University (Persian Department).

2. Excluding the first volume of the work in which an outline of the history of India from earliest times to the death of Aurangzeb has been presented; it is entirely based upon other, earlier, works and has not been translated into English.
3. A Frenchman turned Muslim, Raymond translated the *Siyaru'l Muta'-akhkhirin* in English under the pseudonym Nota Manus originally published in 1789, it was reprinted in Calcutta in 1902 and again in 1926. All references hereunder are from the 1902 edition, hereinafter cited as *Siyar*.
4. *Siyar*, III, pp. 93-4.
5. Ibid., p. 29.
6. Ibid., p. 162.
7. Ibid., p. 154. The portion in italics differs slightly from Raymond's translation.
8. These Indians did so in order to 'initiate them (English) in those arts of oppressions and rapine which they themselves employed . . . and set up standing rules and customs . . . doubtless to the end that not a jot of former tyranny might be abated or lost by disuse'; ibid., p. 27.
9. *Siyar*, III, p. 38.
10. Ibid., pp. 154-5, 164, 184-5, etc.
11. Ibid., section xiv, pp. 156-213; Persian text compiled by Hakim Abdul Majid, Mujeed, Calcutta, 1833, pp. 402-20.
12. All references and quotations are from the English translation, Calcutta edition, 1902, referred to above. The Persian text, cited above, has also been consulted. While slight changes may be made in Raymond's translation here and there, no substantial change is necessary, so far as this potion is concerned.
13. *Siyar*, III, p. 185.
14. Ibid., p. 185; Persian text, pp. 403-4.
15. Ibid., III, pp. 185-6.
16. Ibid., p. 186.
17. Ibid., p. 196.
18. Ibid., p. 197.
19. Ibid., p. 199.
20. An important figure in the history of Bihar in late 18th century, Shitab Rai, took a leading part in the negotiations for the grant of Diwani to the East India Company. As *Naib Diwan* of Bihar from 1765 to 1772, he was in-charge of collection of land revenue. Like Muhammad Reza Khan in Bengal, he performed a useful service in acquainting the

Company's administration with the technicalities of the previous administrative system. Gradually, he ran himself out of usefulness. He was removed in 1772, charged with embezzlement and put to trial but subsequently acquitted. An excellent discussion of his career is available in the unpublished thesis of Dr. F. Lehmann, *vide* infra, p. 15, n. 2.

21. *Siyar*, III, p. 199.
22. Ibid., p. 187.
23. Ibid., also see pp. 193-4.
24. Ibid., p. 207.
25. It is to be noted that this refers to a period *before* the introduction of Cornwallis' policy of Europeanisation, when plenty of experienced Indian officials were available to assist. However, it appears from Ghulam Husain's remarks in an earlier portion of the work that he did not think highly of such Indians (ibid., pp. 154, 163).
26. *Siyar*, III, p. 200.
27. The cases of Muhammad Reza Khan & Raja Shitab Rai show that it was not only the common man who suffered under the system. Ghulam Husain himself refers briefly to the plight of Reza Khan, ibid., pp. 42-3.
28. Ibid., pp. 210-11; Persian text, pp. 419-20.
29. Ibid., p. 29.
30. Ibid., pp. 161-2; Persian text, p. 405.
31. *Siyar*, III, p. 27.
32. Ibid., p. 27.
33. *Siyar*, III, pp. 191-2; Persian text, p. 414. Italics mine.
34. These insults and humiliations must have been rendered more galling by the fact that they came from persons belonging to the lower social order.
35. *Siyar*, III, p. 191.
36. Ibid., p. 202.
37. Ibid., p. 205.
38. Ibid.; Persian text, p. 418.
39. *Siyar*, III, p. 202.
40. Ibid., pp. 202-3.
41. Ibid., III, pp. 203-4.
42. Ibid., III, p. 192, see also p. 204.
43. Ibid., p. 194.
44. Ibid.
45. Elliot & Dowson, op. cit., p. 195.
46. *Siyar*, III, pp. 154-5, 185.
47. *Calcutta Review*, April 1916, pp. 113-28.
48. Unpublished thesis, entitled 'The Eighteenth Century Transitions in India: Responses of Some Bihar Intellectuals', submitted by Dr. Fredrick Louis Lehmann to the University of Wisconsin (USA) in 1967. It is to be published soon.

I utilised the opportunity of his recent visit to Patna to discuss the draft of this paper with him and I am grateful to him for his very useful comments and suggestions.'

49. *Siyar*, III, pp. 153-4.
50. Ibid., p. 28.
51. For detailed citations see N. Dhar, *The Administrative System of the East India Company in Bengal 1774-1786*, vols. I-II, Calcutta, 1964, 1966; Tarachand, *History of the Freedom Movement in India*, vol. I, 1961, Chapters 7, 9 and 10.
52. Ibid.
53. *Siyar*, III, pp. 153, 205, etc.

CHAPTER 6

Calcutta, 1806: Observations of an Iranian Scholar–Traveller*

QEYAMUDDIN AHMAD

The city of Calcutta is advantageously placed in many ways in the matter of its historiography. Ever since it was purchased by the English East Company in 1698,[1] it had formed a part of the English Settlement in Bengal, and its administrative control had remained in the hands of the Council of Fort William, the proceedings of whose consultations and decisions are fairly recorded and well preserved. Subsequently, as the seat of the rising British power in India, Calcutta has been the subject of published works of a wide variety[2]—historical accounts of the Settlement, memoirs, diaries, travel-accounts, handbooks, guides, Selections from Records, Collections of Letters, List of Inscriptions, etc. Additionally, and more importantly, there are old maps[3] and plans, views and portraits, the Gazettes and periodical literature. All these make the history of Calcutta well-covered and documented. The coverage, however, is almost exclusively from one angle, the British, and based on one category of source-material, English.

It is, therefore, all the more necessary to make use of whatever supplementary information is available in other types of source-materials, particularly that in Persian and in Bengali. Information obtained from such sources is valuable not only content wise, but more so from the different perspective it provides. It gives us an idea of the Indians' perception of, and responses to, a new developing situation.

In this paper, a portion of one such Persian work is being introduced. The work is a travel-account of a Persian *mujtahid*,[4] named Ahmad bin Muhammad Ali bin Muhammad Baqir al-

**Indo-Iranica* (Calcutta), vol. 50, nos. 1-4, 1997.

Isfahani, better known as al-Behbahani, and the work is entitled *Mir'atul Ahwal-i-Jahan Numa.*[5]

Several copies of the work in India, and outside, are available. The Khuda Bakhsh Public Library has three copies.[6] One copy, written in the city of Azimabad, 'appertaining to Bihar', is listed in the Catalogue,[7] and is dated AH 1225 (1810-11). Another copy, also listed in the Catalogue,[8] does not bear the exact date of transcription but is ascribed by the Cataloguer to the 19th century. The third copy of the work is dated AH 1236 (1820-1).[9]

Among the copies available at other places inside Patna, mention may be made of the copy in the Madrasa (Waqf) Sulaimaniyah, Patna City, which is the earliest one, being dated 1811.[10] Copies are also available in the Patna University Central Library (Mss. Section), the Asiatic Society of Bengal Library, Calcutta, and Maulana Azad Library, Aligarh Muslim University, Aligarh.

There are two copies of the work in the British Museum, London,[11] and four copies in Teheran (Iran).

The first published edition of a portion of the text was edited by Aqai Ali Dawwani.[12]

A published edition of the complete text of the work,[13] with an introduction and notes, was brought out by Wahid Behbahani in 1994. This is based on a copy of the work which is different from the other copies noticed above. It contains a reference to the marriage of Jahangir (reigned 1605-27)with Nur Jahan. The event belongs to a much earlier period, and Behbahani either copied it from some other historical work, or narrated what he came to hear about it during his stay in India. Some of the Indian names are also misprinted in it.

Earlier, in 1992, the Khuda Bakhsh Library published the text of one of its manuscripts under the title 'India in the Early 19th Century: An Iranian's Travel Account'. There is a brief Introduction in it incorporating copies of the description of the work given in the Khuda Bakhsh Library Catalogue, and that given in the Catalogue of the British Museum, London, mentioned above.[14]

Finally, an English translation of the work,[15] with an introduction and notes based on the manuscripts in the Khuda Bakhsh Library, collated with two other copies of the work,[16] is shortly to be published by the Khuda Bakhsh Library. It covers the whole account, from the starting of the journey in Iran to the landing at Mumbai[17] (May 1805) and visits to diferent cities in India. Only the account of the author's family and an Ijaza[18] in Arabic, and the portion containing short accounts of England and some other European countries have been left out. The translator, Prof. A.E. Haider, points out that there are slight variations, and some omissions and commissions by the scribes in the three copies colllated and translated by him.

Al-Behbahani was born in Kirman Shahr (Iran) in 1777, and belonged to the well-known Majlisi family of Iran. He was the author of several other works, mostly religious tracts, some of which were written here in India during the course of his travels, and these have been mentioned in this work. He visited several areas in western, central and eastern India. Among the places he stayed at, and has written about, are Mumbai, Hyderabad, Calcutta, Murshidabad, Jahangir Nagar (Dhaka), Azimabad, Patna[19] (where he stayed more than once), and Faizabad. He wrote his account in Patna in 1809, and returned subsequently to Iran.

The portion presented here is based on an Ms. copy belonging to the Khuda Bakhsh O.P. Library, Patna,[20] and it relates to the author's visit to Calcutta in mid-1806, and his observations about the city and about the way in which the English had gained entrance into the country and obtained an upper hand in its affairs as a result of the negligence of the rulers and nobles, and, partly, the miscalculations of the former.

The observations are in two parts; the former relating to 'Kalkutta' the port, the Fort (William), the town, its houses, cleaning of the streets, the numbering of houses in different streets/lanes, the drainage system, etc. The later portion relates to the internal organisation of the English East India Company and some of its departments. Of this latter portion, only that relating to 'Kalkutta', or having a bearing on it, has been examined.

As usual, the original text is in a running account, but this has been divided into suitable paragraphs. The first part of the paper presents a free English translation of the concerned portion,[21] and the second discusses some of the more thoughtful and significant portions. This has not been attempted either in the published edited texts, or in the English translation of the text.

I

'On Thursday, the 15th of the month of *Rabi'us Thani*, the year mentioned above (AH 1221, or 3rd July 1806) we arrived at the port of Kalkutta.[22] Aqa Abu'l Hasan Behbahani, *Mu'tamid* (superintendent) of the estate of Khan-i Mu'azzam (household in-charge of the mother of Nawab Asafud'd Dawlah), and his brothers, Haji Haider Ali, son of the deceased Amir Ahmad Bandariqui and Aqa Muhammad Qummi (?), Sayyid Abdul Latif and some others came to the other side of the river to receive me. The Khan-i Mu'azzam (Muhammad Darab Ali Khan Bahadur) had a house arranged for myself and Mirza Muhammad Husain. I put up in the house which Aqa Muhammad had arranged on rent for one month on my request for which I had written to him from Cuttak. Since he had arranged it on rent, I did not consider it right to leave it and stay in some other house. I stayed there for 9 days, and paid him Rs. 57/- as rent. Men of consequence kept on coming to meet me and Mirza Sahib went to meet the Khan aforementioned (Khan-i Mu'azzam) but I did not go, and sought to be excused for it. A short account of the port (city) is being written here.

'Kalkatta, (the pronunciation of) which rhymes with the word "Albatta"[23] is at present one of the most flourishing ports in the whole of Bangla, nay India, and it is the seat of the dominion of the English. Formerly, the ports of Bangala were Hugli and Chachra, pronounced with the two Persian letters . . . (Che) (Chinsura). Both have now fallen from their prime, and the Dutch ships occasionally go to them.

'The place, where the populous (city) is now situated, was formerly a ditch, filled with dirty water, and a few families of the poor people and beggars had their dwellings in its neighbourhood. The English set themselves to build it up, and now it is a magnificent town, full of lofty buildings and pleasant abodes. Men of means belonging to different groups from all over the world have assembled here.

'The grounds of all the streets, mahallas, and market-places and the courtyards of most of the houses, have been dug up to a man's height, and it has been paved with brick and mortar and brought up to the gorund-level, and shaped like a cow's tail (thick at one end and thin at the other), so that the drain-water from both sides is drawn into the channel and flows into the big river, close to the city. In the streets no trace of filth and mud is to be found. 700 double-bullock-driven carts have been provided by the sarkar (government) of the Company, which collect the garbage every day early in the morning and carry it outside the city, to the ditches. In sum, the whole of Hindustan has been rendered desolate, so that this port (city) prospers.[24]

'On the gate of each house is written the name of the owner of the house, the rent of the houses and also the number of the house in the street concerned. Anyone who want to know the name of the owner, or the amount of rent, need not inquire (about these) from anyone. (Further) at the head of each street/lane is written its name, as also the number of the street/lane. If anyone is in search of someone's house, he should inquire about the name of the street, and the number of the house in that street; (and thus) go to that place on his own without anyone's help, or taking a guide along.

'Most of the houses are three-storeyed, or four-storyed, but the climate is unwholesome. In the two seasons of the summer or the rains, there are hordes of mosquitoes, so much so that one cannot sleep without a mosquito-net (pashsha bund). In the day, however, they (mosquitoes) are not to be seen so much. In this respect, it (city) is very similar to the village of Nushaiyyab, situated at a distance of four farsakhs from the holy city of Karbala.[25]

'The major rivers in the area of Bangala, or rather Hindustan, such as the Ganga, Ghaghra, Gomiti, Lakhna(?) and Brahamputra join each other near Kalkatta,[26] and flow past, close to it, into the Bay of Bengal (Darya-i-Shor). On account of the tides, the water (of the river) is heavy (thaqil), and of bad taste; hence it is not used for drinking purposes. At some places they have constructed water-reservoirs in which the rain-water accumulates, and they call it a talab (pond). Also, there are many sweet-water wells, the water of which they drink. In the whole of Hind, *Dakhkhin* (the south) and Bangala people, especially those living on the banks of the river, depend upon wells and ponds (for their water supply), which they have constructed, or are God-made.

'The Fort of the port (city) is situated in one (farther) side of the town. I have heard that it has been designed on geometrical pattern, having a network of winding passages, so much so that many of the people residing in it often lose their way. Its gate is a plank of wood, which when raised in the night, serves the purpose of a gate, and when thrown open it falls upon the moat and serves as a bridge. The fort is of the ground-level, so that nothing of it, or of its buildings, can be seen from a distance of an arrow-throw, but as one gets closer it can be seen bit by bit. It has places (?) for setting up cannon. It looks as if the doorway and the walls are all full of cannon. There are some cannon-making workshops in it, which are always at work, casting and making cannon. At the foot of each cannon, gun-powder and balls are piled up in large quantities, and soldiers are standing, ready-at-arms, so that anyone who sees them would think that the enemy is near at hand and they (the British soldiers) are ready for the combat. Inside (the fort), there are lofty buildings. All of these, from the ground upwards, have been pallisaded with wooden planks, in such a way that the planks are not touching the walls. Nearly three lakh guns have been arranged in such a way that anyone of these can be easily picked up, and if they want to inspect all of them together it can be easily done. At the head of each bunch of 50 guns, a few persons have been deputed to upload (cleanse?) them each day, and then re-load them and put them in their proper places.

'The water supply in the Fort is from wells and (also) from the tidal waves of the river flowing into the moat. Some war ships are always standing in the river. In sum, if the provisions (inside the fort) do not fall short, (even) the armies of Shallam and Tur[27] cannot take the fort by assault, even after the lapse of a long time. They imprison the Indian nobles and dignitaries in that Fort. In the matter of imprisoning they follow variegated methods, and at present there is no occasion to describe them.

'It is commonly said that at the time when Alamgir (Aurangzeb, reigned 1658-1707) granted a *mauda* (village) to them for the purpose of constructing a house of trade (*Baitul Tijarat*), they had dug up a moat around it. When the news reached the Emperor, he ordered that it should be immediately filled up. These people, on account of the fear of incurring royal displeasure, acted so promptly in filling up the moat that their Chief and senior (officers) filled up their hats with the earth and dumped it in the moat, so that it was filled up very quickly. Now, with the passage of time, the slovenliness of the rulers and rivalries of the nobles have brought matters to such a state that they (the Englishmen) have built up such a fort and such resources. As opposed to the olden days, the (Mughal) king and nobles are so afraid of them (the English) that they cannot build a fort with a moat in their own realm; rather they cannot even equip their soldiers.

Verse: Such are the ways of the Hunch-back (the Heaven)
Sometimes, you sit on the saddle, at others the saddle is on [your] back.

'In all I stayed for 9 days in that port (city). Although the elite and the gentry kept calling upon me, on account of the bad water, the putrid and offensive stink, the mosquitoes, the heat and, further, the sound of the temple bells which ring in the morning and at dusk in this abode of infidelity (*daru'l kufr*), the spectacle of the uncultured (ones from) amongst the Armenians and the Hindus[28] and others who, with flowing hairs and faces exposed, with the embellishments, throng the road in such large numbers that it is difficult to avoid them, I felt distressed, and seeking leave from my friends, hastened my departure. Mirza Muhammad Husain stayed back on account of some works. . . .[29]

'Aurangzeb[30] Alamgir Baburi, the ruler of India, following the example of that family,[31] adopted this method, in order to counter the dominance of Portuguese,[32] who had become powerful in many ports of India, and gave a place to the English in Kalkatta. They are engaged in trade in that port and render more obedience than the people (*ri'aya*) of this country. They pay the customs and other dues on the goods of trade into the Treasury of king in a more regular way than the others. When Alamgir went to the Deccan, they rendered help in the supply of provisions to the troops and gained further approbation of the king. . . .

'During the reign of Muhammad Shah (1719-48), when the affairs of the state had fallen in disarray, and the king and the nobles were indulging in frivolities, this group with the passage of time set themselves to conciliating the hearts of the people of Bangala and made acquaintance with the leading persons in that area. By generosities and liberalities, they won over the people in and around (that area). They fortified their place of residence at Kalkatta and called it a *kothi* or a trade-house. On the pretext of protecting their goods they installed their cannon and guns, along with soldiers, according to their need; they also called in some soldiers from their country, and were secretly engaged in promoting their own interests.

'As opposed to them, each one of the rulers and chiefs of this country, according to his own means, was engaged in merry-making, and totally lost in frivolities, being oblivious of the fact that the control of the English people is (increasing) over Hind. If ever they come to know about the activities of these people they paid no attention to it, whatsoever. Whenever they made some inquiries from these people (the English), they behaved with humility, gratified them by offering presents and gifts made in England. Thus, these people have by now become the masters of many parts of this country.

'They have given up the ways of coaxing men, which is the road to security and prosperity. In fact, they are well-versed in it, for most of the people of this country, particularly the nobles and grandees, are the buyers of this commodity (servility, or being kept in good humour), and are willing to pay with their fortune, *life and even the country* (italics are mine) and are averse to acknowledge the stark Reality. In short, the affairs of these people prospered gradually, and they contracted close intimacy with the officers and nobles, and by the time of Nawab, High-Titled and Centre of Forgiveness, Mahabut Jung (Alivardi Khan), *Nazim* of the territories of Bihar, Orissa and Bangala, who was a chivalrous and intrepid noble, and was strict in the matter of not doing the Forbidden things, and not indulging in intoxicants, and was zealous in the matter of revering the *'Ulama*, the Sayyids and men of atainments, (their affairs prospered) because these people were more obedient in the payment of customs and other dues, and in paying the customary dues and making presents, than traders of this country.

'I have heard that some seditious people had represented to the Exalted Court that these people (the English), after being reprimanded, be ousted from the country. He (Alivardi Khan) replied that [at present] the blaze of a war is raging between us and the Marathas; hence it would be against prudence to create commotion and tumult in the serene water, and against protecting the interests of the Creatures of God.[33] Irrespective of this, nothing except subservience and obedience from these people have come to our notice. To ill-treat them without any apparent cause is against the norms of civility and governace.[34] in addition to this, my age is now past seventy (years) and the time of my passing away is near at hand. If I wage a war against these people and I drive them out from the country, after me there is none who can obstruct and prevent (their coming back). In short, after some time due to the ill-fortune of the well-wishers and the friends of the Nawab, Centre of Forgiveness, Death overtook him on the 9th of the month of *Rajab*, year (Hijri) one thousand sixty-five (1654-5); he passed away from this temporary abode.'

There follows an account of the succession of Nawab Siraju'd Dawlah, the capture of Calcutta by him, and final overthrow by the English.[35]

II

Some of the observations of Behbahani are very significant and deserve a closer attention. One is struck by the sort of things he thought fit to comment upon, and the perspicacity of some of his remarks. If, on the one hand, he writes about some aspects of the civic administration of Calcutta, he also takes note of the construction of the Fort, with the eyes of a military strategist, on the other. That he was a keen observer, and had a tendency for details, is evident from what he writes about the number of carriages used for removing the city's garbage, the system of numbering the houses, the water-supply, the swarms of mosquitoes, etc.

More significant is the remark about Calcutta's prosperity having been built at the cost of the growth of other parts of the country. Though cryptic, it is not an isolated remark. Later, when he visited Monghyr on his way to Patna, he wrote that it was a great town but in state of decay. *That was because the English did not want any other town, except Calcutta, to flourish.*[36] The point to be noted here is not as to whether one can talk of a British policy of de-urbanisation, but that there was a common impression to that efect, so strong and widespread that even a foreign visitor could come to know of it, and comment on it.

The political insight of Behbahani is also remarkable. He writes candidly about the way in which the English had worked their way up, partly due to their tactful behaviour and, partly due to the indifference and frivolities of the ruling class. To say that this is a very simplistic explanation is beside the point. What the account brings out is that the people thought like this. It is also evident that a section of the more politically conscious people were not oblivious of the rising power of British, and of the need to check it. The reported remarks of Alivardi Khan Mahabat Jung about the reasons why he did not think it prudent to initiate action against the British are revealing. The reference to protecting the interests of the Creature of God as a factor in the formulation of state politics is also a significant remark. One comes across such references in other sources, too.[37] Again, the point to be noted is not as to whether Nawab Alivardi Khan actually used these words or not, or whether the points adduced by him were valid or not, but that the people thought like this. It is clear from Behbahani's account that the Nawab realised the perils of the situation but felt handicapped in taking counter-measures due to his advanced age. It is also clear that though he loved Siraju'd Dawlah much, he did not think highly of the capabilities of his successor.

Also to be noted is the comparison Behbahani makes with the situation in Persia after the advent of the Portuguese in the Persian waters and their control over the trade in that area. The Persian rulers wanted to counter the dominance of one European power with the help of another. The Mughals, writes Behbahani, wanted to adopt the same method. He refers to Aurangzeb in this connection. True, the Portuguese had all but disappeared by that time, but earlier they had been a source of troubles to the English. Their intrigues had led to the expulsion of Hawkins from Agra. Clashes had occurred between the two and the English had defeated a Portuguese naval squadron at Swally near Surat in 1612, and again in 1614. These English victories might have made the Mughals think of using them against the Portuguese.

It cannot be said that Behbahani suffered from some kind of Anglophobia. The traditional account he recalls about Alexandar the Great thinking of conquering the British Islands, and of his tutor, Aristotle, advising him against the step on the grounds that the very climate of the place was such that it would nurture a love of independence, shows that he shared the impressions about the bravery and sagacity of the British.

At the same time, he refers frequently to the tactful, if not cunning, ways of the British in India. He underlines the changes which had occurred in their position and attitude since the time of Aurangzeb (d. 1707) to that of Muhammad Shah (d. 1748). The episode he mentions about the English being ordered by Aurangzeb to fill up immediately the moat they had dug unauthorisedly around the Fort at Calcutta, and their doing so in a frantic hurry (their Chief and seniors filling up their hats with the earth and dumping it in the moat) builds up a vivid image, even if it may only figuratively be true. He contrasts this with the situation in Muhammad Shah's time, when the Mughal rulers were so afraid of the English that they could not build a fort in their own realm. The contrast is both interesting and instructive.

The concluding portion of Behbahani's observations, where he speaks of Culcutta being an abode of infidelity, and the crowds of Armenians and Hindus thronging the streets, which made him feel ill-at-ease, is indicative more of a feeling of cultural alienation. It was not just the multitude of the non-Muslims on the streets but many other things too—the bad water, the oppressive climate, the swarms of mosquitoes, etc., which made him feel rather uncomfortable, and keen to move on to the next part of his journey.

To conclude, Behbahani's account is a valuable source-material which helps us to see some aspectsof the situation in India in the second half of the 18th century from a new angle. It enables us to have a glimpse of what the Indians themselves thought of a new developing situation.

NOTES

1. The villages of Deh-i Kalkatta and Sutanuti, *pargana* Amirabad, village Gobindpore, *pargana* Paigan, *sarkar* Satgaon, were sold by, 'obedient to Islam', Manohar Dutt, son of Basudev, son of Raghu; Ramchand, son of Vidyadhar, son of Jagdish; Ram Bhadr, son of Ramdeo, son of Keshav; Pran, son of Kasheeshar, son of Gauri; and Manohar Singh, son of . . ., to the English Company for a sum of Rs. 1300/- on the 19th Jamadiu'l Awwal, AH 1110 (9 November 1698).

   This and some 50 other Mughal documents in Persian, bearing on the activites of the English East India Company in Bengal, Bihar and Orissa have been translated into English, and annotated by Mr. Fathat Husain in his unpublished M.Phil. dissertation, Aligarh Muslim University, 1988.

   Attention may be drawn to the practice of noting in the sale-deeds the name of not only the father, but also grandfather of the seller.
2. To mention only a few of the earlier ones; Rev. W.H. Hart, *Old Calcutta: Its Places and People, 100 Years Ago*, 1895; Maria Graham, *Journal of a Residence in India (with views)*, 1812; J.H. Stocqueller, *Hand-Book of British India*, 1845; E. Mitshell, *Guide to Calcutta*, 1890; Rev. J. Long, *Selections from Unpublished Records of Government, 1748-67*, 1869; Hon. Emily, *Letters from India*, 1872; *List of Tombs, Statues and Monuments, Bengal*, 1896.
3. Lt. Col. Mark Wood, *Plan of Calcutta, Reduced from the Original Executed in 1784-85* (published by W. Baillie, 1792); A. Upjohn, *A Map of Calcutta and its Environs Taken in 1792 and 1793*; W.J. Wood, *Panoramic Views of Calcutta*.
4. It is a technical term in Islamic jurisprudence, denoting a person capable of exercising personal judgement, based on the Qur'an and *Hadith* in matters of law and theology.
5. For biblographical notes on the copies available, see paras below.
6. Another copy of the work has been selected for purchase in a meeting of the Selection Committee on 20 March 1997. It is in the process of acquisition.
7. A reprint, Patna, 1977, Cat. no. 629 (Handlist no. 276), fol. 276. The cataloguer gives a detailed folio-wise account of the contents of the work.
8. Ibid; Cat. No. 628 (Handlist no. 275) fol. 382, bound in two volumes, marked A and B.
9. Handlist No. 4498, dated AH 1236 (1820-1).

10. No. 52, Sulaimaniyah Library, Patna City.
11. Charles Rieu, *Catalogue of the Persian Mss. in the British Museum*, vol. 1, London, 1879, p. 385, No. Add. 24052, fol. 348, dated Azimabad, AH 1225 (1810-11). A summary of the contents, drawn up by the author, covering 27 pages is prefixed to the volume. Another copy, Addl. 23546, fol. 127 (probably incomplete), dated early 19th century.
12. Inasharat-i Amir Kaboi, Tehran, 1991.
13. *Miratu'l Ahwal-I Jahan Numa, Travelogue*, by Allama Wahid Behbahani, vols. I & II, The work is available in the Khuda Bakhsh Library, Accession nos. 95559-60.
14. Khuda Bakhsh Library *Catalogue*, vol. VII, no. 628 (Handlist no. 275), pp. 180-5, and Rieu, *Catalogue*, vol. 1, pp. 385-6.
15. A.H. Haider, formerly, Director, Arabic and Persain Research Institute, Patna, *India in the Early 19th Century, An Iranian Traveller's Account, English translation of Miratu'l Ahwal-i Jahan Numa by Ahmad Behbahani, d. 1819 AD*. The work was done with the help of the award of a Senior Research Fellowship by the Indian Council of Historical Studies, New Delhi, and published by the Khuda Bakhsh Library, Patna.
16. Khuda Bakhsh Library Ms. Handlist no. 4498, and the Madrasa-i Sulaimaniyah Library, referred to above.
17. This is how the name is spelled in the Ms. The name, Bombay, has now, officially, been changed to 'Mumbai'.
18. A technical term, meaning certification by the leading *'Ulama* to the effect that the recipient is well-versed in religious sciences.
19. For a discussion of Behbahani's comments on Patna and some other towns of Bihar, see Imtiaz Ahmad, 'Foreign Travellers' Observations in Bihar: A Comparative Study', S.H. Askari, ed. *Comprehensive History of Bihar*, vol. II, part II, Patna, 1987, pp. 547-67.
20. *Catalogue*, rpt., Patna, 1977, Cat. no. 628 (Handlist no. 275), ff. 382.
21. I am thankful to my friend Mr. Faiyyazuddin Haider, former Head, Dept. of Persian, Patna University, for his help and comments.
22. Behbahani had proceeded from the south, and arrived at Calcutta from Mausalipattam.
23. In the Persian lexicons, the pronunciation of a word was usually indicated in this way. The word, 'Albatta' means 'although'. That, however, is not relevant here; but the pronunciation of the corresponding rhyming word.
24. For comments on this significant remark, see *infra*, p. 10.
25. The holy city in Iraq, containing the mausoleum of Imam Husain, grandson of Prophet Muhammad.

A useful feature of Behbahani's account is that he often compares a particular situation/feature here with that in Iran. For example, after visiting the famous warm-water spring at Sitakund, near Monghyr, he recalls similar water-springs in Iran, whose water possessed medical properties.

26. He seems to be referring here to the major tributaries of the Ganga, not all of them join the Ganga near Calcutta.
27. These are the names of the sons of the famous Iranian ruler, Faridun. Tur was the younger of the two, and one who gave his name to the area called Turan. The point being emphasised here is that place was so well-fortified that, short of a scarcity of provisions inside, it was virtually unconquerable.
28. For comments on this, see *infra*, p. 12.
29. Khuda Bakhsh Library Ms. Cat. no. 628 (Handlist no. 275), Part A, fol. 143b-146.
30. This portion occurs later (ibid. Part B, ff. 305-7). Behbahani begins it by stating that the Portuguese had become very powerful on the Persian coast, and controlled the trade passing through some of the Persian ports. So, in order to counter the Portuguese dominance, the Persian rulers had allowed the English to settle in Bandar Abbas. Subsequently, the need was felt to push out the English too, but that did not prove to be easy because of the superiority of the British guns over the swords of the Persian *sawars*.

    Behbahani is showing here an awareness of the crucial factor of the military and technological superiority possessed by the British. Writing at another place, Behbahani, while referring to Lord Lake's campaigns against the Maratha chief, the Holker (1805), attributes Holker's defeat to the superiority of the guns over the swords.

    For a similar awareness of this important point, shown by the Wahhabis in India in their pamphlet literature, see my *The Wahhabi Movement in India*, 2nd rev. edn., Manohar, New Delhi, 1994, p. 287.

    To return to Behbahani, he recalls a tradition about Alexandar the Great thinking of conquering the British Islands, and decimating all its inhabitants, and of Aristotle advising him against such a step because the very climate of the islands was such that it nurtured a love of independence among the people, and the new settlers, who would come in, would soon imbibe that quality.

    The remarkable insight shown by Behbahani, as well as the Mughal and Persian rulers, in the mutual rivalries of the European trading companies deserves attention.
31. I.e. the Safavids of Iran. Aurangzeb was trying to a similar method of using one European power against another. This deserves notice in the context of the largely unexamined question of the Indian ruling circle's response to the rising power of the European trading companies. It appears that they were quite as dumb spectators as they are often taken to be.
32. See *infra*, p. 11
33. See *infra*, p. 11.

34. This throws light on the norms of chivalry, and concept of kingship at the time.
35. Khuda Bakhsh Library Ms. under reference, f. 307b.
36. Italics are mine.
37. See my article, 'Works on Mughal Administrations: A Survey', in *The Indian Historical Review*, vol. XIV, nos. 1-2, 1987-8, p. 147.

CHAPTER 7*

Lucknow

AN OLD INDIAN

. . . Returning through the wide, clean, and extensive thoroughfare Huzrut Gunge, we pass the wholesome-looking market-place, and several large Mahomedan buildings with imposing painted gateways, one of which we will enter. It is the resting-place of Amjad Ali Shah, the father of the ex-King of Oudh. It consists of a large double square enclosing a considerable area; but the interior is in a very neglected state. A little below is the Begum's Kotee, now used as a post-office, which was the first line of defence taken by Outram's troops when making their way towards the Kaiser Bagh. A breach was formed through the walls parallel with the Imambarra, and the troops thus enabled to advance free of the enemy's fire, which had been arranged to command only the road.

At the back of Amjad Ali's tomb, removed from the Huzrut Gunj Road, in an immense irregular pile called the Zuhoor Buksh, is a very extensive native printing-office, where missionary works, school books, &c., are printed in the vernacular, and where some one or two hundred men may be seen busily engaged in practising Guttenberg's mighty art in the most stolid manner possible; troubling themselves but little as to the results which are likely to flow from so wide-spread a diffusion of knowledge amongst an uneducated people. The seed, it is true, falls on hard ground, but some, nevertheless, takes root, and ultimate good cannot but accrue. Lucknow boasts its vernacular paper printed at this press. It is very extensively circulated, and eagerly read; but, unfortunately, the native press does not, as a rule, set about its teachings or discussions in the way necessary to insure respect and attention.

Moving on in an easterly direction you next come to the Kaiser Bagh, which was erected by the ex-King of Oudh, in 1850, at a cost,

*An Old Indian, *Calcutta to the Snowy Range* (London, 1866).

it is stated, of 80 lacs of rupees. Its shape is that of a series of quadrangles, approached through massive painted gateways, adorned with the regal emblem, 'two fish embowed, and respecting each other', as the heralds have it. Incongruous as is the architecture of the place, and erratic as is the plan of its courts, gardens, pavilions, and avenues, it must have presented, in the days of its founder, a truly brilliant spectacle, surrounded with all the gaudy and striking appurtenances of an Eastern court, which knew no bounds to its extravagance.

The following is a very correct circumstantial account of the place, which I extract from a brief Lucknow Guide:

The Kaiser Bagh, the great work of the ex-King's reign, was commenced in 1848, and finished in 1850 A.D., at a cost (Wajid Ali's), including furniture and decorations, of eighty lacs. Kaiser is the same word as Caesar, a title adopted by the kings of Oudh, and used by them on the royal seal to describe this palace. It will be best to suppose the visitor to enter at the north-east gateway, which faces the open space in front of the Tarawallie Kothie. Through this gate, and through a small gateway on the right hand, which is now closed up, the captives were conducted to their prison. We, however, pass up the open court in front of the gate called the Jillokhana, or place where the royal processions used to form and prepared to start from; and turning to the right, through a gateway covered by a screen, we cross the Cheenie Bagh (so called from the large China vessels with which it was decorated), and going under a gate flanked by green mermaids, we come to the Huzrut Bagh. On the right hand we have the Chandiewallie Baradurrie, which used to be paved with silver, and the Kas Kukam and Badshah Munzil, which used to be the special residence of the king. His vizier, Nawab Ali Nukie Khan, used to reside above the mermaid gateway we have just passed under, in order that he might be close to the king, and obtain instant information of all he was doing. On the left we have the large confused pile of buildings called the Choulukie, built by Azeemoolah Khan, the royal barber, and sold by him to the king for 4 lacs. It formed the residence of the chief muhuls and of the queen. The rebel Begum held her court here, and it was in one of the stables near this that our captives were kept for weeks. Proceeding along the road-way, we pass close by a tree paved round the roots with marble, under which Wajid Ali used to sit in the days when the great fair was held, dressed in the yellow clothes of a Fakeer. Moving onwards, we pass under the great Lukhee-gate (so called from having cost a lac in building), and come into the magnificent open square of the Kaiser Bagh proper, the buildings round which were occupied chiefly by ladies of the Harem. In the month of August, a great fair used to be held here, to which the whole town was admitted. Proceeding past the stone

Baradurrie, fitted up as a theatre (but at present the assembly-rooms of the British Indian Association), and under the western Lukhee-gate, which corresponds to the eastern one just described, we have on our left the building known as the Kaiser Pusond, surmounted by a gilt semicircle and hemisphere. It was built by Roshun-o-Dowla, the vizier of Nuseer-od-deen Hyder, confiscated by Wajid Ali Shah, and given by him as a residence to a favourite muhul, Masook-ul-Sultan (it is now used for public offices). On the right is another Jillokhana, corresponding to the eastern one, by which we entered the palace; and turning down it, we find ourselves outside the Kaiser Bagh and opposite the Sher Durwaza, or Neill gateway, under which General Neill was killed by a discharge of grape-shot from a gun posted at the gate of the Kaiser Bagh, which we have just left. [Marshman, in his Memoirs of Havelock, says he was shot from an upper room.]

Between the great quadrangle of the Kaiser Bagh and the Cheenie Bazaar stand the two tombs of Sadut Ali Khan (called after his death, by a sort of apotheosis, Jinnut Aramgah, or the one whose soul is in Paradise) and of his wife Murshid Zadie. Both these tombs were built after their death by their son Ghazee-ood-deen Hyder, who thereby displayed a very uncommon amount of filial affection. The spot on which the Sadut Ali's tomb now stands was formerl y occupied by a house in which Ghazee-ood-deen Hyder lived during his father's reign, and it is reported that, when he came to the throne and occupied Sadut Ali's palace, fully appreciating the change in their respective situations, he remarked that, as he had now taken his father's house, it was but fair that he should give up his own to his father. Accordingly, he gave orders to destroy his former abode, and raise on the site a tomb to Sadut Ali Khan.

Almost facing the Kaiser Bagh, on the other side of the road and separated by an enclosed green plot neatly railed in, is the Tarawallee Kotie, formerly the Observatory, and now the Bank of Bengal. The enclosed space in front is memorable as the spot where, during the mutiny, the massacre of the English captives sent in by the Dhowzear Rajah and the Mithowlie Rajah took place, after they had suffered a dreadful series of indignities and hardships. The memorial erected on the spot gives the names of most of the sufferers. It is satisfactory to know, however, that the prime instigators and abettors of these deeds, Rajah Joylal Singh, Bundeh and Futteh Ali, were ultimately discovered and hung in sight of the very spot they had made infamous by their sanguinary cruelty.

You now get a very pleasing view of the river Goomtee, which is crossed here by a bridge of boats, and lower down by an iron and stone bridge. The former is a not inelegant structure, commenced in the time of Nusser-ood-deen, but not completed until the reign of Mahomed Ali Shah (about 1840). The stone bridge is a clumsy edifice, built by Asf-o-Dowla, about AD 1780.

It was along the stone bridge that the rebels escaped on the capture of Lucknow. Our troops were insufficient in number to occupy both this and the iron bridge, at which latter, however, we had guns posted, playing on the former, and these did terrible execution amongst the flying rebels.

A short distance in advance of the Residency stands—The Muchee Bhowan Fort.— This was formerly the stronghold of the Seikhs in years long gone by, and is situated on the main road leading from the Residency towards the Hoseynabad. At the wish of Sir Henry Lawrence, an attempt was made to fortify and provision it on the first serious indication of disturbances, in 1857. It was at this time closely surrounded by houses, and considered by the engineers of the time (as it ultimately proved to be) quite untenable. It was abandoned, in great part blown up, and the guns spiked, on the night of the 30th of June 1857; the garrison effecting this, and their junction with the residency troops, without the loss of a single man. It is believed that had the attempt to hold both the Muchee Bhowan and Residency been persevered in, both must have fallen, from the numerical weakness of the defensive force. The fort has since been repaired, enlarged, and altered, and all surrounding houses cleared away from its vicinity; but it is not even now much relied on as capable of any prolonged defence. A strong military position is in course of construction at Char-Bagh, the southern entrance to the city, which will enclose the railway station, the arsenal, and enough accommodation for the European residents in case of an emeute.

We now arrive at the great architectural gem of Lucknow. Entering through a pair of lofty imposing double gates, and passing from an inner court under a large gateway on the left, you enter the enclosure of the Great Imambarra. This truly magnificent hall, said to be the largest in the world, stands on an elevated terrace approached more immediately from two vast square courts, richly laid with tesselated pavements, the innermost court being elevated considerably above the other, adding thus to the effect of the building as viewed from below. It is described as

The crowning work of Nawab Asf-o-dowla's reign. He is said to have spent incredible sums on it, and the native report, always prone to exaggerate, puts the cost at a million sterling. The architects were invited to submit their plans to a competition, Asf-o-dowla only stipulating that the building should be no copy of any other work, and that it should surpass anything of the kind ever built in beauty and magnificence. Kyfeeut-ool-lah was the name of the successful competitor, and it would be hard to say that its conception, as it stands before us in the present day, falls at all short of the large and liberal stipulations of the monarch. The building is as solid as it is graceful, built from very deep foundations, and no wood-work is used throughout.

The Great or Royal Imambarra is now used as an arsenal, and, fitted with the stern implements of war, it presents a striking contrast to what it must have done when in the time of its splendour. The great hall is 162 ft. long by 53 ft. 6 in. wide, and lofty in proportion, with carved and highly ornamented roof. On the two sides are verandahs, respectively 26 ft. 6 in. by 27 ft. 3 in.; and at each end is a fine octagonal apartment, 53 ft. in diameter, the whole interior dimensions being thus 263 ft. by 145 ft. At the death of its founder he was interred here, but during his lifetime it was probably used as the grand celebration place for the Mohurrum; since Knighton, in his *Private Life of an Eastern King,* observes that an Imambarra is a building raised by the sect of Moslems called Sheeahs, for the celeberation of the Mohurrum; and he describes in another chapter the Mohurrum as kept in the time of Nusseer-o-deen in, as I take it, this very building—'The Imambarra on this day was fitted up, of course, with extraordinary splendour, and when the preparations were complete, the public were admitted to gaze upon the glittering, although somewhat *bizarre,* scene. They crowded the vast hall in thousands; some admiring the strangely-varied collection of chandeliers, one of which alone, as I well remember, contained more than a hundred wax-lights.'

On the capture of the Imambarra by Sir Colin Campbell, at the taking of Lucknow, these chandeliers, mirrors, and the like, were ruthlessly destroyed by our infuriated troops; and Mr. Russell describes the marble floor as having been three inches thick with the debris of the valuable decorations it contained. To the right of the Imambarra stands a copy of the Delhi Jumma Musjid, having two lofty four-storied minars or towers, an ascent to the upper galleries of which is rewarded by a truly superb view of the city and surrounding country.

The great Imambarra stands near the Room-i-Durwaza or Constantinople Gate of Lucknow—a gate built, it is asserted, on the model of that which gave to the court of the Sultan of Turkey the title of 'The Sublime Porte'. The gate is grand and elegant in style, and well harmonizes with the Imambarra itself. Much of the effect, however, which would otherwise be produced by the magnificent structures in Lucknow, is lost from very sameness. The architecture all partakes more or less of the same character, as do also the decorations of the buildings. The designs are pure Moresque in most cases, and the Palace of the Alhambra will give, in its various parts, a copy of almost all the styles of stone carving and decoration in Lucknow.

It is stated that both the Room-i-Durwaza and the Great Imambarra were undertaken in a year of great famine, to provide the starving population with bread; but judging from the system of forced labour then prevailing, and from the capricious acts of the kings of those times, I should be inclined to attribute the origin of these works to a far more personal ambition.

The next notable building, and one closely adjoining the Great Imambarra, is the Hoseinabad Imambarra. It was erected by Mahomed Ali Shah, the successor of the 'Eastern King' described by Knighton. This man, the uncle of Nusseer-o-deen, reigned only four years, and does not appear to have performed any other noteworthy act than the building of this place, and of a large tank adjoining. He commenced, however, close by, a Musjid, which was intended to surpass anything of the kind, as well as a seven-storied watch-tower. But his death interrupted both, and the unfinished remains are still as they were at that time. The Hoseinabad Imambarra is, in comparison with its grander neighbour, insignificant, but nevertheless of great beauty of execution and finish in detail. It stands in a large quadrangle, occupied in the centre by a marble reservoir of water, crossed by a fanciful iron bridge. On the water floats an ugly punt, with a very admirably executed model, made in England, of the Nawab's favourite charger. The quadrangle is, for its size, injudiciously crowded with buildings and contains a very poor model of the Taj at Agra. The Hall itself is filled with massive but old-fashioned mirrors and enormous upright chandeliers, standing ten feet high, and hung with all kinds of coloured glass globes. A great number of chandeliers also hang from the roof, and with the crystal and coloured globes and glass ornaments with which the place is filled, and the stained and painted windows, the effect when illuminated must be wondrously brillant. The throne of the King, covered with beaten silver, and his Begum's divan of solid silver supports, velvet hangings, and silver ceiling-work, are also seen here.

In the open court, along the parapet of the fountains, up the pillars, across cornices, and on every conecivable inch of brickwork and plaster, are iron sconces for lamps, which, in the Mohurrum, are duly lighted. It must truly, at that time, be a sight worth seeing, and I only regretted I could not stay for it.

Tired almost with gazing at the gorgeous effect of the pure white marble and lofty ornamented roofs of these wonderful structures, we returned to our hotel, having made arrangements, through the kindness of Major Chamberlain, to see the native quarter of the town in the only way that it can properly be seen, viz., from the back of an elephant.

It takes, properly speaking, three days fully to explore the city of Lucknow. I had already spent two in viewing the various places of interest here described, and the third day I devoted to a visit to the bazaars, to the Secunderabagh, Shah Nujeef, and to a charming country ride through a diverging road leading behind the town towards that point where the Alumbagh forms the apex of the junction of this road with the Grand Trunk Road from Cawnpore. It now only remained, therefore, to make this visit to the native city.

CHAPTER 8

Muslim Culture and Religious Thought

YUSUF ALI

Educated in Wilson College, Bombay, and St. John's College, Cambridge, the author of this paper was called to the Bar from London's Lincoln Inn in 1896. He joined the Indian Civil Service in 1906, and held various positions in government. He was also connected with various Muslim organizations, including the Muhammadan Educational Conference, and the Islamia College in Lahore. A member of the Royal Asiatic Society, Abdullah Yusuf Ali wrote a fair number of books, including *Life and Labour of the People of India* (1907), and translated the Koran, in three volumes.

In considering the interactions of the civilizations of India and the West, especially on the religious side, it should be borne in mind that the Indian Muslims stand on a somewhat different footing from their Hindu fellow-citizens. The differences are due partly to historical causes, partly to the sociological structure of the Muslim community, and partly to a difference in the nature of their religious ideals. The historical causes as they affect Islam generally are of world-wide significance. Islam is a world religion. From its origin it has been in intimate contact with Christianity and Judaism. Its contact with Greek and Roman ideas has been constant. Its earliest exponents clothed their systematic expositions in methods developed in the defunct schools of Alexandria and in the cosmopolitan philosophies which they borrowed. In the age of Charlemagne the more characteristic ideas of the modern West were enshrined in

*Yusuf Ali, 'Muslim Culture and Religious Thought' in L.S.S. O'Malley (ed.), *Modern India and the West: A Study of the Interaction of their Civilizations,* London, 1941.

Arabic works, and the practical arts and sciences were cultivated by the Muslims. Cordova in Spain and Palermo in Sicily were centres at which the West met and commingled with the Islamic East. The medical school of Salerno in Italy, to which may be traced the germ of the university system of Europe, looked back traditionally to four masters as its founders—a Greek, a Latin, a Jew, and a Saracen. In politics, in commerce, in navigation, and in the warlike enterprises of the Crusades, there were intercourse and interactions, conflicts and borrowings, which left their marks deep on the history both of Islam and of Europe. The *Ilm ul Kalam* of Islam and the medieval theology of the schoolmen of Christianity, the Neoplatonists and the Sufis, show subtle interrelations, sometimes direct and sometimes unconscious, which indicate how religious influences acted as between East and West.

In India Islam was subject to certain special influences. The Muslims, coming as conquerors, consciously borrowed little from India itself, though learned men, like Albiruni, studied deeply Hindu sciences, Hindu philosophies, and Hindu ethics. But they could not help being indirectly affected by their environment, and the bulk of the Indian Muslims, who came into Islam by conversion, brought with them their ethnic heritage in the form of customs, domestic traditions, ingrained ideas of social schemes like the joint-family system, and certain customs relating to marriage, inheritance, and priestly ceremonies. On the other hand, the Arabs, Persians, Turks, and other Muslims of non-Indian stock brought with them their inherited instincts and ideas, which included ways of thought and life cast in a more western mould.

Even on the soil of India itself the Muslims were not as isolated as the Hindus from the rest of the world. A constant stream of Persians, Afghans, and Turks was attracted to India all the time that the Muslims held sway there. When Vasco da Gama landed at Calicut, on 20 May 1498, a messenger whom he sent ashore was met, and accosted in Spanish, by a Moorish Muslim merchant from tangier (or Tunis), who introduced the Portuguese to the Zamorin's Court and acted as an intermediary between the Portuguese, who knew no Indian language, and the people of Malabar, who knew no western language.[1] Vasco da Gama's pilot from the east coast of Africa to the west coast of southern India was an Arab. Arab commerce and shipping had been till then predominant in the Indian Ocean, and there was a considerable Arab colony in southern India.

The Muslims have been particularly susceptible to outside influences on account of their sociological structure. However, great the pull exerted by local factors, they have on the whole resisted any tendency to racialism. The absence of a feeling of racialism prepared the Muslim mind freely to receive impressions and influences from outside. 'Seek knowledge,' said the Prophet, 'even though as far as China.' This principle has gone a long way towards the formation of the religious ideals of Islam, which have always tended towards cosmopolitanism. And religious ideals with Muslims include social and intellectual ideals. An interesting instance of this spirit of receptivity is mentioned by the French traveller Bernier, who visited India from 1659 to 1667. He held a salaried post as physician in the Court of Aurangzeb and a similar position with Danishmand Khan, who was Governor of Delhi and directed the affairs of the Mughal foreign department. Bernier was a philosopher and had been a disciple of Gassendi. He was a welcome exponent to his Agha of the philosophy of Descartes (1596-1650), which rejected scholastic theology and opened a new horizon by the use of the recent discoveries in experimental science. Danishmand Khan was eager to learn about Harvey's theory of the circulation of the blood and Pecquet's explanation of the conversion of chyle into blood, and got Bernier to translate for him into Persian the works of Gassendi and Descartes.[2]

The wide horizon created by historical, sociological, and religious influences was, however, narrowed for the Indian Muslims by other causes which operated in the eighteenth and nineteenth centuries. In their conquest of India a handful of foreign origin, drawn from the most vigorous races of Islam, had been reinforced by Indian elements. These latter were numerically strong and their psychological heritage very considerably modified the practical working of Islam among them. There had been mass conversions, especially in Kashmir and in eastern Bengal, mainly at the bottom of the social scale. In Islam the converts found a status of equality, but their minds still ran in the old grooves. Muslim saints were worshipped almost like Hindu gods and godlings. The Prophet and (among some Shias) Hazrat Ali were raised almost to divine rank. The Buddhist worship of relics insidiously crept into Islam. Religious processions and Muharram celebrations began to partake of the character of *rath jatras* (Hindu car festivals). The mystic teachers known as *pirs*, ascetics, and holy men began almost to create a priesthood and a hereditary sacred caste. Necromancy and a belief in omens and magic gained ground, in spite of the Koranic protest against them. Pure monotheism and the moral fervour of a society based on social equality began in practice to recede into the background.

These tendencies were much strengthened with the decline of Muslim power in India, because (a) the recruitment of the Indian Muslim community from brother Muslims outside India ceased; (b) the higher classes of Muslims began to sink into poverty and to be submerged in the lower social strata; (c) Muslim education began to contract both in quantity and quality; (d) learned men began to connive at popular practices, and, as the lamp of their learning began to burn less brightly, were themselves caught in the mesh of the influences that surrounded them; and (e) the loss of political power to the British made the former Indo-Muslim governing classes bitter against the British and against the western civilization which they represented.

The result was that the intellectual and religious leadership of Muslim India fell from its early standards. A people who might have been expected from their antecedents to be most favourable to the new civilization became bitterly and implacably hostile to it. Politics and economics reacted on ethics and religion. And it must be confessed that there was much in the British attitude, conscious and unconscious, that fanned this hostility. To cite one instance, the Marquess Wellesley, in writing to the Secret committee of the Company's Court of directors on 28 September 1801, used these words;[3] 'It is not consistent with the dignity of the British Government to employ any native of this country as its representative at a foreign court, nor could the British interest be with any degree of safety confided to any person of that description.' Many of the finer and more skilled industrial arts of India had been in the hands of Muslims, and they were ruined by the fiscal policy of the East India Company. The higher posts in pre-British India, in the army, in the administration, and in the learned professions, had been in Muslim hands. Many of the higher and middle classes were reduced to beggary and joined Pindari bands and seditious movements aimed at the British power. The Christian missionaries found no field for their propaganda among the Muslims, and their main influence, direct and indirect, was exerted on the Hindu mind. Hence we find such progressive movements as that of Raja Rammohun Roy among the Hindus, but they had no counterpart among the Muslims. On the other hand we have the Faraidhi and the Wahhabi movements of the early nineteenth century, which were hostile to the British, politically and culturally, and caused great searchings of heart in Muslim circles. Other movements, too, aimed at reform, but, as we shall see, their inspiration was not Western until we come to the days of Sir Saiyid Ahmad Khan.

A glimpse into the Indian Muslim mind of the end of the eighteenth century is afforded in the book of travels written in Persian by Mirza Abu Talib Khan, of Oudh and Bengal, who travelled in England, Europe, Asia, and Africa, in 1793-6.[4] He praises many good qualities in the English people, but he condemns three features: their want of religion, their luxurious living, and their contempt for other nations. He had in his mind of course not only what he saw in his travels, but also his experiences in contemporary India. He was not peculiar in his views. Thousands of his co-religionists in India would have slurred over the virtues which he praised, and merely pointed to the vices which he condemned. Their general mental attitude was one of opposition to the West and little was done to effect a *rapprochement*. The Calcutta Madrasa founded by Warren Hastings (1781) and Fort William College, which the Marquess Wellesley, in 1800, established in Calcutta for the training of British civil servants, did, however, gather a few learned Muslims together at the capital of India and had some slight influence on Muslim cultural development. The casting of type and the printing of Indian writings by movable type was also a contribution to cultural progress. Charles Wilkins, a 'writer' in the Bengal service, was the first to caste types in the Bengali and Persian characters. Urdu uses the Persian character, and it is noticeable that the so-called Wahhabi literature, to be mentioned presently, was type-printed;[5] and it is probable that the type it used derived its origin from Wilkins's type. Neither Urdu nor Persian type-printing has caught on in India, much to the misfortune of the Indian Muslims. They are still content in the main with lithographic printing. Had the first type been cast, not in imitation of calligraphic writing, in which the letters change shapes and merge into each other, but in distinct unchanging shapes, Urdu type-printing and the evolution of modern Indo-Muslim culture might have had a different and more favourable history.

We have tried to analyse the causes of the hostility of the Indo-Muslim mind to British education and British culture at the beginning of British rule in India. Let us now consider some of its consequences. There is no doubt that the Muslim mind at the beginning of the nineteenth century entertained the deepest suspicion of the British, who had destroyed their power, and of western culture, which was in their mind associated with the British. The hatred of Tipu Sultan to the British is well known. It induced him to accept the French Revolution, call himself 'Citoyen Tipu', and correspond with the directory in France. It cost him his throne and his life. The Nawabs of the Carnatic, though nominally friendly to the British, sympathized with Tipu, and their State was annexed in 1801. About the same time the British relations with the Nawab-Wazir of Oudh were not happy; and all the resources of British diplomacy were required to suppress the anti-British party that raised its head again and again in the Court of the Nizam of Hyderabad. The feelings of suspicion and distrust which prevailed in such fragments of Muslim power as remained drifted across to British territory. British rule was still new, and none of the agencies to explain the higher side of British culture and British character had yet taken root in the country. Such as there were, were gladly used by the Hindus, Government by non-Hindus was nothing new to them and, in spite of their caste exclusiveness, the new commercial regime opened out to them avenues of employment and gain. They readily took to the language of their new rulers—as readily as they had taken to Persian, the official language of the Muslim rulers. The Hindu College in Calcutta (now Presidency College), which was founded in 1861, disseminated English knowledge among the Hindus and made their reform movements (and even to some extent their reactionary movements) follow western lines in a manner which was then impossible for the Muslims.

There were four reform or reactionary movements in Indian Islam which we may now consider in some detail. They have often been confused by English writers on account of their contact at certain points and because they seemed in a way all directed towards resisting the onrush of western ideas. But when they are examined they will be found to have originated in different circumstances, to have been fostered by men of very different characters, and to have left their mark in quite different degrees on Indian Islam. These four movements we shall group under the names of their four respective leaders, Shah Abdul Aziz of Delhi, Saiyid Ahmad of Bareli, Shaikh Karamat Ali of Jaunpur, and Haji Shariat-ullah of Faridpur. I have named Shah Abdul Aziz first, as I consider that his influence has been the most lasting of all and persists to the present day. Doctrinally, it inspired at least two of the other movements, though the practical shape they took was outside the scope of Shah Abdul Aziz's school of thought.

Shah Abdul Aziz taught the need for reforming Islam in India by purging it of superstitious practices which it had borrowed from Hinduism and restoring the creed of early Islam as taught by the Prophet. His disciples and followers started puritan movements, which may be called 'Back to the Quran[6] movements', as their object was to make the Quran take its proper place as the foundation of belief and guide of conduct. A militant propaganda was set on foot by Saiyid Ahmad, who proclaimed that India, being under non-Muslim powers, was a *dar ul harb* or war zone, in which a *jihad,* or holy war, should be waged against unbelievers. He and Muhammad Ismail took for their field of action not British India, where there was religious toleration, but the then non-British Punjab, where Muslims were oppressed and persecuted by the Sikhs. They made their base in the Swat Valley, where from 1824 to 1831 they kept up a militant campaign against the Sikhs, capturing Peshawar itself in 1830. They brought a large number of their followers from India, but the backbone of their fighting strength was the sturdy Afghan. Valour and enthusiasm, however, availed them nothing against the disciplined armies and European equipment of Ranjit Singh, and they fell fighting at Balakot in 1831. The movement continued for some years, with its head-quarters at Sittana on the Swat frontier, and after the British annexation of the Punjab it became anti-British. But it became a mere frontier political movement and has no further interest for us in this connexion.

The movement led by Sheikh Karamat Ali, who was born at Jaunpur early in the nineteenth century and was also a disciple of Shah Abdul Aziz of Delhi, had a wholly peaceful and religious aim. He was able to bring a large number of ignorant Muslims to abandon the extreme doctrines by which they were being led into dangerous paths of political irredentism. One of these doctrines was that as India was no longer a Muslim country, the Muslims should consider themselves as in a war zone (*dar ul harb*), in which the celebration of the congregational Friday prayer and the celebration of the two joyful festivals of Id were unlawful. He taught that on account of the prevalence of complete religious liberty India was not a *dar ul harb,* and that the celebration of the Friday congregational prayer and of the two Id festivals was not only lawful but obligatory. He did much to stabilize Muslim opinion in Bengal, and indirectly facilitated the movements which brought the Indian Muslims again into the circle of western education and western ideas.[7]

The most popular movement which Karamat Ali's school had to contend with was the Faraidhi (pronounced in India *Faraizi*) movement of eastern Bengal. This was partly religious and partly agrarian. It was founded by Haji Shariat-ullah of Faridpur. He performed the Mecca pilgrimage in 1802, at a time when the Wahhabi ferment was beginning to show itself, but he himself belonged to the Shafii school. On his return to Bengal he began to preach purity of faith and conduct, and obtained a large following among the peasantry. He declared the country to be a *dar ul harb*. Therefore, he argued, Friday congregational prayers and the celebration of the two Id festivals were unlawful, and Muslims should exert themselves to bring about normal conditions in which they could exercise these important rites of their religion. The tenantry of Eastern Bengal were mostly Muslims, whom the exactions of their Hindu landlords had reduced to great poverty, and the propaganda was as much agrarian as religious. Under Shariat-ullah's son, Dudhu Miyan (Muhammad Mohsin), the Faraidhi organization was further tightened up, and a sort of Jacquerie movement, with a no-rent campaign and a regular fund, was set in full working order. This resulted in riots in 1838, but the peasantry were well-protected by their boycott of British courts, the absence of witnesses making legal process impracticable. The religious side of the movement slowly toned down, and it has nearly lost its force with advancing education. But other forces, and from other parts of India, have since brought the eastern Bengal Muslims into the circle of modern western ideas, especially since the foundation of the Dacca University in 1921.

Puritan movements in India are loosely spoken of as Wahhabi. In official literature the frontier movement and the seditious movements of the 1860s are so labelled, as well as Shaikh Karamat Ali's movement and that of the Faraidhis. But this is without warrant. None of them was organically connected with the movement started in Arabia by Muhammad ibn Abdul Wahhab (1707-87), which sought its inspiration from Imam ibn Taimiya of the Hanbali school of Muslim theology, was literalist and puritanical in tendency, and had for its chief practical aim the abolition of tribalism in Arabia. Many of the Indian movements followed the Hanafi and the Shafii schools and expressly disclaimed or even criticized or attacked the Wahhabi rejection of *Tasawwuf* or orthodox Sufi philosophy, though they sympathized with the reform which seeks the abolition of extraneous customs and forms and rites. Perhaps the only Indian school of thought which may legitimately be called Wahhabi is that known as the Ahl-i Hadith. This, however, has no importance either numerically or doctrinally, and its main general principle, that nothing should have authority in Islam except the Quran and the Hadith traditions, is practically universally accepted in theory by all schools.[8]

We have hitherto spoken of the negative side of our inquiry, of the resistance to western civilization rather than receptivity of its influences, salutary or otherwise. But the resistance may itself be considered one of the factors due to the circumstances in which western influences had impinged on Muslim institutions and Muslim thought in the eighteenth and early nineteenth centuries in India. Owing to loss of power and dignity, loss of honourable employment and the comforts of material life, owing to poverty and injured pride, there was a degradation in Muslim standards, which prevented curative forces from coming into operation, as they did later. In British India this continued till after the Mutiny. But there were favoured spots like Oudh, where the Muslim court, raised to the dignity of a royal court by the Marquess Hastings, was the focus of a very active convergence of influences. It is true that there was much evil as well as much good introduced on both sides. The private life of some of the Oudh kings may not bear strict investigation, but we are concerned more with general influences than with particular lives, and there is no doubt that there was in Lucknow a general 'European Mania',[9] as an anonymous writer calls it, in the reign of King Nasir-ud-din Haidar (1827-37). Even now, after the lapse of a century, the appearance of Lucknow, with its spacious undulating parks, its Italian statuary, and the Martinière recalling memories of General Claude Martin, the French soldier of fortune, speaks of an early Europeanization that extended from outward things to inner thought and current literature.

Bishop Heber visited Lucknow in 1824 in the reign of Ghazi-ud-din Haidar and has recorded his impressions in his *Narrative of a Journey through the Upper Provinces of India*. He found the appearance of Lucknow more like 'some of the smaller European capitals (Dresden for instance) than anything I have seen in India'.

He spoke of 'a very handsome street indeed, wider than the High Street at Oxford, but having some distant resemblance to it in the colour of its buildings, and the general form and Gothic style of the greater part of them'. Speaking of a wedding breakfast at the Residency, at which the king of Oudh was present, he gives a glimpse of the mind of the king.

> At this breakfast he was more communicative than he had been, talked about steam-engines, and a new way of propelling ships by a spiral wheel at the bottom of the vessel, which an English engineer in his pay had invented, mentioned different circumstances respecting the earthquake at Shiraz which had been reported to him, but were not named in the Calcutta newspapers, and explained the degree of acquaintance which he showed with English books by saying he made his aides-de-camp read them to him in Hindoostanee.

Bishop Heber tells in another place that the King had 'a strong taste for mechanics and chemistry', and retained a good English painter, whose son was his equerry and European aide-de-camp. His successor, Nasir-ud-din Haidar, inherited his scientific and artistic tastes and often wore European dress and a European hat. He built an observatory, which was in the charge of an English Astronomer-Royal, a Colonel Wilcox, and he had a German painter and 'musician in his entourage; the royal palace was full of good pictures, including portraits by Zoffany.'[10] Altogether the atmosphere of the Lucknow court was brilliant and cosmopolitan.

These external influences were reflected in literature. The Urdu literature of the best Lucknow period is full of joy and pride. New ideas took root and new methods were adopted, which made original contributions to it, though it would be far-fetched to suggest that all this was due directly to Western influences. The fine development of *marthiya* (or *marsiya*) poetry under Anis and Dabir went far to introduce an epic element into Urdu literature.[11] The new impulse given to Urdu drama with plays like the *Indar Sabha* of Amanat almost gave a glimpse of European opera to the Urdu-speaking public.[12] Wajid Ali Shah, the last king of Oudh, was full of ideas on art and literature, and his court attracted a galaxy of foreign artists. He had a press where books in Urdu and Persian were printed with movable types; he maintained a museum; and his library contained not less than 200,000 rare books and manuscripts.[13] With the end of the Oudh kingdom in 1856 was extinguished the last bright spot of Muslim cultural development on the old lines as modified by the new civilization from the West.

The tragedy of the great revolt in 1857-8 marks the death of the old order, and brought political, economic, and cultural disaster to the Indian Muslims. It made their sullenness, their aloofness, their suppressed hatred for the new order more marked than ever. For many years afterwards the Muslims steadily lost ground in education, in the public services, and in general leadership in India. But no great community can commit suicide in that way. The key to the whole situation was adaptation to the new environment, use of the new forces that had come into play, acceptance of the new instrument of progress that had been created through English education. Sporadic efforts were made in this direction in many places, but the concentrated effort that won the field was the Aligarh movement and the All-India Muslim Educational Conference. The Aligarh movement is so called after the college, the opening of which in 1875 as the Muhammadan Anglo-Oriental College forms a landmark in the history of Indian Muslim education, but it was much more than that. It was a comprehensive reform movement. Its leader, the man who gave it life and soul, was undoubtedly Sir Saiyid Ahmad Khan, but it attracted to its orbit some of the most brilliant contemporary Muslims of northern India, such as the poet Khwaja Altaf Husain Hali of Panipat (1837-1914), the novelist, lecturer, legist, and educationist Maulvi Nazir Ahmad of Bijnor (1836-1912), and the professor, intrepid traveller, and researcher Maulvi Shibli Numani of Azamgarh (1857-1914), a younger man who for sixteen years (1882-98) taught at the college. These are only three of the greatest names on the Indian side, each of them representing a particular phase of the movement, and there was a vast army of support in all parts of India. On the English side, three names stand out and are household words in Aligarh: Mr. Theodore Beck, the first Principal of the college and the right-hand man of the founder in working out the administrative details and putting them into operation; Sir Theodore Morison, who continued to interest himself in the college and the cause long after he had relinquished formal connexion with them; and Sir Thomas Arnold, the scholar and Arabist, who did so much to elucidate by his writings some of the less known features in the history and art of Islam.

Among the objects and ideals of the movement the first place should, I think, be assigned to the desire to make modern knowledge a living force among Muslims, as it was in their palmy days. It has been, and still is, the fashion among Indians to use rhetorical language about the discoveries, inventions, and progress of their ancestors. But rhetoric is not of much practical value, and may even make the community ridiculous and retard their actual progress. The Aligarh school aimed at the practical and fruitful method. The first step was to make the Muslim mind eager for the best modern knowledge in science and art, which is undoubtedly to be found in the West, and to dispel the false notion that it was in any way inconsistent with the Islamic religion. The next step, which was practically simultaneous—the one helped the other—was to use this knowledge in its practical applications to all departments of life and thought.

The Saiyid saw that the way to modern knowledge in India was through the English language, but he felt that English as a language of thought and an instrument of culture could only be the language of a select few in India. The main hope of Indian progress should lie in the presentation of modern ideas and facts through the Indian languages themselves. Persian was still used as the cultural language of upper-class Muslims all over India, but Urdu had wider scope and immensely greater possibilities for the masses. He therefore wrote largely in Urdu and encouraged the growth and cultivation of that language. He may himself be regarded as one of the precursors of a practical, modern, Urdu prose. He even drew up in 1867 a scheme for an Urdu university, which was submitted to government. It came to nothing then; but the idea has since found favour with the Hyderabad State, where His Exalted Highness the Nizam in 1919 established the Osmania University, in which all instruction is given in Urdu.

We now come to education. College education in India is subject to the curricula and the regulations of the university to which the college is affiliated. At the time when the Aligarh College was founded the colleges in the United Provinces were under affiliation to the distant University of Calcutta, as the Allahabad University was not incorporated till 1889. The Calcutta University originated and worked in a milieu totally different from any that suited the Muslims, but at any rate it granted degrees that brought employment in government services and in the learned professions, and to that extent a college of any kind was helpful to the Muslims. But there were two defects which could be cured in a separate Muslim college even under the Calcutta University. Those defects were the lack of residential and social life and the lack of religious education.

It was from the beginning intended that at Aligarh there should be residential hostels or, as they were called, boarding-houses, and that a closely knit residential and social life should be provided, in which not only should the students learn self-discipline among themselves but have opportunities of meeting their professors in informal contacts. A number of Englishmen were intentionally chosen, and Mr. Beck, with his experience of the residential University of Cambridge and his honours as president of the Cambridge Union, proved an admirable choice, none the less admirable because he was appointed Principal of the college at the formative age of 24. The Debating Union of Aligarh became one of the foremost college debating societies in India. Manly English games were also encouraged; Aligarh College was in its conception meant to be a great public school, like the public schools of England, and was sometimes called the Eton of India. Common dining in hall was insisted on. All this was possible in a Muslim institution, because sports and games, common social life, and common meals were among the most rooted of Islamic traditions. For though Aligarh admitted non-Muslim students, its traditions and management were Islamic. These features were absent from the ordinary schools and colleges of India, of mixed composition, because caste and exclusive dining customs were observed among the Hindus and could not be broken without offence to the Hindu students.

Religious instruction was an element which was considered even more vital. The Muslims did not want godless and soulless education, such as ordinary education without religious instructions was apt to become. The State schools were bound to religious neutrality and by their very constitution barred religious education. The missionary institutions gave instruction in the tenets and principles of Christianity, which was unacceptable to Muslims. Instruction in the religion of Islam was what most Muslim parents earnestly desired. The crucial question was what was to be its precise nature. It was easy to provide that attendance at the college mosque was to be compulsory for Friday congregational prayers. But in a graded course of instruction in religious tenets certain difficulties presented themselves. The chief religious cleavage among the Muslims is that of Shias and Sunnis. Even here a common basis could have been found, and has been found elsewhere. But Indian Islam had got into a narrow groove, and a new institution or movement could not afford to offend one side or another. India had not passed through a religious educational history such as has evolved the Cowper-Temple clause in England. It was decided that separate worship and separate religious instruction should be provided for Shias and Sunnis. Separate theological professors were appointed, and religious instruction was not, and has not yet been, distinguished from theology. The majority of the students belonged, and belong, to the Sunni persuasion. Though there is an occasional outburst of *odium theologicum,* there is on the whole mutual toleration of the four recognized orthodox schools of theological thought.

But what about modernism, or anything outside the pale of the four recognized schools? In Aligarh this presented a real difficulty. The founder of the college held views on the interpretation of the Quran which were not acceptable to the community generally. Some of his own lieutenants, staunch in support of his educational policy, dissented from his religious interpretations, based as they were on the right of private judgement, which challenged the accepted standards of authority in matters of doctrine and practice. These he had published in numerous papers and in his commentary on the Holy Book. Among the Maulvis, or recognized religious leaders, there were two classes of men. One consisted of the ordinary bazaar Maulvis, very ignorant outside the narrow circle of their religious knowledge, and as intolerant of new views as they were ignorant. The other consisted of really learned men, but men whose horizon was bounded by the theological writings of the Middle Ages of Islam and who looked upon the new learning with suspicion if not with positive horror.

These various hostile forces pronounced the Saiyid Saheb to be an unbeliever, or worse still, a *kafir,* one who rejected the true religion. What then was to be done? Religious instruction could not be abandoned, or the funds that were necessary would not be forthcoming. Either English education was to be jeopardized by the preaching of religious views obnoxious to the community, or orthodox religious views were to be taught inconsistent with the promoter's views. The latter course was chosen, without bringing the matter to a definite issue. Religious instructors were appointed, to teach on the old lines, which did not really appeal to the students but which appealed to their parents and to the community generally. No definite lines were laid down. Committees were appointed from time to time to give greater definition to religious instruction, but their members often held opposite views, and even the compromise reports which they presented were mostly merely recorded and then forgotten. To this day the nature of religious instruction remains undefined. And this is so, not only at Aligarh, but in other Muslim institutions.

The religious views propounded in Saiyid Ahmad Khan's commentary,[14] and supposed to be held by the Aligarh school, were dubbed *Nechari*, a word which was an importation from English, meaning that they followed Nature rather than Revelation. Those views, it is true, followed a rationalistic line of thought, but they lost sight of historical perspective, and were wanting in the devout fervour of the Sufi schools. They explained away miracles, but it would be a mistake to suppose that they followed the precept of the Stoic school of philosophy 'Follow Nature'. The Stoic practically eliminated God, and his wise man was either a materialist or a pantheist. If a label is to be applied at all to Saiyid Ahmad Khan's scheme of interpretation, it might possibly be called deistic. But it gave a prominent place to Revelation as the main source of religious knowledge, which the eighteenth century of English deism did not. In any case his views never crystallized into a system, or sect, or school, and in spite of personal attacks on him there was never a schism. This was fortunate. The religious views were almost forgotten in the educational effort with which the Aligarh school is identified.

With the testing of religious forms and customs by ethical standards and social behaviour are bound up questions of social reform and the development of sound popular literature. And it is in these matters that the interactions of the East and West appear to the best advantage and are most readily recognized. Aligarh did a great deal in both directions. It evolved a distinctive dress—a national dress if the Indian Muslims can be called a nation—viz., the Turkish cap for a headdress, and the *sherwani*, or closefitting coat, a compromise between the old loose *achkan* or *angarkha* and the short European coat. Boots and shoes of English leather or English fashion also came into vogue. It evolved a less formal code of manners and more businesslike forms of address in correspondence. A higher material standard of living was adopted, with more modern forms of houses. Dinner parties, with the use of forks and knives, chairs and tables, tea parties, and 'At Homes' became fashionable. Customs deriving their origin from Hinduism, which were enforced in the case of Muslims by British courts of law, especially in the

Punjab, came gradually to be disowned. These related mainly to questions of inheritance, in which Muslim law gave definite shares to women as well as men, while Hindu law excluded women. Certain Muslim families, which, on account of these legally enforceable customs, were handicapped in following the Muslim law, made statutory declarations, adopting the full provisions of the latter; and this principle has now been recognized in all-India legislation by the enactment of the Muslim Personal Law Application Act, 1937. The bar against the remarriage of widows, which was observed among the higher castes of Hindus, had been tacitly accepted in Muslim families of Hindu descent. Much literature was produced against it, and a public opinion was created which almost stamped out the objections to it. There was also opposition to plural marriages. They were condemned in Maulvi Nazir Ahmad's novel *Mubtala,* which is only one of a number of social novels which the Maulvi Saheb wrote with a purpose. In *Taubat un Nasuh* he dealt with social life and the moral questions involved from a man's point of view, and in *Mirat ud Urus* with similar problems from a woman's point of view. On the other hand, in *Ibn ul Waqt* (1888) he condemned not only the views of those who took to the new fashions and new civilization, but the excesses to which imitation in dress and manners was carrying the new generation. He had some shrewd thrusts at the smoking of cigars and cigarettes and the off-hand manners of the younger people, as they appeared to the older generation.

Hali, besides writing a strong plea for women's education, wrote his famous poem, the *Musaddas* (1879), which takes us to the wider questions of the rise and fall, the progress and decline, of nations. The last work marks an epoch in the modern awakening of the Muslims of India. Hali's argument is not perhaps historically accurate in details. But in flowing verse he draws graphic pictures of pre-Islamic Arabia and its fallen condition; of the rise of Islam and the elevation of the Arabs to a lofty eminence; of the progress which the early Muslims made in the arts and sciences, in which they led the world; of their subsequent neglect of the manly virtues which Islam had taught them, and their consequent loss of power, position, wealth, and honour. 'With my unskilful hands,' he says modestly in his preface, 'I have built a house of mirrors, in which our people can see their face and form reflected', and he makes a strong and effective appeal to Indian Muslims to give up their ignorance, selfishness, intolerance, and want of cohesion.

The work done by Maulvi Shibli Numani in making the results of modern research available to the Muslim public in their vernacular calls for special mention, and since his death it has been continued under the competent leadership of Saiyid Sulaiman Nadwi in the institution, *Dar ul Musannifin,* which he founded in his native place Azamgarh. His researches into the past history of Islam were not merely for the abstract acquisition of knowledge. He wished to spread knowledge in order that contemporary ignorance might be removed and contemporary life made more intelligent, fuller, and richer. He aimed at teaching the teachers, especially the religious teachers, whose shortcomings and narrowness were a scandal that leapt to the eye in Muslim India.

In devoting so large a part of our attention to work done in connexion with the Aligarh movement, we do not suggest that all credit for modernism in Muslim India should be attributed to it. What we do suggest is that Aligarh was typical of the modernist movement which was spreading in all parts of India in different forms, particularly in the Punjab, in Hyderabad (Deccan), and in Bombay. And many other movements allied themselves with Aligarh, or lent Aligarh their support and countenance. Since the death of Sir Saiyid Ahmad Khan the prestige of Aligarh has to some extent suffered a decline, both in education and in cultural leadership, even though the college was raised to the status of a university in 1920. There are more Muslim centres now, and the leadership of the Punjab in modernist Muslim India has been silently achieved within this generation.

Some of the men whom we have already mentioned belonged to the Punjab, which lent very great support, both financial and moral, to the ideas and impulses affiliated to Aligarh. While Urdu seems to have lost some ground in the United Provinces and other provinces of British India, on account of political currents and cross-currents, it still retains a strong position in the Punjab, where, alone of the provinces in British India, it remains the predominant official language. The vigour and directness of the Urdu writers of the Punjab reflect the Punjabi character. They deal with concrete things. Even if they do not soar into the highest regions, they give a touch of actuality to the modern life and the western ideas surging around them. Perhaps the greatest credit in this connexion is due to Maulvi Muhammad Husain Azad of Delhi, who, during his twenty-five years' work in Lahore (1864-89), laid firm the foundations of Urdu in the Punjab and took a leading part in the organization of Urdu education in that province. He was a man of marvellous memory and intellect and had travelled extensively in Iran, Afghanistan, and Central Asia. He spoke the living Persian of his day, and not merely the language learnt from books. In the same way he made Urdu a language of living interest, not merely a record or following-up of previous tradition. Urdu poetry he purified, both from old forms and old traditional subjects, and he brought back poetry from exaggerated similes, far-fetched metaphors, and too finely drawn-out word-conceits to subjects of nature and human life. Artistic embellishment, he pointed out, was 'like salt to food, but what should we think if food was all salt and nothing else?'[15] His *mushairas* (meetings which were the occasion of poetical contests) had definite subjects given out to them, like 'Rain', 'Patriotism', 'Bigotry', &c., and not mere rhymes to cap. His *Ab-i-Hayat* was a fine literary history of Urdu on modern lines. It was a pioneer piece of work, and in spite of inaccuracies in detail, for which he relied too much upon memory, it holds the field as a popular presentment of the growth of Urdu literature.

The Punjab literary movement claims Sir Muhammad Iqbal (1876-1938) as its best-known international figure. In the early days of his career he was connected with Punjab education, and his European education, in England and Germany, makes him representative in many ways of the interaction of eastern and western civilizations. His activities were many-sided. He took some interest in current politics, having presided over the All-India Muslim League at Allahabad in 1930 and served a term in the old Legislative Council of the Punjab. But provincial politics afforded too narrow a field for him, and in all-India politics he was more of a philosopher than a practical statesman. His genius lay in the direction of developing a mystical interpretation of Islam as the final form both for the development of human personality and for the working out of a great and eternal State coextensive with the whole of humanity. In the only book which he wrote in English, his chapters on the Spirit of Muslim Culture and on the Principle of Movement in the Structure of Islam have a direct bearing on the subjects we are discussing. While he welcomes the reform in Turkey as 'creating new values' instead of 'mechanically repeating old values', his attitude to reform generally is expressed as follows:

We heartily welcome the liberal movement in modern Islam; but it must also be admitted that the appearance of liberal ideas in Islam constitutes also the most critical moment in the history of Islam. Liberalism has a tendency to act as a force of disintegration, and the race-idea, which appears to be working in modern Islam with greater force than ever, may ultimately wipe off the broad human outlook which Muslim people have imbibed from their religion. Further, our religious and political reformers in their zeal for liberalism may overstep the proper limits of reform in the absence of a check on their youthful fervour.[16]

He wholly approves of the spirit of the second Khalifa Umar, 'the first critical and independent mind in Islam, who at the last moments of the Prophet had the moral courage to utter these remarkable words: "The Book of God is sufficient for us." '[17] This implies that Iqbal would prefer an independent and progressive interpretation of the Quran itself to the many glosses put upon it by medieval commentators. It does not imply that he would go to the lessons of European experience except as a warning. For to him European civilization was bad, fraudulent, chaotic, unjust, and greedy. For comments on European civilization, he would go to such writers as Schopenhauer, Nietzsche, Spengler, or Karl Marx, who take a pessimistic view of it. He looks upon political and economic stability, peace, and justice as essential elements in religions, but he thinks that Europe has deserted them. His criticism of European civilization is expressed in many scathing lines and passages in his poetry, both Persian and Urdu. The following two couplets will suffice as a specimen:

The glitter of modern civilization dazzles the sight;
But it is only a clever piecing together of false gems.
The wisdom or science in which the wise ones of the West took such pride
Is but a warring sword in the bloody hand of greed and ambition.[18]

The boasted power of the West is nothing but imperialism to oppress the weak, and the League of Nations is a mere society of robbers to parcel out the graves of those they have killed. The western freedom of women is not real freedom. The unwomanly virgin on the planet Mars in the *Jawid-nama* is an importation from Europe. Woman's true sphere is in a secluded life of love and family. Modern civilization is a godless civilization and can lead to nothing but self-destruction.

Though Iqbal's literary genius and his philosophic interpretation of Islam brought him his immense popularity, he was yet an isolated figure. He founded no school of literary thought, as his principal works were written not in Urdu but in Persian. In public affairs, and in building up the 'new temple' (*naya shiwala,* to use his own words), his influence was negligible. To the conservatives he appeared as a man speaking a new language, and he trod on some of their cherished convictions. To the advanced school with a nationalistic tinge, his attacks on the West seemed to furnish an argument for their patriotism. But in other matters they remained cold. If there is an advanced school of any other tinge, it is silent in literature and daily life.

In the emancipation of women, though the Punjab is now fairly advanced,[19] it has by no means led the way. Bombay, under the lead of the Tyabji family, was a pioneer two generations ago. In the United Provinces Shaikh Abdul Halim Sharar (1860-1926) of Lucknow, the talented novelist and playwright, was an uncompromising opponent of purdah, and published a periodical to further his views. On the other hand, writers holding advanced views on other questions have been conservative in this respect, notable examples being Sir Muhammad Iqbal and Khan Bahadur Saiyid Akbar Husain of Allahabad, who have been caustic critics of purdah reform. In spite, however, of the protests of the more conservative elements western modes of life are being gradually adopted; there are now several Muslim women's periodicals in the Punjab and in Hyderabad (Deccan), and though they do not all advocate the abolition of the purdah system, they are distinctly feminist in their outlook. Indeed, feminism, if it means the legal and social rights of women, was the essence of the reforms introduced by Islam. These reforms were obscured or suppressed by selfishness or ignorance, and there were not wanting Muslim writers in the ages of decline, who misinterpreted ancient texts to conform to the usages and customs which had since grown up. In the process of reinterpreting the spirit of Islam, none has rendered truer service than Nawab Chirag Ali Azam Yar Jang of Meerut and Hyderabad (1844-95) and the Right Hon. Ṣaiyid Ameer Ali, a judge of the Calcutta High Court and the first Indian member of the Judicial Committee of His Majesty's Privy Council in London (1849-1928), though *The Spirit of Islam* written by the latter had perhaps more influence outside India than in India itself.

In the matter of marriage customs there is satisfactory progress. The age of marriage has risen, and plural marriages are fortunately becoming rarer and rarer. Cousin-marriages, leading to inbreeding, are still, however, common among the propertied classes. The leading incentive is the desire to 'keep the property in the family'.

In the Muslim marriage the bride does not bring a dowry to her husband, but the husband has to give or promise a dower to the bride. The abuse of the system was to fix an impossibly high dower because it was not immediately payable, and to demand it in case of death or divorce or where there were dissensions between the families. In many cases the dower was taken by the bride's family instead of being left (as it should be in law) at the sole disposal of the wife. There is much awakening in this matter. The simpler rule of a reasonable *sharai* dower is being adopted more and more. The wedding ceremonies are being curtailed and simplified, and the bride, and not her family, is being recognized as having the right to control and dispose of the dower property.

Education is still in a backward stage, both among men and women, but especially among women, as the figures for literacy make abundantly clear. At the last census (1931) the figures for literacy per cent were 10.7 for males and 1.5 for females, compared with 15.6 and 2.9 respectively for all India. Special efforts have been, and are being, made for Muslim education, and the movement has not left out of its purview the education of girls and women. Nearly every Islamic *Anjuman* (i.e. society or association) in every province devotes some attention to this subject. The All-India Muslim Educational Conference, which meets annually at different centres, collects funds for the purpose, and has passed a number of resolutions urging it on the attention of the community. Along with the Conference a separate Women's Conference is usually held in purdah. Muslims themselves have started a number of girls' schools and women's colleges, in which the purdah custom is observed and religious education is combined with secular education, while general educational institutions are open for those whose parents do not insist on these two features. As a matter of fact, modern education, culminating in a university degree, has a distinct and graded market value in the marriage market. There are some Muslim Inspectresses and Deputy Inspectresses of schools, and special efforts have been made to adapt curricula to the needs and prejudices of the people. If the progress has been and is still slow, it is because of certain special features in Muslim social organization and also because of the paucity of Muslim teachers.

Having brought under review the western influences that have operated on the Muslim mind in India from an historical point of view, and noted the names of the leading characters who have helped in evolving the present situation, we now proceed to sum up the different departments of life and thought in which these influences have operated. The quickening effect of new contacts is to be judged not only by direct influences but also by indirect results and resistances. If we take account of this we shall find that there is scarcely any department of life which has not been affected by western influences.

Take religion first. The Christian missionaries have reaped no harvest worth considering among the Muslims. But their propaganda has produced a number of most interesting reactions on the side of the Muslims themselves. The apologetics which were followed by Shah Abdul Aziz and his circle were very different from those of Sir Saiyid Ahmad Khan and Maulvi Chirag Ali. The latter appealed to reason and modern thought, and in many ways departed from the orthodox interpretation of ancient texts. Mirza Gulam Ahmad of Qadian (1838-1908) founded a new sect, which has a considerable number of followers, called Mirzais by friends and Qadianis by critics. They met the propaganda both of the Christian missionaries and of the Arya Samaj, which was itself organized among the Hindus on modern lines. The movement took definite shape in 1890. The Mirza Saheb claimed to be the promised Messiah of the Jews and Christians and the Mahdi of Muslim tradition. He believed in verbal revelation and claimed that God spoke to him in words. He also claimed to work miracles, to prophesy, and to be, in himself and in the events around him, a fulfilment of previous prophecies. He claimed not to be the bearer of a new dispensation or *shariat* but to be an exponent of the real teachings of Islam. In the words of the present head of the movement, 'Ahmadiyat is Islam itself, and not a mere offshoot of Islam, as Christianity was not an offshoot of Judaism, but was pure Judaism in a plain and simple form'. The Quran 'contains a complete code of teachings suitable to the needs of every age, and provides a remedy for the ills, and means for the moral and spiritual development, of all ages'.[20] The sect is strong in organization, and has an active missionary propaganda both at home and abroad.

Apart from sectarian movements, a much broader spirit prevails among the Muslims as a whole. Urdu and English translations of the Quran have been multiplied, and translations are found in many of the vernacular languages of India. Sufiism is found in some parts, especially Sind and the North-West Frontier Province, but the most recent trends in religious opinion are in a direction away from mysticism. The approach is more and more to the practical simplicity of early Islam.

The influence of western ideas is apparent in two directions. Among intellectuals the indifferentism of modern secular life is not uncommon, and there is occasionally but rarely agnosticism. The majority of them remain faithful to the tenets of Islam, but hold that it is not immutable and favour a liberty of interpretation of the Quran which will enable Islam to be adapted to modern conditions in consonance with modern ideas. Such an interpretation, however, is opposed by the conservative school of thought, which finds support for its attitude in a well-known saying—*La bidaat fil Islam,* i.e. let there be no innovation in Islam. Reaction against western domination led after the conclusion of the Great War of 1914-18 to the Khilafat agitation, but this is now practically dead. In any case it was more a political than a religious movement, though its religious phraseology attracted the Muslim masses. The Hijrat movement of 1920, which was one of its products, recommended a migration of Muslims to Muslim lands, but never commanded wide support. For the few whom it misguided, it ended disastrously, as the Afghans treated the migrants unsympathetically (to use a mild term). The Moplah rebellion of 1921 ended even more disastrously, as it cost many lives and ruined thousands of homes. These, however, were frankly political moves. In more recent times the stress of politico-religious moves has shifted towards organization. The attitude is more communal than religious. The Muslim mind in India is content to remain in the traditional grooves of religion rather than be stirred by any great religious emotions. It follows with admiring interest the political movements in Turkey and Egypt, but is cold towards the modernist religious movements in those countries.

In education Western influences are more positive. Modern education has been standardized in government schools and universities; and private and communal schools and colleges, whatever special distinguishing features of their own they may have, are yet made to conform to general standards by systems of grants-in-aid and general supervision. Even old institutions have tended slightly in the direction of modernization. Modern influences affect even the Dar ul Islam at Deoband, a theological college in the United Provinces, which is one of the homes of extreme orthodoxy. It sends out preachers and emissaries both within and outside India, but in recent years its influence seems to have waned, and its orthodoxy is coming more into line with modern tendencies. The Calcutta Madrasa, which is controlled by government, has a modern side, and the Delhi Arabic College has to submit to the standards of the Delhi University. The *Nadwat ul Ulama* in Lucknow owes a great deal of its modernization to the efforts of Maulvi Shibli Numani. The Jamia Millia of Delhi was started under the impulse of Muslim nationalism by the late Mr. Muhammad Ali as a rival to the Aligarh University, but is, under its present competent management, of a severely modern and practical type. The Firangi Mahall used to be a stronghold of extreme orthodoxy, but its politics are coming into the orbit of the Indian National Congress under the distinguished lead of Maulvi Abul Kalam Azad, who, in his Urdu commentary on the Quran, has not disdained to use the results of the researches of modern European archaeologists in support of some of his arguments. It may be said generally for the whole of India that 95 per cent of the students of this generation receive an education, even if it is not in English, of a kind wholly different from the traditional education of a century ago. There is also a strong reaction against this spirit of modernization, and it has several counts of well-founded criticism. It is not, however, for us here to go into the merits of the question on one side or another.

In literature the influences are still more patent. And here the results have been achieved not so much by the co-operation and help of western people, as by the assimilation by Indians themselves of tendencies, characteristics, methods, and ideas, which their western education has instilled into their mental fibre. All the vernacular languages and literatures of India have been affected in this way. Speaking of Muslims we are concerned chiefly with Urdu The structure of the language and its syntax have undergone some modifications owing to its contact with English. Its vocabulary has been largely enriched with modern terms derived from English. The attempt to stem this process by coining learned words of Perso-Arabic origin has to a large extent been neutralized by the logic of facts. In Urdu literature the influence of English has been studied in sufficient detail by Saiyid Abdul Latif.[21] We may not agree with his finding that there was no Urdu prose before the era of English influence, but there can be no doubt that Urdu prose has undergone considerable modifications under that influence, as can be seen at once on glancing at the columns of any modern Urdu newspaper.

The Urdu novel has made great progress in lightness, flexibility, and unity. The pioneer publication, the *Fasana i Ajaib* by Rajab Ali Surur (*obiit* 1867), was overburdened with old mannerisms and a rigid style of rhymed prose. The story rambled on without any relation to the facts of life, and there was hardly any delineation of character. Since then the novel has gradually undergone a complete transformation in form and style. There is now more attention paid to psychological characterization and the actualities of life. There is also a truer and more flexible prose. New forms of literature have come into vogue, such as the short story, the detective novel, essays, biography, history, and travel. The short stories of Prem Chand (United Provinces) are admirable, and a number of young Punjab writers are devoting themselves to this form of fiction.

The whole of the modern political movement is based upon western ideas, though their working in Indian conditions has led to considerable modifications in theory and practice. Separate communal electorates were insisted upon by the Muslims when the present electoral system came into vogue, and they have been claimed by, and granted to, other minorities in India, such as the Sikhs, the Indian Christians, the Europeans, and the scheduled castes. The possession of a vote, either in local bodies or in provincial or central legislatures, has tended to alter the balance of social forces in the country as a whole and within the different communities. It is not only in the political field that the effects are seen. They are gradually transforming social ideas and habits and the customs of everyday life. The extension of the franchise has touched large classes of people. It is estimated that the new constitution of 1937 granted the vote for the legislatures to 30 millions of persons, of whom the majority are illiterate. The vote is used for other purposes besides politics, and the evils which Ibsen denounced in *The Pillars of Society* may be seen in action. What the ultimate results in the lives of the people may be, it is difficult to say. But in many of the private bodies and *anjumans*, the 'vote' figures as an important feature, and '*party-bazi*' (the play of a factious party spirit) has become an element to reckon with.

The irresistible force of example, opportunity, and environment in bringing in western influences is seen every day in such matters as houses, dress, furniture, sports, subjects of conversation, and modes of entertainment. The old-fashioned *haveli* (mansion), with its separate quarters for men and women (*mardana* and *zanana*), is fast becoming *démodé*. Even in the houses of the old design there is usually now a room or rooms where guests sit at chairs and tables, and smoke cigars and cigarettes, instead of reclining on carpets on the ground, supported by thick cushions, with a *hookah* (hubble-bubble) to smoke or a *pan-dan* on which to serve betel leaves and betel nut. The modern young Muslim considers a turban a bore and affects a fez (or Turkish cap so-called), or, if he is sufficiently advanced, a European hat out of doors and a bare head indoors. It is difficult to get tailors now who can cut and make old-fashioned dresses for men. Women, it is true, still adhere to *saris,* but they wear beautiful brooches of western make to keep them in position, and they wear underclothing of western style, though in this matter Western fashions are also somewhat approximating to eastern. No one sees palki or *duli* (dooly) in cities nowadays; the motor-car is the rage for those who can afford it, and the plebeian motor buses and lorries crowd urban thoroughfares.

The schools and colleges, though they still support some of the eastern games, are keenest about cricket, football, hockey, and tennis. The general run of talk is picked up from newspapers, and the old bazaar gossip is turned into the new journalistic sensationalism. The theatre itself was remoulded a century ago on western models. It has now given place to the cinema. In any large city there are ten or twenty vernacular picture houses, with 'sound' films; and quite a number of people, innocent of English, go to English picture-houses, 'to see English manners and morals'. The wireless, helped and encouraged by official agency, has established a secure position in India. In the towns most well-to-do homes and educational institutions now have wireless sets, and there are community or public receiving sets in the villages. It is true the items which most interest the community are those which relate to their own familiar interests. But the broadcasting stations provide catholic programmes (of music, lectures, speeches, &c.), to serve both eastern and western tastes; quite often eastern ears listen to western programmes, and western ears to eastern, and quite a good few sample both impartially. If again you visit a modern Indian fine arts exhibition, you will find that the eastern pictures and exhibits are a mannerism, and the normal exhibits are western in tone, method, and subjects.

On the other hand, movements of reaction against western influences are not absent, though they are sporadic and, owing to the logic of facts, not very effective. Journals like *Al-Irshad,* a monthly issued from Amritsar, avowedly aim at waging war against 'Westernism' (*magrabiyat*) among other things. Probably the other aims of such publications have a more direct appeal than the war against Westernism, but in any case neither their circulation nor their influence is to be compared with the force of the rising tide of Westernism that is flowing into men's minds and habits consciously or unconsciously. The periodical meetings at which westernism is denounced from pulpit or platform are attended by way of religious or communal duty, but the very people who do lip service to such propaganda are often found among the foremost of those in the other camp. The literature of anti-Westernism is growing more and more feeble, as it is usually completely divorced from the actualities of modern life. Perhaps its most caustic verse-exponent was the late Saiyid Akbar Husain, whose *nom de plume* was Akbar. He attacked modernism from many points of view. Of the 'Young Party's' social reform he said that 'the remedy was worse than the disease'. Their politics he compared to 'an owl teaching the hawk to be a nightingale'. Laughing at science and materialism, he says: 'The days are past when they searched for the light of God in their hearts; now they test what phosphorus there is in the bones.' Modern progress he thinks evil: 'the devil invented a new way to bring down men; he said, Let us give them a taste for "Progress"'. The decline of religion is thus satirized: 'He teaches us courage by saying, "It is cowardice to be afraid of Hell".' Elsewhere he says: 'Not through books or colleges is religion to be attained, but only through those venerable (in faith).'

The old issues debated by Maulvi Chirag Ali, such as *jihad*, slavery, captives of war, the position of Muslims in a non-Muslim State, and of non-Muslims in a Muslim State, and the controversies about the precise meanings to be attached to texts, are now matters of historical academic interest, discussed by the learned, rather than matters of present concern. Attention is now focused on the practical issues of social and economic problems, e.g. how far exorbitant dowers are permissible in marriage; how far usury (which is forbidden) is to be distinguished from economic interest, which is in the nature of a share in profits; how far purdah tends to injure the health of women, to affect mothers in the upbringing of their children, or in the management of their households, and to prejudice the evolution of the larger interests of society; and how far plural marriages, which on principle are condemned, can be prohibited, as they are in Turkey.

In all these matters, the actual trend of events is more important than theory or argument, and the trend has decidedly set, in circles that count, in the direction of the usages of the West.

NOTES

1. See the graphic picture of this incident drawn in the seventh book of the *Lusiad*, which here closely adheres to historical facts.
2. *Bernier's Travels*, ed. Constable and V.A. Smith (1914), p. 324.
3. *Despatches &c., of the Marquess Wellesley,* ed. M. Martin (1836), vol. II, p. 580.
4. An English translation was published by Charles Stewart, 2 vols. (London, 1810). Quotations will be found in my *Angrezi 'Ahd men Hindustan ke tamaddun ki tarikh* (Allahabad, 1936), pp. 131-4.
5. *Angrezi 'Ahd*, Chapter 2.
6. Anglice Koran.
7. See my article on Karamat Ali in the *Encyclopaedia of Islam.*
8. Sir Willam Hunter's account in his 'Indian Musalmans' (1872), is, of course, accurate as regards the facts elicited from official documents and state trials for treason, but as regards doctrinal discussions it is an unconscious travesty. Unfortunately it has been followed in some articles in the *Encyclopaedia of Islam.*
9. *Private Life of an Eastern King* (1855), by a Member of the Household (ed. W. Knighton), p. 113.
10. See *Private Life of an Eastern King.* pp. 13, 253.
11. See my remarks on this subject in Chapter 7 of *Angrezi 'Ahd.* The Marthiya is a specialized form of literature describing the tragic events of Muharram and the martyrdom of Imam Husain.
12. See 'The Modern Hindustani Drama' in the *Transactions of the Royal Society of Literature,* vol. XXXV, 2nd series (1917).
13. *Dacoitee in excelsis, or the Spoliation of Oude*, p. 145.
14. The commentary has been discussed by Khwaja Altaf Husain Hali in his life of Sir Saiyid Ahmad Khan, *Hayat i Jawid* (Agra, 1903), part II, pp. 165-94.
15. The quotation will be found in *Siyar-ul-Musannifin* by Muhammad Yahya Tanha (Delhi, 1928), vol. II, p. 169.
16. *Six Lectures on the Reconstruction of Religious Thought* (Lahore, 1930), p. 227.
17. Ibid., p. 226.
18. *Nazar ko khira karti hai chamak tahzib hazir ki;*
Yih sanna'i magar jhute nagon ki reza-kari hai.
Wuh hikmat naz tha jis par khiradmandan i Magrib ko
Hawas ke panja i khunin men teg i karzari hai.

19. Two Muslim ladies are members of the Legislative Assembly of the Punjab, and one of them, Begum Shah Nawaz, who is as conversant with western social life as with eastern, is a Minister in the government formed in 1937.
20. I have based my account of the Ahmadiya movement on a paper written for the Conference on Religions of the Empire, 1924, by Hazrat Mirza Bashir-ud-din Mahmud Ahmad: see W.L. Hare, *Religions of the Empire* (1925), pp. 106-32.
21. See his book, *The Influence of English Literature on Urdu Literature* (1924). See also Ram Babu Saksena, *History of Urdu Literature* (Allahabad, 1927), pp. 206-10.

CHAPTER 9

The Cause of the Indian Revolt

SAYYID AHMED KHAN BAHADUR

During the revolt of 1857, Sayyid Ahmad Khan (1817-98) served in Bijnor, and wrote an account of the happenings (*History of Bijnor Rebellion,* translated with notes and introduction by Hafeez Malik & Morris Dembo). His best known book on that tumultuous event is *Asbab-i Baghawat-i Hind*, a candid account of the grievances against British rule. This is what he wrote in his preface to the book: 'The following pages though written in 1858 have not yet been published. I publish them now, as although many years have elapsed since they were indited, nothing has occurred to cause me to change my opinions. An honest exposition of Native Ideas is all that our Government requires to enable it to hold the country with the full concurrence of its inhabitants and not merely by the sword.' Major-General Graham and Auckland Colvin translated the *Asbab* in 1873.

IN THE NAME OF GOD, THE MERCIFUL,
THE COMPASSIONATE

"Obedience and submission become the servant;
Forgiveness is the attribute of God:
If I should do amiss
Reward me as seemeth right in Thine eyes",

Since I began this essay on the causes of the rebellion in Hindustan [India] I have been tempted to keep silence on the events of the past, and even to wish my remembrance of them should be blotted out. The proclamation issued by Her Majesty contains such ample redress for every grievance which led up to that revolt, that a man

*'The Cause of the Indian Revolt', Written by Sayyid Ahmed Khan Bahadur, C.S.I. in Urdu, in the Year 1858, and translated into English by his two European Friends, 1873.

writing on the subject feels his pen fall from his hands. Why enter further into the matter when the cause of all the dissatisfaction has been discovered and provided against? Yet I think that loyal men, and such as really wish well to their government, should not content themselves with reflection: but explain with all possible fidelity, their views on the origin of this rebellion. Although, therefore, the causes of complaint have been met, and the grievances redressed, I think it my duty to record my opinion on the subject. That many well-informed, able, and experienced men have written on the causes of the disturbance, I know; but I am not aware that any native of the country has hitherto been among their number. I venture therefore, publicly to express my opinion.

What Were the Causes of the Rebellion in Hindustan?

Definition of 'Rebellion': exemplified with instances

Before answering this question, let us ask what is the meaning of the word, rebellion. To fight against the Government, to aid and assist those who are resisting the authority of Government, to set at nought, and to disobey the orders of Government with a view to resist its authority or with contempt and disrespect to infringe the rights of Government, and disregard it prerogations in any, or in all of these, I take it that rebellion consists.

Let us Clearly Recapitulate the Above

1. To fight with, or oppose, the servants, or subjects of Government.
2. To neglect, and set at nought the orders of Government, with a view to resist its authority.
3. To aid and assist or in any way take part with those who are in open opposition to Government.
4. To shew a turbulent disposition, and such as is likely to lead a lawless riot, and disregard of the authority of Government.
5. To swerve at heart from respect and loyalty to the Government; and in times of trouble, to withhold from it an active support.

In that said year, 1857, there was not one of these forms of rebellion which did not find a place. There are but few men in truth, even amongst the best of us, who may not be connected under the latter head; which though in appearance of little import, is in reality of no small weight.

Why it is resorted to

The primary causes of rebellion are, I fancy, everywhere the same. It invariably results from the existence of a policy obnoxious to the dispositions, aims, habits, and views of those by whom the rebellion is brought about.

From this it follows that widely-spread disaffection cannot spring from any solitary, or local cause. Universal rebellion must arise from universal grounds for discontent or from streams deriving from many different sources, but finally merging into one wide-spreading, turbulent water.

The Rebellion of 1857 did not originate from a single cause, but from a complication of causes

As regards the rebellion of 1857, the fact is, that for a long period, many grievances had been rankling in the hearts of the people. In course of time, a vast store of explosive material had been collected. It wanted but the application of a match to light it, and that match was applied by the mutinous army.

The distribution of 'Chuppaties', had not league for its object

In the course of the year 1856, and almost simultaneously with the outbreak, chuppaties were passed from hand to hand in many districts. Cholera happened at that time to be raging in Hindustan. Some have imagined that these chuppaties were used as a kind of Talisman to keep off the cholera, the superstitious Hindustanees [Indians] being in the habit of using such talismans. The fact is that even at the present day we do not know what caused the distribution of those chuppaties. We may be very sure, however, that they could never have been used with the object of spreading a conspiracy. We have, in Hindustan, I know, a custom of passing messages from tongue to tongue in this way; but with these chuppaties there is no such message passed. Had there been, it would have been sure to have leaked out; known as it would have become to every native, to all races and tribes, and to men holding every kind of opinion. The manner in which the rebellion spread, first here, then there, now breaking out in this place and now in that, is alone good proof that there existed no widespread conspiracy.

Russia and Persia not chargeable with a league in this matter

Nor is there the slightest reason for thinking that the rebels in Hindustan received any aid from Russia or from Persia. The Hindustanees have no conception of the views of Russia, and it is not probable that they would league themselves with her. Nor can I think that they would ever be likely to receive any help from Persia. As between Roman Catholics and Protestants, so between the Mussulman [Muslims] of Persia and of Hindustan, cordial co-operation is impossible. To me it seems just as credible that night and day should be merged in one, as that these men should ever act in concert. Surely, if such were the case, it is very strange that during the Russian and Persian wars, Hindustan should have remained completely tranquil. Nor on the other hand is it less strange that while Hindustan was in flames, there should have been in those countries no visible stir whatever. The notion of an understanding existing between these countries must be set aside as preposterous.

The subject of Proclamation which was found in the tent of a Persian prince discussed

The proclamation found in the tent of a Persian Prince is no proof of a secret understanding with Hindustan. It was evidently written with the view of animating and encouraging the Persians. The mutinies are spoken of in order to keep up the spirit of the Persian soldiers. There is nothing whatever to imply the existence of an understanding with the mutineers.

The despatch of a farman by the ex-king of Delhi to the king of Persia not improbable, but not the origin of the rebellion

I see nothing strange in the fact, if fact it were, of the ex-king of Delhi having written a farman to the Persians. Such an imbecile was the ex-king that had one assured him that the angels of Heaven were his slaves, he would have welcomed the assurance, and would have caused half a dozen farmans to be prepared immediately. The ex-king had a fixed idea that he could transform himself into a fly or gnat, and that he could in this guise convey himself to other countries, and learn what was going on there. Seriously, he firmly believed that he possessed the power of transformation. He was in the habit of asking his courtiers in Durbar [Court] if it were not so, and his courtiers were not the men to undeceive him. Is there anything wonderful in the fact of such a dotard writing a farman to any person, or at any man's instigation? Surely not: But it is perfectly incredible that such a farman should have formed the basis of any league. Strange that such wide conspiracies should have been for so long hatching, and that none of our rulers should have been aware of them! After the revolt had broken out, no volunteer, whether soldier or civilian, ever alluded to such a thing; and yet had any league existed, there could then have no longer been any reason for concealing it.

The annexation of Oudh not the cause of the general rise

Nor do I believe that the annexation of Oudh was the cause of this rebellion. No doubt, men of all classes were irritated at its annexation, all agreed in thinking that the Honourable East India Company had acted in defiance of its treaties, and in contempt of the word which it had pledged. The people of Oudh felt on this occasion much as other men have felt whose countries have been annexed by the East India Company. Of this, however, more hereafter. But what I mean here is that the men who would be the most irritated and dismayed at such a step, were the noblemen, and the independent princes of Hindustan. These all saw that sooner or later such a policy must lead to the overthrow of their own independence and confiscation of their own lands. Nevertheless, we find that there was no one of the great landed princes who espoused the rebel cause. The mutineers were for the most part men who had nothing to lose, the governed not the governing class. To cite in contradiction of what I say the cases of the nawab of Jhujjar, and the rajah of Bulubgurh, and other such petty feudatories would shew little else than ignorance of the status of the various Hindustanee chiefs.

The national league not framed with the view of overthrowing the government of strangers

So too we must reject the idea that the natives of this country rose of one accord to throw off the yoke of foreigners, whom they hated and detested. The English did not obtain the Government of Hindustan in a day. By little they have spread their authority. They date its commencement from the year 1757: the year in which Siraj-ud-dowlah was overthrown on the plains of Plassy, from that day until a comparatively recent date, all men, high or low, have remained well-affected to the English Government. They have long been accustomed to hear of the good faith, the clemency, the consideration, and the leniency of the Government, of the noble qualities of the high moral character of those by whom it has been conducted. Hindoo and Mussulman, all who have been under English rule have been well content to sit under its shadow. Foreign princes have relied implicitly upon the English: A promise given, or an agreement made by them has been looked upon as graven on stone. The Government is twice as strong in these times as it was in the earlier years of the century; while the native princes, the subahdars and the nobles do not retain one tenth of the power they then had. The Government was continually engaged at the period in wars with every race and religion in India, with Hindu and Mussulman alike. Its career was one long victory. All natives of the country saw that some day the English sway would extend itself over the whole of Hindustan and that all races, religions alike must sooner or later be held within the English grasp. And yet during those early years we hear of no attempt at revolt, no striving against English authority. Find if you can any mention of such in the History of India. Had a national hatred been the cause of this rebellion, should we not have found it betraying itself in the former times; in times, as I have said, when the relative power of the nations gave far greater facilities for such an outbreak? During the wars which commenced in 1839, there was not a single attempt at a revolt in Hindustan, and yet for a hundred years Hindustan had been governed by the race from which sprang the princes against whom those wars were conducted. It was to those princes that the Mussulman owed their very preference and influence in India. How then can it be supposed that the present revolt originated from hatred on the part of the Mussulman against those who had wrenched the kingdom from them?

The position of ex-king of Delhi well-known within the town, and its environs, but overrated in the district provinces

No one ever had the slightest hope that the King of Delhi would revive the Empire. The eccentricities and follies of the king and of his house had lost him all respect in the eyes of the world. It is no doubt true that people outside the walls of Delhi, who were less well informed as to his conditions, his mode of life, and his general incompetence, did look on him as emperor. The Hon'ble East India Company, they believed to be his viceroy. But those who lived in and about Delhi held him in no esteem whatever. Hence it happened that when the king was virtually deposed, no Hindustanee felt the slightest regret.

Declaration of Lord Amherst in 1827 to the effect that the sovereignty of India belongs to the British Government

It will be remembered that in the year 1827 Lord Amherst openly declared that our Government was no longer in any way subservient to the house of Timour [Mughal emperors], and that the East India Company was *de facto* the sole sovereign power in Hindustan, and that when this declaration was made, the natives expressed no dissatisfaction. The only men probably who felt any chagrin were the relatives and personal attendants of the king

The Muhammadans did not contemplate jehad against the Christians prior to the outbreak

There are again grounds for supposing that the Muhammadans [Muslims] had for a long time been conspiring or plotting a simultaneous rise, or a religious crusade against the professors of a different faith. The English Government did not interfere with the Muhammadans in the practice of their religion. For this sole reason it is impossible that the idea of a religious crusade should have been entertained. Thirty-five years ago a celebrated Moulvie Muhammad Ismael [died in 1830] by name preached a religious crusade in Hindustan and called upon all men to aid him in carrying it out. But on that occasion he distinctly stated that natives of Hindustan subject to the British Government could not conscientiously take part in a religious war within the limits of Hindustan. Accordingly while thousands of jehadees [Muslim fighters] congregated in every district of Hindustan, there was no sort of disturbance raised within British Territory. Going northwards, these men crossed the Punjab frontier, and waged war in those parts of the country. And even if we should imitate the know-nothings in the various districts and call the late disturbances a religious war, it is very certain that no preparations were made for it before the tenth of May 1857.

None of the acts committed by the Muhammadan rebels during the disturbances were in accordance with the tenets of the Muhammadan religion

It must be remembered that the men who in those times raised so loud the cry of 'jehad' were vagabonds and ill-conditioned men. They were wine drinkers and men who spent their time in debauchery and dissipation. They were men floating without profession or occupation on the surface of society. Can such fellow[s] as these be called leaders of a religious war? It was very little that they thought about religion. Their only object was to plunder Government treasuries and to steal Government property. To be faithless to one's salt is to disregard the first principle of our religion. To slaughter innocents, especially women, children and old men would be accounted abominable. Can it possibly be imagined then, that this outbreak was of the nature of a religious war? The fact seems to be that some scoundrels, prompted by greed and hoping to gain their end by deceiving fools and increasing their own numbers, gave the disturbances the title of a religious war. The project was worthy of the men, but there was no crusade.

The futwah of jehad printed at Delhi was a counterfeit one

I know that the futwah which was printed at Delhi is looked upon as a convincing proof that the rebellion was in fact a crusade. I have gone into the question, and I find very strong proof to the effect that this futwah was a forgery. I am told that when the mutineers arrived at Delhi from Meerut, some persons expressed a wish for a futwah as to the expediency of a religious war. Every opinion given was against such a step. I have only seen a copy of the futwah I allude to. The original has been lost and it is impossible to say how far the copy may be authentic. But I may mention that on the arrival of the Bareilly mutineers at Delhi, a second futwah was published with the object of instigating a religious war, and there is not the smallest doubt that this second futwah was a forgery. The man who had it printed, and who was a turbulent fellow, and a noted scoundrel, attached certain names to it in order to deceive the public, and gained for it thus a degree of credit. He stamped it, by the way, with the seal of a man who had died before the commencement of the mutinees [*sic*]. It may be added that some of the Bareilly mutineers, and their rebel brethren caused several seals to be forged. This fact has become a matter of notoriety.

A large number of the moulvies who considered the king of Delhi a violator of the law left off praying in the Royal Mosque

Many of the Delhi moulvies and their followers considered the King little better than a heretic. They were of the opinion that it was not right to pray in the Mosques to which he was in the habit of going and which were under his patronage. These men never read prayers in the Jumma Musjid. Long before the mutiny broke out, they had published a futwah on the point. Can it be thought that men holding such views would give a futwah in favour of a religious war and of placing the king at the head of it? Among the men whose seals were affixed to the futwah above alluded to, were many who have sheltered Christians, and guarded their honour and their lives. Of these men not one took an active part in the rebellion, or shewed himself in the ranks of the rebel army. If they in reality held the opinions which are usually ascribed to them, why did they act in this way? It is my firm belief that the Muhammadans never dreamed of forming a combination in order to carry on a religious war against the Christians. It was ignorant and disaffected men who raised the cry of 'jehad' and 'Haidree'. Presently I shall speak of the causes of discontent among the Muhammadans on the score of religion. I will then show how far such discontent really did exist, that the Muhammadans were, in every respect more dissatisfied than the Hindus, there is little doubt. Hence it was that, in many districts the greater proportions of rebels were found in their ranks. Nevertheless, in districts where the Hindus rebelled, matters were carried to as great extremes.

The Bengal army was not previously in league for an outbreak

A conspiracy, or concerted league never existed in the army. It is well known that after the mutiny had broken out, no sepoy [Indian soldier] ever mentioned such a thing. True that after the affair at Barrackpore, and especially in the Punjab, on the introduction of the new drill, men of several regiments used to meet together and declare they would never allow the use of the new cartridges. But they formed no plan whatever; on the contrary, they believed that Government would not insist on carrying out the order. The order was not carried out. But after the 2nd of May, when it had been withdrawn, the mutinies had broken out, and could no longer be checked by such means; a flame had been lit, that was not to be thus quenched.

Nor was there any league between the army and the ex-king though it is not improbable that some Sepoy or non-commissioned officer may have been his disciple

So too there never existed a previous understanding between the rebel army and the ex-king. The idea is entirely without foundation. No one looked upon the king as sovereign or as consecrate; men used to flatter him to his face, and laugh at him behind his back. The people clung to him from no feeling of loyalty, but with a view to their own advantage. Very likely privates, and subahdars in some of the regiments were in communication with him. This however does not prove that there was any general understanding between him and the mutineers. The rebel army collected at Delhi, it is true, but after it had thrown off its allegiance to the Government, there was no one but the king of Delhi round whom it could rally. The fact of their gathering at Delhi is in itself no proof of a conspiracy. It was impolitic and unwise of Government to keep up the semblance of a king at Delhi. Lord Ellenborough's views on this point were sound and it is a pity they were not put more thoroughly into practice. The king of Delhi was a spark from a furnace which, wafted by the wind, eventually set all Hindustan in a blaze.

The non-admission of a native as a member into the Legislative Council was the original cause of the outbreak

I believe that this rebellion owes its origin to one great cause to which all others are but secondary branches so to speak of the parent stem. I do not found my belief on any speculative grounds or any favourite theory of my own. For centuries, many able and thoughtful men have concurred in the views I am about to express. All treatises and works on the principles of Government bear me out. All histories either of the one or the other hemisphere are witnesses to the soundness of my opinions.

Most men, I believe, agree in thinking that it is highly conducive to the welfare and prosperity of Government: indeed is essential to its stability that the people should have a voice in its councils. It is from the voice of the people only that Government can learn whether its projects are likely to be well received. The voice of the people can alone check errors in the bud, and warn us of the dangers before they are burst upon [us] and destroy us.

A needle may dam the gushing rivulet. An elephant must turn aside from the swollen torrent. This voice however can never be heard and this security never acquired, unless the people are allowed a share in the consultations of Government. The men who have ruled India should never have forgotten that they were here in the position of foreigners, that they differed from the natives in religion, in customs, in habits of life and thought. The security of a government, it will be remembered, is founded on its careful observance of their rights and privileges. Look back at the pages of history, the record of the experience of the past, and you will not fail to be struck with the differences and distinctions that have existed between the manners, the opinions, and customs of the various races of men: differences which have been acquired by no written rule or prescribed by any printed form. They are in every instance the inheritance of any peculiar race. It is to these differences of thought and customs that the laws must be adopted, for they cannot be adopted to the laws. In their due observance lies the welfare and security of Government. From the beginning of things, to disregard these has been to disregard the nature of men, and neglect of them has ever been the cause of universal discontent. Can we forget the confusion that ensued on the acceptance of the Dewannee by the British Government in the year 1760, a confusion brought about by the ignorance then prevailing? If one wishes to recall those times, he can read of them in Marshman's History. Who on the contrary, does not remember the prosperity of Bengal under the rule of Lord Hasting [*sic*]? I attribute it to the knowledge of its peculiarities and the acquaintance with the vernacular which obtained in those days.

To form a Parliament from the natives of India is of course out of the question. It is not only impossible, but useless. There is no reason however why the natives of this country should be excluded from the Legislative Council, and here it is that you come upon the one great root of all this evil. Here is the origin of all the troubles that have befallen Hindustan. From causes connected with this matter sprang all the evil that has lately happened.

I do not stay that Government has made no attempt to acquaint itself with the characteristics, and economy of the country. I am well aware that serious efforts have been made. The regulations of Government, the circulars of the Board of Revenue, and Mr. Thomanson's directions to revenue officers are sufficient proof of this. But I do say that Government has not succeeded in acquainting itself with the daily habits, the modes of thought and of life, and likes, and dislikes, and prejudices of the people. Our Government never knew what troubles each succeeding sun might bring with it to its subjects, or what sorrow might fall upon them with the night. Yet day by day troubles and anxieties were increasing upon them. Secret causes of complaint were rankling in their breasts. Little by little a cloud was gathering strength, which finally burst over us in all its violence.

The non-admission of such a member proved a hindrance to the development of the good feeling of the Indian subject towards the Government

The evils which resulted to India from the non-admission of natives into the Legislative Council of India were various. Government could never know the inadvisability of the laws and regulations which it passed. It could never hear as it ought to have heard the voice of the people on such a subject. The people had no means of protesting against what they might feel to be a foolish measure, of or giving public expression to their own wishes. But the greatest mischief lay in this, that the people misunderstood the views and the intentions of Government. They misapprehended every act, and whatever law was passed was misconstrued by men who had no share in the framing of it, and hence no means of judging of its spirit. At length the Hindustanees fell into the habit of thinking that all the laws were passed with a view to degrade and ruin them, and to deprive them and their fellows of their religion. Such acts as were repugnant to native customs and character, whether in themselves good or bad, increased this suspicion. At last came the time when all men looked upon the English Government as slow poison, a rope of sand, a treacherous flame of fire. They learned to think that if today they escaped from the hands of Government, tomorrow they would fall into them; or that even if they escaped on the morrow, the third day would see their ruin. There was no man to reason with them, no one to point out to them the absurdity of such ideas.

When the governors and the governed occupy relatively such a position as this, what hope is there of loyalty or of good-will? Granted that the intentions of Government were excellent, there was no man who could convince the people of it; no one was at hand to correct the errors which they had adopted. And why? Because there was not one of their own member among the members of the Legislative Council. Had there been, these evils that had happened to us, would have been averted. The more one thinks the matter over, the more one is convinced that here we have the one great cause which was the origin of all smaller causes of dissatisfaction.

I see no force in the argument that the Government has allowed a perfectly free press, forbidding it merely to print abusive or seditious language or language of an inflammatory nature. Nor was it of any use to circulate laws before they were finally passed so that every man should have an opportunity of speaking his mind out about them. It was not by such measures as these that evils such as I am writing about could be remedied. Far from it, these half measures were useless.

I do not wish to enter here into the question as to how the ignorant and uneducated natives of Hindustan could be allowed a share in the deliberations of the Legislative Council; or as to how they should be selected to form an assembly like the English Parliament. These are the knotty points. All I wish to prove here is that such a step is not only advisable, but absolutely necessary, and that the disturbances are duc to the neglect of such a measure. As regards the details of the question, I have elsewhere discussed them and those, who wish to enter into it can read what I have said.

The outbreak of rebellion proceeded from the following five causes

This mistake of the Government then made itself felt in every matter connected with Hindustan. All causes of rebellion, however various, can be traced to this one. And if we look at these various causes separately and distinctly we shall, I think find that they may be classed under five heads.

1. Ignorance on the part of the people: by which I mean misapprehension of the intentions of Government.

2. The passing of such laws and regulations and forms of procedure as jarred with the established custom and practice of Hindustan, and the introduction of such as were in themselves objectionable.
3. Ignorance on the part of the Government of the conditions of the people; of their modes of thought and of life; and of the grievances through which their hearts were becoming estranged.
4. The neglect on the part of our rulers of such points as were essential to the good Government of Hindustan.
5. The bad management, and disaffection of the army.

I shall now proceed to consider these five heads, and under them may be classed their sub-heads, distinctly, and in detail.

Cause I

Ignorance on the Part of the People, That is, Misapprehension of the Intentions of Government

I would here say that I do not wish it to be understood that the views of Government were in reality such as have been imputed to them. I only wish to say that they were misconstrued by people, and that this misconstruction hurried on the rebellion. Had there been a native of Hindustan in the Legislative Council, the people would never have fallen into such errors.

Interference in matters of religion

There is not the smallest doubt that all men whether ignorant, or well-informed, whether high or low, felt a firm conviction that the English Government was bent on interfering with their religion and with their old established customs. The believed that Government intended to force the Christian religion and foreign customs upon Hindu and Mussulman alike. This was the chief among the secondary causes of the rebellion. It was believed by every one that Government was slowly but surely developing its plans. Every step it was thought was being taken with the most extreme caution. Hence it is that men said that Government does not speak of proselytising Muhammadans summarily, and by force; but it will throw off the veil as it feels itself stronger, and will act with greater decision.

Events, as I shall presently show, increased and strengthened this conviction. Men never thought that our Government would openly compel them to change their religion. The idea was that indirect steps will be taken, such as doing away with the study of Arabic and Sanskrit, and reducing the people to ignorance and poverty. In this way, it was supposed, the people would be deprived of a knowledge of the principles of their own faith, and their attention turned to books containing the principles of the Christian creed. It was supposed that Government would then work on the cupidity, and poverty of its subjects and on conditions of their abjuring their faith, and offer them employment in its own services.

Secundra Orphan Asylum

In the year 1837, the year of the great drought, the step which was taken of rearing orphans in the principles of the Christian faith, was looked upon throughout the N.W.P. as an example of the schemes of government. It was supposed that when Government had similarly brought all Hindustanees to a pitch of ignorance and poverty, it would convert them to its own creed. The Hindustanees used, as I have said, to feel an increasing dismay at the annexation of each successive country of the Hon'ble East India Company. But I assert without fear of contradiction that this feeling arose solely from the belief in their minds, that as the power of Government increased, and there no longer remained foreign enemies to fight against, or internal troubles to quell, it would turn its attention inwards, and carry out a more systematic interference with their creed and religious observances.

Religious discussion being carried to a great height during the present time

In the first days of British rule in Hindustan, there used to be less talk than at present on the subject of religion. Discussion on this point has been increasing day by day and has now reached its climax. I do not say that Government has interfered in these matters; but it has been the general opinion that all that was done was according to the instructions and hints of Government, and was by no means displeasing to it. It has been commonly believed that Government appointed missionaries and maintained them at its own cost. It has been supposed that Government, and the officers of Government throughout the country were in the habit of giving large sums of money to these missionaries with the intention of covering their expenses, enabling them to distribute books, and in every way aiding them.

The covenanted officers assumed the Missionary functions

Many covenanted officers, and many military men have been in the habit of talking to their subordinates about religion; some of them would bid their servants come to their houses, and listen to the preaching of missionaries and thus it happened that in the course of time no man felt sure that his creed would last even his own life time.

Preaching of the Gospel by the Missionaries

The missionaries moreover introduced a new system of preaching. They took to printing and circulating controversial tracts, in the shape of questions and answers. Men of a different faith were spoken of in a most offensive and irritating way. In Hindustan these things have always been managed very differently. Every man in this country, preaches and explains his views in his own Mosque, or his own house. If any one wishes to listen to him, he can go to the Mosque, or house, and hear what he has to say. But the missionaries' plan was exactly the opposite. They used to attend the places of public resort, markets for instance, and fairs where men of different creeds collected together, and used to begin preaching [to] them. It was only fear of the authorities that no one bid them off about their business. In some districts the missionaries were actually attended by policemen from the station. And then the missionaries did not confine themselves to explaining the doctrines of their books. In violent and unmeasured language they attacked the followers and the holy places of other creeds: annoying, and insulting beyond expression the feelings of those who listened to them. In this way too the seeds of discontent were sown deep in the hearts of the people.

The establishment of Missionary schools and the covenanted officers attending examinations of them

The missionary schools were started in which the principles of the Christian faith were taught. Men said it was by the order of Government. In some districts covenanted officers of high position and of great influence used to visit the schools and encourage the people to attend them; examinations were held in books which taught the tenets of Christian religion. Lads who attended the schools used to be asked such questions as the following: 'Who is your God?' 'Who is your Redeemer?' and these questions they were obliged to answer agreeably to the Christian belief; prizes being given accordingly. This again added to the prevailing ill-will. But it may be said with some justice, 'If the people were not satisfied with this course of education, why did they let their children go to the schools?' The fact is that we have here no question of like or dislike. On the contrary we must account for this by the painfully degraded and ignorant state of the people. They believed that if their children were entered at the schools they might have employment given them by Government, and be enabled to find some means of subsistence. Hence they put up with the state of affairs in reality disagreeable enough to them. But it must not be thought that they ever liked those schools.

Village schools

When the village schools were established, the general belief was that they were instituted solely with the view of teaching the doctrines of Jesus. The Pergunnah visitors, and Deputy Inspectors, who used to go from village to village and town to town advising the people to enter their children at these schools, got the nickname of native clergyman. When the Pergunnah visitor, or Deputy Inspector entered any village the people used to say that the native clergyman had come. Their sole idea was that these were Christian schools, established with the view of converting them. Well-informed men, although they did not credit this, saw nevertheless that in these schools nothing but Urdu was taught. They were afraid that boys while reading only Urdu would forget the tenets of their own faith, and that they would thus drift into Christianity. They believed also that Government wished such books as bore upon the doctrines of the former religions of Hindustan, to fall into entire disuse. This was to be done with the view of ensuring the spread of Christianity. In many of the Eastern districts of Hindustan where these schools were established, boys were entered at them by compulsion, and by compulsion only. It was currently reported that all this was in pursuance of the orders of Government.

Introduction of female education

There was at the same time [a] great deal of talk in Hindustan about female education. Men believed it to be the wish of Government, that girls should attend, and be taught at these schools, and leave off the habit of sitting veiled. Anything more obnoxious than this to the feelings of the Hindustanees cannot be conceived. In some districts the practice was actually introduced. The Pergunnah visitors and Deputy Inspectors hoped by enforcing the attendance of girls, to gain credit with their superior. In every way, therefore, right or wrong they tried to carry out their object. Here then was another cause of discontent among the people, through which they became confirmed in error.

Alterations in the system of education in large colleges

The large colleges, established in the towns, were from the first a source of suspicion. At the time of their establishment Shah Abdul Aziz, a celebrated moulvie of Hindustan, was alive. The Muhammadans asked him for a futwah on the subject. His answer was distinct. 'Go', he said, 'Read in the English colleges, and learn the English tongue. The laws of Islam admit it.' Acting on this opinion the Muhammadans did not hesitate to enter these colleges. At that time, however, the colleges were conducted on a Principle widely different from that which is at present adopted. Arabic, Persian, Sanskrit, and English were equally taught. The 'Fickah', [Fiqh, i.e. Islamic jurisprudence] 'Hadees' [Hadith, i.e. The Traditions of the Prophet Muhammad] and other such books were read. Examinations were held in the 'Fickah' for which certificates of proficiency were given. Religion was not in any way thrust forward. The professors were men of worth and weight: all scholars of great reputation, wide knowledge and sound moral character. But all this has been changed. The study of Arabic is little thought of. The 'Fickah' and 'Hadees' were suddenly dropped. Persian is almost entirely neglected. Books and methods of teaching have been changed. But the study of Urdu and of English has greatly increased. All this has tended to strengthen the idea that Government wished to wipe out the religions which are found in Hindustan. The professors are no longer men of weight or acquirements. Students at the college, in whom people have not gained confidence, have for some time past been appointed professors. And hence it is that throughout the country these colleges have fallen into disrepute.

Government proclamation on the subject of admitting Government college English students to appointments in preference to other candidates

Such was the state of the village schools and colleges. Such was the general feeling of distrust throughout the country as to [the] view of Government about conversion, when a proclamation was issued by Government to the following effect. Whoever had studied and passed an examination in certain sciences, and the English language, and had received a certificate to the effect, was to be considered as having prior claims for employment in the public service. Petty appointments were granted on the production of certificates from the Deputy Inspectors: the very man who had hitherto been nicknamed native clergyman. This came as a blow to everyone. Suspicion increased tenfold. The rumour again arose that Government wished to deprive the Hindustani [ees] of all means of subsistence and by impoverishing them gradually, to substitute its own religion in the place of theirs.

Introduction of the messing system in the jails

It was at this time, that the practice was introduced in some district jails, of making prisoners eat food which had been cooked by a single man; such a measure as this was fatal to the caste of Hindus. To the Muhammadan creed it was not actually obnoxious, nevertheless Muhammadans were annoyed at its introduction. They looked upon it as another proof that Government wished to meddle with all creeds alike. They saw in it but another part of one huge plan.

Circulation of Mr. E. Edmond's letters from Calcutta

Whilst all these discontents were at their height, there suddenly appeared in 1885, a letter by Mr. Edmond which was circulated publicly from Calcutta, and a copy of which was sent to all the principal officials of Government. It was to the effect that all Hindustan was now under one rule, that the telegraph had so connected all parts of the country that they were as one; that the rail road had brought them so near that all towns were as one; the time had clearly come when there should be but one faith; it was right therefore, that we should all become Christians. It is no metaphor to say that men were blinded with fear at the receipt of this circular. The ground seemed at last to have given way beneath their feet. They cried out that the long-expected hour had indeed arrived. The servants of Government were first to be made Christians, then the mass of the people. This circular, it was said, was written by order of Government. Natives in Government employ were asked whether they had received the circular, and this was in fact to taunt them with having turned Christian, on the condition of getting Government employ. The native officials were so ashamed of the circular that those to whom it had been sent used to hide the fact, from fear of being ridiculed and abused, and would deny having ever received it. They used to say, 'It has not been sent to us': and the answer used to be 'Well, well be sure that it will come. Are you not in government employ?'

Looking into the subject, one feels that this unhappy circular set the finishing stroke to the public suspicion and ill-will. And yet against this crisis there was no one to find that there should have been something very like conspiracy and more or less disturbance about this time. This was in fact the case. But the Lieutenant Governor of Bengal soon heard of it, and issued a Proclamation which soothed men's minds and put suspicion to sleep for a time. It was, however, but a temporary relief; men still thought that Government had given up its project only for a while, but that when it found itself a little stronger, it would resume them.

Interference in religious matters more repugnant to the feelings of the Muhammadans

All these causes rendered the Muhammadans more uneasy than the Hindus. The reason of this, I take to be that Hindu faith consists rather in the practice of long established rites and forms, than in the study of doctrine. The Hindus recognise no canons and laws, or appeals to the heart and conscience. Their creed does not admit of such things. Hence it is that they are exceedingly indifferent about speculative doctrine. They insist upon nothing, excepting the strict observance of their old rites, and of their modes of eating and drinking. It does not annoy or grieve them to such rites and observances, as they consider necessary, disregarded by other men. Muhammadans, on the contrary, looking upon the tenets of their creed as necessary to salvation and upon the neglect of them as damnation, are thoroughly well-grounded in them. They regard their religious precepts as the ordinances of God. Hence, it was that the

Muhammadans were more uneasy than the Hindus, and that, as might have been expected, they formed the majority of the rebels. It is wrong and impolitic on the part of a government to interfere in any way with the faith of its subjects. But of all courses, the most unjust is to hinder the study of the tenets of their religion: and especially of such as is heartily believed by its votaries to be true. But be this as it may, all I wish to prove is that, whatever the intentions of Government might be, matters were so managed that the people were left to stumble on in error, suspicion, and ill-will.

Cause II

The Passing of Such Laws, Regulations and Forms of Procedure as were Inconsistent with the Established Customs and Practices of Hindustan: And the Introduction of Such as were in Themselves Objectionable

Promulgation of objectionable laws

The Legislative Council is not free from the charge of having meddle [d] with religious matters. Act XXI of 1850 was without a doubt prejudicial to the professors of other creeds. This act was thought to have been passed with the view of converting men into Christianity. The Hindu faith, as is known, allows of no converts. To the Hindus, therefore, this act brought no benefit. If a man becomes a convert to Islam, he is forbidden by the Laws of his new religion from inheriting property left to him by men of another creed. No Muhammadan convert, therefore, could profit by this act. To such men, however, as became Christians it offered great advantages. Hence this act was said not only to interfere with people's religion but to hold out strong inducements to convert.

Act XV of 1856, again related to Hindu widows, was opposed to [the] practice of the Hindu religion. There is, I grant, much controversy on this point, and there always has been; but it is none the less a fact that the Hindus, who cling particularly to the forms and customs of their faith, were greatly annoyed at this Act. They thought that its provisions were little less than an insult to them. The suspicion arose that this act was intended to free widows from all restraint and to give them the power of doing whatever they might think proper. So, too, it would be impossible to overstate the disgust which was felt by all Hindustanees at the licence given to women in criminal actions, even married women were recognized in the Criminal Courts as competent. To give a married woman such a liberty was simply to deprive her guardian of all power over her: and not only this, but the measure was altogether opposed to the spirit of the existing religions. The remedy provided for such cases by a suit in the Civil Courts was little better than useless. Cases of this kind which, according to our belief and practice should have met with prompt attention, were so delayed and deferred that the remedy was nearly as bad as the grievance. The decrees of the Civil Court for the restoration of married women are very often waste paper. It often happens that a woman has borne two or three children to the man who abducted her, before her husband can find a trace of her whereabouts.

Promulgation of certain acts in cases wherein the parties are of one religion

Moreover, certain acts and laws were passed which led to decision[s] in the Civil Courts opposed to the religious practice of litigants, even where they happened to be of the same faith. I would not have the Government show a partiality for any creed whatever. When parties to a suit are of different creeds, Government should be careful, provided due respect is paid to the religious practice of the litigants, to ensure equal justice. When, however, the litigants are of the same creed, it is but right that decrees affecting rights, issued by the Courts, should be in accordance with the religious practice of the parties.

This resumption of mafis [revenue free land]

The laws providing for the resumption of revenue free lands, the last of which was regulation VI of 1819, were most obnoxious. Nothing disgusted the natives of this country more with the English Government than this resumption of revenue free lands. Sir T. Munro and the Duke of Wellington said truly enough that to resume lands granted revenue free was to let whole people against us, and to make beggars of the masses. I cannot describe the odium and the hatred which this act brought on Government, or the extent to which it beggared the people. Many lands which had been held revenue free for centuries were suddenly resumed on the flimsiest pretexts. The people said that Government not only did nothing for them itself, but undid what former governments had done. This measure altogether lost for the government the confidence of its subjects.

It may be said that if revenue free lands were not resumed, some other source of income would have to be sought or some new tax imposed to meet the charges of Government: so that the people would have still to bear the burden. This may be so: but the people do not see it. It is a remarkable fact that, wherever the rebels have issued proclamations to deceive and reduce the people, they have only mentioned two things: the one, interference in matters of religion; the other, the resumption of revenue free lands. It seems fair to infer that these were the two chiefs causes of the public discontent. More especially was it the case with the Muhammadans, on whom this grievance fell far more heavily than on the Hindus.

Public sales of Zamindari rights

Under former rules, and in old times, the system of buying and selling rights in landed property, of mortgage, and of transfer by gift, undoubtedly prevailed. But there was little of it, and what little there was [was] due to the consent and wishes of the parties concerned. To arbitrarily compel the sale of these rights in satisfaction of the arrears of revenue, or of debt, was a practice in those days unknown. Hindustanee landlords are particularly attached to this kind of property. The loss of their estates has been to them a source of the deepest annoyance. A landed estate in Hindustan is very like a little kingdom. It has always been the practice to elect one man as the head over all. By him, matters requiring discussion are brought forward and every shareholder, in proportion to his holding, has the power of speaking out his mind on the point. The cultivators and the Chowdries of the villages attend on such occasion and say whatever they have to say. Any matter of unusual importance is settled by the headmen of some of the larger villages. You have here, in fact in great perfection, a miniature Kingdom and Parliament. These landlords were as indignant at the loss of their estate as a king at the loss of his empire. But the Government acted in utter disregard of things formerly existing.

Dating from the commencement of English rule to the present, there is probably not a single village in which there have not been more or less transfers. In the first days of British rule, sales of landed property were so numerous that the whole country was turned upside down. To remedy this, Government passed the law which is called Regulation I of 1821, and appointed a Commission of Enquiry. This Commission, however, gave rise to a thousand other evils. After all, the affair was not brought to a satisfactory conclusion, and at last, the Commission was abolished. I shall not here enter into the question as to how Government could ensure the payment of the land revenue, if it gave up the practice of sales or its right to enforce sales as arising from the fact of the land being pledged for the payment of revenue. All that I now say is that, whether this system of sales was the result of necessity or of ignorance, it has at all events had a hand in bringing on the rebellion. If any one wishes to see what my views are on this question, he will find them in my work on the Government of Hindustan.

I will only mention here that it is open to grave doubt whether the land pledged for the payment of revenue. The claim of the Government lies, I take it, upon the produce of the land, not upon the land itself.

So, too, the practice of sale in satisfaction of debt has been most objectionable. Bankers and money-lenders have availed themselves of it to advance money to landlords, resorting to every kind of trickery and roguery to rob them of their property. They have instituted suits without end in the Civil Courts, some fraudulent, some correct enough. The consequence has been that they have very generally ousted the old landlords and insinuated themselves into their properties. Troubles of this kind have ruined landlords throughout the length and breadth of the land.

Heavy assessments of lands

The system of Revenue Settlements introduced by the English Government does it the greatest credit. But it is heavy compared with former settlements. Formerly the revenue was realized by sharing the actual crop with the cultivator. Sher Shah [founder of the Suri dynasty in 1538] claimed for Government one third of the produce of the land, and though this plan had its difficulties and exposed the Government to some little risk, yet the cultivators felt secure and were little liable to loss. Akbar was the first regularly to adopt this plan of taking one third of the produce. It was by him that the system was matured as may be seen in Mr. Elphinstone's excellent work upon India, and in the *Ain-i-Akbari*.

Akbar divided the land into the classes and changed the payments in kind into money payments. The first class, which goes by the name of *Pulich*, was cultivated yearly, and the produce of this he divided with the cultivators according to their respective shares. The second class was called *Paroti* and was not kept in constant cultivation, being occasionally allowed to lie fallow in order to strength it. The produce of this class of land he shared with the cultivators in such years as it was cultivated. The third class, which was called *Chachar*, remained uncultivated for 3 or 4 years and required the expenditure of money in order to make it fertile. In the first year of cultivation, Akbar took two-fifths of the produce from this land increasing his demand yearly, till in the fifth year he received his full share. The fourth class, which was called *Bunjar* and required to lie fallow for more than five years, was treated on still more lenient terms.

The way in which the money value of the crops was calculated was as follows. The crop of every *beegah* and of every different kind of land was reckoned according to the weight of an average amount of grain produced by such land. For example the average crop of a *beegah* would be reckoned at 9 maunds of grain, a third of which, namely, 3 maunds, would represent the demands of Government on the cultivator. The grain would then be valued at the average of the price current; and a money rate fixed on the *beegah* accordingly. The great advantage of this system was that, if the cultivators considered the price fixed by the price tables more than the value of the corn, they had the option of paying in kind.

The assessments imposed by the English Government have been fixed without any regard for their various contingencies. Land lying fallow pays in the same proportion as other land. Such lands as are for a time left uncultivated in order that they may acquire strength are not considered free from assessment. From being cultivated to the same extent year after year, land becomes weak and unfruitful and does not yield an equal amount. It ceases to have the same value as was put upon it at the time of the settlement. In many districts, every settlement that was made pressed heavily, and landlords and cultivators were alike reduced to straight. In course of time they were unable to provide themselves with proper implements. These accordingly became scarce. Land was not properly cultivated. The property became scanty. The cultivators were obliged to borrow money in order to pay the revenue. The interest on these loans ran up. Landlords, formerly men of substance, found themselves suddenly ruined. Villages in which there happened to be land already lying uncultivated became more than ever neglected. Mr. Thomason, in Paragraph 64 of his directions to settlement officers says that the settlements under Regulation IX of 1833 were light on good villages, but pressed heavily on poorer ones.

The landlords, I admit, can no longer extort rent illegally or make illicit profits, but they were entitled to more consideration than has been shown them. Both they and the cultivators have suffered, and hence it is that, notwithstanding the security of life and property which they now enjoy, the landlords look back with regret on the dynasties of former days.

Abolition of Talookdari rights particularity in the Oudh province

I will not say that to crush the talookdars were an unjust measure, but it was one of the chief causes of the rebellion, and especially of the rebellion in Oudh. The talookdars had long enjoyed the rank of Rajas. They exercised the rights of sovereignty in the villages composing their talookdaries. From these villages, their income derived. All these rights and all this income alike were suddenly wrested from them. Here again, I shall not stop to enquire what other steps could have been taken by Government to secure the under-tenants from the oppression of the talookdars. I have elsewhere entered into the matter. I merely say now that the abolition of the talookdars was among the causes of the rebellion.

Introduction of stamped paper

The practice of using stamped papers is peculiar to Europe, where land is scarely looked upon as a means of revenue. The introduction of this practice into Hindustan and the gradual rise in price of stamped paper, which reached its highest amount under Regulation X of 1829, were entirely opposed to the spirit of Hindustanee customs. Taking into consideration the general poverty of the Hindustanees, the measure seems to me to have been very unwise. The question of stamped paper has long been an open one, and strong arguments have not been wanting to show the mischief of the practice and to prove that it is opposed to all sound rules of political economy.

This, however, is a question I shall not discuss here. I would only remark that the question as hitherto argued has had reference to countries where people were educated, wealthy, and intelligent. It is easy to see that the Hindustanees, who are becoming more and more impoverished every day, can never hope to bear up under this expense. This system of using stamped paper is one which has been disapproved of by most men of reflection. They argue that, to whatever extent it may be unjust to levy a tax on lands, title-deeds, and so on, so much the more it is unwise to levy a tax upon papers intended to aid in the furtherance of justice. Besides the heavy expenses which this system entails, it tends greatly to hinder the actual administration of justice. M. Mill, in his book on *Political Economy*, and Lord Brougham, in his work on *Political Philosophy*, have expressed their disapproval of the system, and it must be remembered that all arguments urged against its practice in Europe carry with them a tenfold force when applied to Hindustan.

Civil Administration in Bengal superior to that in the Punjab, but requires revision in certain points

The Civil Courts in the Presidencies of Bengal and Agra deserve much praise. They have had nothing to do with the late rebellion. I know that many Government Officers will differ from me on this point and will prefer the system which has been adopted in the Punjab. But this is a matter which is open to a great deal of doubt. The laws in force in the Punjab are very vague and sketchy. There exist in the Punjab no commentaries or instructions for the purpose of explaining or elucidating the laws or adapting them to practice. Each individual judge is a light to himself; and unfortunately it does not happen that a judge is always right in his interpretation. To what confusion is such a state of things likely to lead in the course of time.

The Civil Court is the tribunal in which the most implicit trust should be placed. It is Civil Court on which depends the internal tranquillity of the kingdom, the safe transport of merchandise, the increase of trade, and the establishment of rights. But Punjab officers pay very little attention to the Civil Courts. They have not, indeed, the time to do so. Cases requiring long and patient investigation regarding transfers of right and a variety of other matters, such as have sprung up in process of time under the English Government and are constantly recurring in the Civil Courts of these Provinces, are as yet unknown in the Punjab. But when, in course of time, such suits are brought into the Civil Courts of Punjab, the laws by which the judges are at present guided will be found altogether inefficient.

The Civil Courts, no doubt, have their share among causes of the rebellion; but only in connection with two subjects: the one, the transfer of rights; the other, the issue of decrees for debt. These led [to] internal riots, but they gave rise to no opposition against Government. They were sores which festered only in the breasts of the parties concerned. Such a state of things might have been expected. Whenever the reins of Government are loosened, the people always begin fighting with each other. Unjust transfers of land and debts, unjustly adjudged due, increased the confusion. Many men, moreover, had fallen victims to trumped up suits and the blame of these fell upon the Civil Courts. But the incomplete and summary modes of investigation which prevail in the Punjab Civil Courts, and the wrong headedness of the judges presiding in them, have been productive of no less mischief. Ten years cannot tell us how the Civil Courts work. Fifty years hence, we may compare the administration of the North West Provinces and the working of its Courts with the administration and Courts of the Punjab; at present the comparison cannot hold. I do not deny that the laws which regulate justice in Bengal and the North West Provinces are capable of improvement. Great delays occur in the decision of cases. The price of stamped paper and various gradations of appeal render appeal too costly for the people. The powers of judges have been in certain respects unduly restricted. Act XIX of 1853 remedied this to some extent, but there is still room for improvement. However, anyone caring to see what I have to say on this subject, can read my book on the Government of Hindustan, in which work my views are given in *extenso*.

Cause III

The Ignorance of Government of the State of the Country and Their Subjects

The ignorance of Government of the State of the country and their subjects

There is no doubt that government were but slightly acquainted with the unhappy state of the people. How could it well be otherwise? There was no real communication between the Governors and the governed, no living together or near one another as has always been the custom of the Muhammadans in countries which they subjected to their rule. Government and its officials have never adopted this course, without which no real knowledge of the people can be gained. It is, however, not easy to see how this can be done by the English, as they almost all look forward to retirement in their native land and seldom settle for good amongst the natives of India.

The people again having no voice in the Government of the country could not well better their condition, and if they did try to make themselves heard by means of petitions, these same petitions were seldom if ever attended to and sometimes never even heard.

Government, it is true, received reports from its subordinate officials, but even these officials themselves were ignorant of the real thoughts and opinions of the people, because they had no means of getting at them. The behaviour of these subordinates as a rule, their pride and their treatment of natives, is well known. In their presence native gentlemen were afraid, and if they had told these officials of their want of knowledge of the people of their Districts, they would only have been summarily ejected for their pains. All the *Amlah* [readers and clerks] and the civil functionaries as well as wealthy native gentlemen were afraid and consequently did nothing but flatter.

New Government, although in name only a government subordinate to a higher government, was in reality the real Government of this country, and as such, it ought to have received the complaints and petitions of its people directly and not, as it did invariably, by reports from its district officers. These are some of the reasons why the real feelings and ways of its people, why the action of new laws passed for the people, their working for good or for bad for the prosperity or otherwise of the countrymen, were unknown or only slightly known to Government. The people were isolated; they had no champion to stand up for their rights and to see justice done to them, and they were constrained to weep in silence.

Overwhelming Poverty of the Indians, particularly of the Muhammadans

There is nothing wonderful in the fact that the natives were poor and in distress. A native's best profession is service. Now although every one felt the difficulty of getting service, this difficulty pressed most heavily on the Muhammadans. It must be borne in mind that the Hindus, the original inhabitants of the country, were never in former days in the habit of taking service, but on the contrary they were each engaged in such work as their forefathers had been engaged in before them. The Brahmins never took service; the Vaishyas were always traders and bankers; the Kshatriyas, once lords of the land, never took service, but each kept his own small portion of land, dividing it amongst his kinsmen and preserving a semblance of authority. They had no standing army, but as occasion required they all united either to resist or to invade, as the case might be, as was the custom in former days in Russia. There was one caste, certainly, that did take service and these were the Kayasths.

The Muhammadans are not the aborigines of this country. They came in the train of former conquerors and gradually domesticated themselves in India. They were, therefore, all dependent on service, and on account of this increased difficulty in obtaining the same, they, far more than the Hindus, were put to much inconvenience and misery. An honourable military service, distinct from that eagerly engaged in by the lower classes of the community, was with difficulty procurable under the British Government. The army, which was composed of sepoys, was not looked upon as a favourable field by the higher class of Muhammadans. True service was obtainable by them in the Cavalry, but the number of posts in that branch of service was small compared with what it had been in olden days. Formerly, besides Government service, employment was obtainable in the private retinues or households of officers of state and large landlords, and these posts were well paid.

It is not so now, as the posts which are now filled by Englishmen do not entail upon the holders the necessity of keeping up a large retinue, and Englishmen, therefore only have their own few private servants.

The same causes induced them to serve the rebels for one anna, one and half annas, or one seer of flour per day

The consequence of this was that, when the mutineers wanted recruits, thousands flocked in, just as in a famine, hungry men rush upon food. Many took service upon one anna or one anna and a half *per diem* and many, instead of cash, received a couple or perhaps three pounds of grain daily. It is evident, therefore, that however much they might desire service, the natives of India were unable to obtain it, the number wanting service being greatly in excess of the number of posts to be filled.

The stoppage of stipends and pensions

Under the old regime there was another thing which contributed to the prosperity of the people, viz., the custom of bestowing *Jagirs* [grants of land or presents]. At the coronation of the Emperor Shah Jehan [1628-58] at Delhi, no less than 400,000 *beegahs*, 120 villages, and tens of thousands pounds of sterling were given away in presents. This is never done nowadays and not only is it not the case now, but even *Jagirs* [grants of land] bestowed on the recipients in former days have been forfeited. Having thus shown the unsatisfactory state into which the zamindars and cultivators have fallen, I must also state that petty artisans have suffered severely by the opening up of trade with England, as they cannot, of course, compete with machinery. No one even thinks nowadays of buying country-made thread or matches, and the country-cloth weavers have been ruined. When, by the Divine Will, Hindustan became an appendage of the Crown of Great Britain, it was the duty of Government to enquire into and lessen as much as possible the sufferings of its subjects. By not doing so, many who would otherwise have been staunch friends of the British joined the rebels.

The investment of capital in Government loan

The issue of government notes is another cause of injury to India, such as was never the case under any former Government. The interest of the money which Government borrowed, the expense of collecting the money to pay for that interest, and the benefit which Government derived from the money borrowed were all taken from the country.

Families, who in former years and under the former rulers of this country were great and powerful, have under this Government been reduced to poverty. This was one great reason for the dissatisfaction felt in India and one great reason, in my opinion, why they were inclined for a change of rulers. When the British were victorious in Afghanistan, the people mourned. Why was this? Because they thought that they would now be compelled to relinquish the cherished faith of their forefathers and become Christians. When, in addition of this, Gwalior was conquered and the Punjab and Oudh annexed, this fear gained ground. In these native states, natives were eligible for high public posts and native wares were always saleable there. When therefore, the native courts of these states were done away with, these openings and aids to the people of India were suddenly cut off.

The English Government had, however, very many good points. I do not condemn it entirely, The feeling of security which the subject enjoys under the British rule, of ease and freedom, the many good roads, the putting down of dacoitee, thuggee and highway robbery, the facilities afforded to travellers, the ease with which merchants could transport their goods to far off localities, the benefit to all, rich and poor alike, which accrued from the extension of the cheap postal system, the decrease of murders and deadly affrays, the protection of the poor from the oppression of the rich, these and many other blessings have never been enjoyed under any former Government, and in all probability never will. But it must be borne in mind that the benefits derived from the above do not efface the feeling that I have above portrayed.

Another thing is that this good government benefits more especially merchants and women, who have always been loud in their praises of it, because it protected them from lawless affrays, from dacoitees, from the *Amils* (men formerly put in charge of Districts by the Sovereign and who exercised great oppression), and from many other numerous evils. They, therefore, deriving benefits as they did from the government, were not against it.

Cause IV

Neglect in Matters Which Should have Received Consideration from Government

I will now proceed to show what duties Government ought to have fulfilled and which it did not fulfil.

Neglect in matters which should have received consideration of Government

I feel it most necessary to say that which is in my heart and which I believe to be true even at the risk of its being distasteful to many of the ruling race. What I am now going to treat of is that which, if only done in a right way, will attract even wild animals, causing them to love instead of to dread, and which, therefore, will in a much greater degree attract men. I cannot here state at length what the benefits of friendship, intercourse and sympathy are, but I maintain that the maintenance of friendly relations between the governors and the governed is far more necessary than between individuals. Private friendships only affect a few; friendship and good feeling between a Government and its subjects affect a nation. As in private friendships two persons are united by the bond of a friendship, so also should a government and its people be knit together in like manner.

Want of cordiality towards the Indians

The people and the Government I may liken to a tree, the latter being the root and the former the growth of that root. As the root is, so will the tree be. What! Was such intimacy impossible under this Government? Most certainly not. We have numerous instances in which foreigners and natives of countries have been brought in contact with each other and of their becoming friends, even when their religions and countries were different and widely separated. And why was this? Just because they wished and did their utmost to become so. How often do we not see strifes and enmities between people of the same race, religion, and customs? Friendship, intercourse, and sympathy are, therefore, not wholly dependent for their existence merely on the giver and recipient being of the same religion, race, or country.

Does not the Apostle Paul admonish us in these beautiful words: 'And the Lord make you increase, and abound in love one toward another, and toward all men, even as we do toward you' (1st Epistle of Paul to Thessalonians Ch. III, Verse 12). And does not Jesus admonish us in these: 'Therefore all things whatsoever ye would that men should do to you, do ye even so to them, for this is the law and the Prophets' (Matthew, VII 12)

These were meant to inculcate friendship and love to all men, and no one, no wise and thoughtful man, will say that the admonition is wrong, that friendship and love to our fellowmen are not beneficial, that their results are nil, and that they do not blot out much that is wicked. As yet, truth compels me to state, government has not cultivated the friendship of its people as was its duty to do. The Creator has instilled it into the heart of man and the instinct of animals that the strong should be kind to and care for the weak.

The father loves his child before the child loves him. The man tries to win the woman, not the woman the man. If a man of low degree try to win the esteem of one in high position, he is liable to be styled a flatterer and not a friend. It was, therefore, for Government to try and win [the] friendship of its subjects, not for the subjects to try and win that of the Government. If it had done so, the results would have been great and the people would have rejoiced. Alas that it has not done so. If Government say that what I say is untrue, that they have tried to cultivate friendship and have only been repaid with enmity, I can only say that, if it had gone the right way to work, its subjects would most undoubtedly have been its friends and supporters, instead of, as in many instances, rising up in arms against it.

Now friendship is a feeling which springs from the heart and which cannot be kindled by admonitions. Men may meet on very friendly terms, but it does not therefore follow that they are friends in the real sense of the word, that they are friends at heart as well as in outward signs. This is a link, as it were, between hearts, a man instinctively feels that he likes a man or the contrary. Government has hitherto kept itself as isolated from the people of India as if it had been the fire and they the dry grass, as if it thought that, were the two brought in contact, the latter would be burnt up. It and its people were like two different sorts of stone, one white and the other black, which stones too were being daily more and more widely separated. Now the relations between them ought to have been close like those between the streaks of white and black in the stone called Abri in which we see the former close alongside of the latter, the one blending with the other. Government was, of course, perfectly right in maintaining special friendly relations with its Christian subjects (the English), but it was at the same time incumbent upon it to show towards its native subjects that brotherly kindness which the Apostle Paul exhorts us to in these words: 'And to godliness, brotherly kindness and to brotherly kindness, charity' (II Peter 1.7).

In ancient times, as long as cordiality was not observed by the reigning powers, tranquillity was not established

It must be borne in mind that the blood of the Muhammadan conquerors and that of the people of the country was not the same; that their faith was not the same; their manners and customs not the same; that in their hearts the people did not like them; and that at first there was little or no amalgamation of the two. What then was the secret of their becoming friends? Let us glance at the former Indian dynasties. First came that of the Muhammadan conquerors. In the reign of the Turks and Pathans, there was no intercourse between the conquerors and the conquered until the government of the former was made firm and easy. A feeling of cordiality was first established in the reign of the Mogul Emperor Akbar I and continued till the reign of Shah Jehan. No doubt owing to many defects in the system of Government, the people were subjected to many evils, but these were lightened by the feelings just mentioned. This feeling, unfortunately, ceased during the reign of [Aurangzeb] Alamgeer, AD 1779, when owing to the rebellion of several Hindus of note, such as Sewajee, the Mahratta, etc., Alamgeer vowed vengeance against them all and sent orders to all his lieutenants to treat them with rigour and harshness and to exempt none from paying tribute. The injury and disaffection which were therefore caused are well known. Now the English Government has been in existence upwards of a century, and up to the present hour has not secured the affections of the people.

Treating the Indians with contempt

One great source of the stability of a government is undoubtedly the treating of its subjects with honour and thus gaining their affections. Though a man's income be but small, treat him with honour and he is far more gratified than if he were presented with three or four times the amount and were treated with contempt. Contempt is an ineradicable wrong. Being treated contemptuously [hurt] sinks deep into a man's heart and, although uninjured by the same as to his worldly goods, he still becomes an enemy. The wound rankles deep and cannot be healed; that given by a sword can be healed, but that inflicted by a contemptuous word cannot. The results of kindness are different: an enemy even, if treated courteously, become a friend; friends by friendly intercourse become greater friends; and strangers, if treated in a friendly manner, are no longer strangers. By kindness we make the brute creature our willing slaves; how much more then would such treatment cement the bonds between a Government and its people? Now in the first years of the British rule in India, the people were heartily in favour of it. This good feeling the Government has now forfeited and the natives very generally say that they are treated with contempt. A native gentleman in the eyes of any petty official is as much lower than that official, as that same official esteems himself lower than a Duke. The opinion of many of these officials is that no native can be a gentleman.

The uncourtly address of local authorities towards the natives

Now, as Government is throughout India represented by its officials, it follows as a matter of course that the natives will judge of the temper of Government towards them by what they see of these officials. However good the intention of the Government with regard to its subjects may be, unless these same officials give practical proof thereof by kind treatment of the natives, the people will not believe in them. Theory and practice are not one and the same. In these days, or rather within the last few years, the feeling of officials towards natives is not nearly so favourable as was formerly the case. In olden days natives were treated with honour and in a friendly manner by these officials and, consequently, to use a native expression, 'they carried their (the natives) hearts in their hands'. They sympathized with them in their joys and sorrows, and this, too, notwithstanding their high position. They were consequently greatly liked, and the natives used to say, 'How wonderful is the treatment from men in the highest position, who, though wielding the reins of empire are still without pride!'

Natives of rank were also treated in a highly honourable manner. They (the officials) really followed the precepts of St. Peter; 'And to Godliness, brotherly kindness, to brotherly kindness, charity.' (II Peter V. 7). The reverse of which is, unfortunately, the case as regards the greater number of the officials of the present day. Has not their pride and arrogance caused them to esteem the Hindustani as nothing in their eyes, and have not their ill-temper and want of solicitude for the natives caused them to be looked upon with dread by the latter? Is it not well-known to Government that even the natives of the highest rank never come into the presence of officials, but with an inward fear and trembling? Is it a secret that the *Amlah* (native court officials) are often addressed harshly and abused by their superiors whilst reading out papers to them? These men, many of them of good birth, often inwardly exclaim, 'Oh! that I could gain my living otherwise, cutting grass by the wayside were better than this.' I do not say that the behaviour of all English officials is like this. There are many who are well known for their kindness and friendly feeling toward the natives and these are in consequence much beloved by them, [and] are, to use a native expression, as the sun and the moon to them, and are pointed out as types of the old race of officials.

These men truly follow the admonition of Christ Jesus who said to Simon called Peter and Andrew his brother when they were fishing, 'Follow me and I will make you fishers of men.' They, by their good character, have drawn the people to them, as it were, in a net; they have not treated them with useless arrogance, without which some think that a high position in the eyes of the natives cannot be kept up. They have earned that blessing which Christ enunciated: 'Blessed are the poor in spirit, for their is the kingdom of heaven' (Matthew, V. 3). They have treated the people with gentleness and leniency and have ruled the land according to the precept: 'Blessed are the meek for they shall inherit the earth' (Matthew, V. 5). They have also let their light shine before men, as Christ enjoined in Matthew (V. 16), 'Let your light so shine before men that they may see your good works and glorify your father which is in heaven.'

Few in number, wherever they are, they are held dear by the natives.

The ill treatment more repugnant to Muhammadans

This treatment before alluded to was most offensive to all people of India, but most especially so to the Muhammadans. The reasons for this are clear. For centuries the Muhammadan's position in India has been an honourable one. There is an element of shame in his disposition. He has no grasping desire for money; he esteems honour above all other things; and there are many proof on record which show that the Muhammadan is not easily brought to do that which, under the influence of temptation, other races in India will do without compunction. It may be that this is wrong, but God having instilled it into him, his views and feelings cannot easily be changed. It may be unfortunate, but it is inculcated into them by their religion and is no fault of theirs. This ill-treatment then it was which pained them grievously and which caused them heartily to wish for a change of Government and to hear with joy of anything that was opposed to the present Government. It is much to be regretted that the

Muhammadans did not know that Government was doing its utmost to further their interests, their education and to uphold their honour. This they did not know, as the intentions and wishes of Government were never made known by their various officials.

Exclusion of natives from high appointments

Another great reason for the dissatisfaction of the natives of India, and more especially of the Muhammadans, was the exclusion of the natives from high appointments. A few short years ago Muhammadans filled the most honourable posts under their Government and the desire and hope for such is still in them. Under the English Government they longed for the advancement of their honour in the eyes of the world, but their was no way open to them. In the early days of this Government, natives of rank were certainly singled out to fill high posts, but by degrees this fell into disuse. The assertion by Muhammadans that the practice of holding examinations is a bad one is a mistaken one. If they have not the qualifications to enable them to pass, they must not blame the system; undoubtedly the examination system goes far towards procuring an efficient staff of public servants, but many natives are appointed to high posts, who, in the estimation of their countrymen, are very small indeed. In the giving of certificates very little [is] thought of family and honour. Lord Bentinck, did most for the advancement of the natives in this respect, but the high appointments which he bestowed upon a select few were utterly inadequate to the wants of the people. English officers of the highest rank have often admitted this of late years. Now, passing an examination is a *sine qua non* in England. Are the best English statesmen invariably those who have passed high examination? Are high diplomatic posts not often given to them on account of their birth and practical commonsense and some times even without the latter qualifications?

The not holding of durbars by the Governor-General of India and not conferring rank and honour due to merit according to the usage of former emperors

The people of India have from time immemorial been in the habit of attending the *durbars* [courts] of their Sovereign and have always enjoyed seeing his pomp and state and influence. This feeling of gladness at the sight of the Sovereign is a feeling instinctively felt by everyone. Man feels the power of the ruler when thus brought face to face with him and acknowledges himself to be his subject. Now although the Governor-General of India was certainly, whilst on tour, in the habit of holding *durbars*, still the few that he did hold were not sufficient for the wants of the country. Lords Auckland and Ellenborough held right regal *durbars*. This perhaps may not have been approved of by the Home Government, but it was a most excellent thing for India, although even their *durbars* were too few in number. May the Almighty always watch over and protect our most gracious sovereign Queen Victoria and Her representation in India, His Excellency the Viceroy and Governor-General. Let us hope that the heart-felt wants of the natives of this country may be listened to and gradually satisfied.

The observation of rules by Lord Auckland and Ellenborough a very proper one

The only real kingdom is that of the Almighty who created the world. He, however, made the kings of this world as a type of what he himself is, in order that man, on seeing his sovereign, should recollect that there is the still greater one who made him. For this reason, many wise and able men have laid down that the good qualities of the Almighty, such as bounty kindness, etc., should also be found represented in earthly kings, hence the title 'Shadowed of God'. It is, therefore, incumbent on earthly kings to treat their subjects with that bountiful liberality with which the Almighty has treated the whole world. It may appear at first sight bad policy to spend the public money in rewarding slight services, but in my humble opinion this practice is calculated to increase the loyalty of the subject and thus to render the empire more stable.

It is a well-known saying that 'kindness and beneficence make slaves of men', therefore, when the people see those virtues in their rulers, true love towards him and a desire to serve him faithfully and loyally are germinated in their hearts. We know from history that this was the case in olden days and under various dynasties in India, and that the nobles and the people at large had honours and gifts, such as titles, money, land, and other valuables, bestowed upon them with no sparing hand. The recipients felt honoured and pleased, were held in greater honour by their brethren, and the nation at large liked the practice as being one which had come down to them from remote ages. Government put a stop to this and no one could expect much in the way of rewards and honours from it. When, therefore, the people heard that the Government of India had been formally assumed by Her Majesty Queen Victoria, they rejoiced, as they were longing for a change.

The expenses of former rulers of India were of two sorts, viz., money spent on their own private luxuries and debauches which were undoubtedly wrong and disapproved of by the people and that spent in rewarding faithful servants, victorious generals, learned men, faqueer [Faqir, men of learning and sanctity], poets, beggars, or deserving poor, which latter expenditure was very popular. The discontinuance of the same by the British has displeased the people, especially the recipients, who from being always well cared for were unable to work for their bread. Now this system is undoubtedly bad as it makes the people lazy and not induced to help themselves; and much better is it that the rewards be discontinued and freedom be granted to the subject, that, thus he may earn his daily bread himself; but this boon of freedom can only be appreciated when the people become educated and contented and not all at once. It is like taking the reins out of a horse's mouth, turning him loose, and turning him out into the jungle to find his food for himself. What is the result? He either dies or remains a wild animal all his days, giving the rein to his passions. If a man be thus treated he will either rob, murder or rebel.

The facts of the rebellion in India appeared more serious to the authorities than they in reality were

Men's minds under the influence of anger are apt to lose sight of the true causes of any event and to be warped by a desire for vengeance. The events of the year 1857 were no doubt so dreadful as to justify the feelings of anger and desire for vengeance which had full possession of the hearts of the English during that awful year; but at the same time we must find out what, at that time, was the condition of Hindustan, how the rebellion really commenced, why it attained such a height, and why, in certain districts, more misled Muhammadans rebelled than in others.

It must be borne in mind that for centuries past the condition of India has been unsettled, that from time immemorial, its people have been accustomed to flock in thousands to the standard of any powerful noble (Ameer) who attained any success in the field and that they never held their doing so to be criminal, accepting responsible posts in the administration of his country for the time being. It is well known in India that the taking of service is no offence. Whoever pays is served. It is thought wrong not to tender allegiance to a king who may have been proclaimed king in the place of another deposed. The various kings and princes of Hindustan have never, on conquering an enemy's country, attached any blame to the servants, whether civil or military, of that enemy, and the people were aware of this.

When the leaders of the rebellion called for recruits, thousands of poor men wanting service flocked in and took it. They thought there was nothing wrong in doing so, as their livelihood was procured by such service. Many thought that the British rule in Hindustan was at an end and that, therefore, it was their duty to tender their allegiance to the reigning powers, i.e. to the rebels. Many officials also thought that lives would be spared by feigning to be on the rebel side and that when the British rule was re-established, they could throw off the mask. These men were, however, found guilty, although, undoubtedly, many amongst them were true subjects of the British. Many also there were, servants of government and others, who, under compulsion, or through ignorance, or from being merely mortal, committed themselves, and then, thinking that their sin, committed perhaps under great temptation or perhaps under compulsion, would not be pardoned and would meet with severe punishment, cast in their lot entirely with the rebels. Others there were who had really done nothing; but through fear, etc., joined the rebels. Many also, as before stated, joined them, thinking it no crime to do so.

If the whole facts regarding the rebellion be thoroughly sifted, I feel certain that we shall find that just as many Hindus were concerned therein as Muhammadans, and the proof of this will be found in what took place all over Hindustan. It must not be supposed that the reason why, in some districts, the Muhammadans who rebelled were greater in number than the Hindus was that the king of Delhi, who was their head, claimed the throne of Delhi or that they were in reality as rebellious as they seemed to be. No! small acts said to have been committed by them were seized upon and magnified by their enemies, and the minds of the officials were worked upon and poisoned against them. The breach was thus widened, the English becoming more and more angry and the Muhammadans more and more afraid and hopeless. It was their fate to have their actions misrepresented and to have the minds of their rulers poisoned against them. There were, no doubt, many

Muhammadans who did rebel and whose rebellion we must enter in the V Class. These men were delighted at the prospects of a change of government for reasons already shown. Nevertheless Government are no doubt well aware what race it was and what men that proved most faithful even unto death. All men are guilty, in His eyes, who is the only true Ruler. They are also guilty in the eyes of earthly kings, temporarily put into authority by Him.

The Psalmist has truly said, 'Enter not into judgement with thy servant, for in thy sight shall no man living be justified' (Psalm cxliii, 2). 'Have mercy upon me, O God, according to Thy loving kindness; according unto the multitude of Thy tender mercies, blot out my transgressions. Wash me thoroughly from mine iniquity, and cleanse me from my sins' (Psalms li, 1 and 2).

The Almighty is the preserver of our Most Gracious Majesty, Queen Victoria. Words of mine cannot sufficiently praise the most merciful and considerate proclamation issued by Her Gracious Majesty.

Her Majesty's proclamation highly commendable, indeed may be said to have originated under divine inspiration

The hand of the Almighty is on Her Gracious head and this proclamation has been inspired by God. There is an ancient custom in Hindustan which is that, whenever a new king ascends the throne, rightly or wrongly, all the nobles of the land present themselves to pay their respects. This was the case in rebellion. When the people heard that the emperor of Delhi had ascended the throne, they presented themselves, and when he was deposed and imprisoned, men knew perfectly well that the same people would tender their allegiance to the English. The rebel army itself might perhaps not to do this, but the reasons for their not doing so need not be treated of here.

CAUSE V

THE INSUBORDINATE STATE OF THE INDIAN FORCES

The paucity of the English forces

The English army system in India has always been faulty and one great fault was the paucity of English troops. When Nadir Shah conquered Khorassan and became master of the two kingdoms of

Persia and Afghanistan, he invariably kept the two armies at equal strength. The one consisted, or rather was composed, of Persians and Kuzul Bashies, and the other was composed of Afghans. When the Persians Army attempted to rise, the Afghan army was at hand to quell the rebellion and vice versa. The English did not follow this precedent in India. The sepoy army was no doubt faithful in its day and served the Government well, but how could Government feel certain that it would never act contrary to its orders? What measures had Government for quelling at once on the spot any emeute in that vast army, such as that which happened last year?

The employment of Hindus and Muhammadans in the same regiment

Government certainly did put the two antagonistic races into the same regiment, but constant intercourse had done its work and the two races in regiment had almost become one. It is but natural and to be expected that a feeling of friendship and brotherhood must spring up between the men of a regiment, constantly brought together as they are. They consider themselves as one body and thus it was that the difference which exists between Hindus and Muhammadans had, in these regiments, been almost entirely smoothed away. If a portion of the regiment engaged in anything, all the rest joined. If separate regiments of Hindus and separate regimens of Muhammadans had been raised, this feeling of brotherhood could not have arisen, and, in my opinion, the Muhammadan regiments would have refused to receive the new cartridges.

The pride of the India forces and its causes

Owing to the paucity of the European element, the people of India only stood in awe of the sepoys, who thus became puffed up with pride and thought that there were none like them in the world. They looked upon the European portion of the army as a myth and thought that the many victories which the English had gained were gained entirely by their own prowess. A common saying of theirs was that they enabled the English to conquer Hindustan from Burmah to Kabul. This pride of the sepoys was most marked after the Punjab was conquered. So far had it gone that they made objections to anything which they did not like and, I believe, even remonstrated when ordered to march, consequent on the yearly reliefs.

It was precisely at this time, when the army was imbued with this feeling of pride and the knowledge or rather conjecture that Government would grant anything they stood out for, that the new cartridges were issued, cartridges which they really believed were made up with fat and the using of which would destroy their caste. They refused to bite them. When the regiment at Barrackpore was disbanded and the general order announcing the same was read out to each regiment, the deepest grief was felt throughout the army. They thought that the refusal to bite the cartridges, the biting of which would have destroyed their caste, was no crime at all; that the men of the disbanded regiment were not in the least to blame and that their disbandment was an act utterly devoid of justice on the part of the government. The whole army deeply regretted ever having had anything to do with Government. They felt that they had shed their blood in its cause and conquered many countries for it, that in return it wished to take away their caste and had dismissed those who had justly stood out for their right. There was, however, no open rebellion just then, as they had only been disbanded and had not been treated with greater severity; but partly from feeling certain that the cartridges were mixed with fat, partly from grief at seeing their comrades disbanded at Barrackpore, and still more by reason of their pride, arrogance, and vanity, the whole army was determined, come what might, not to bite the cartridges.

The impropriety of punishing the non-commissioned officers at Meerut which touched the vanity of the Indian forces

Correspondence was undoubtedly actively carried on in the army after the events at Barrackpore, and messages were sent telling the men not to bite the cartridges. Up to this time there was a strong feeling of indignation and irritation in the army but, in my opinion, there was no intention of rebelling.

The fatal month of May 1857 was now at hand in which the army was punished in a manner which thinking men knew to have been most wrong and most inopportune. The anger, which the news of this punishment created in the minds of the sepoys, was intense. The prisoners, on seeing their hands and feet manacled, looked at their medals and wept. They remembered their services and thought how they had been recompensed, and their pride, which as I have before said was the feeling of the whole army, caused them to feel the degradation all the more keenly. Then the rest of the troops at Meerut were fully persuaded that they would either be compelled to bite the cartridges or undergo the same punishment. This rage and grief led to the fearful events of the 10th of May, which events are unparalleled in the annals of history. After committing themselves thus, the mutineers had no choice left but to continue in their career of rebellion.

Want of confidence in the Indian forces towards Government after the occurance of Meerut

When the news of the outbreak became known, the irritation of the sepoys increased. The whole army felt that their confidence in Government was at an end, that Government was only waiting for an opportunity to punish them all and hence it was that their confidence in what their officers did and said was scattered to the winds. They used to say, 'Government says this and that just at present, but when all is quiet again it will not do what it says it will do.'

I state on the best authority that thousands of the sepoys who composed the rebel army in Delhi were sorry for the acts that had been committed and for having rebelled so insanely. Whilst the siege was going on, they used to say with tears in their eyes that fate had caused them to do this. 'What could we do,' said they, 'except rebel?' We were never sure what punishment was in store for us, as Government had no confidence in us. On an opportunity offering, we should have been compelled to do everything. At the commencement of the rebellion, when it was known that a force was going to be sent out, many stated it to be their conviction that when the two opposing forces met, the whole of the native portion would desert from the British. This was verified by the results; and the reason for it was that, when it came to fighting against their brethren, no one would remain true as they said when with our aid the English conquer our comrades, they will then turn their attention to us! All therefore joined in the rebellion, even those who wished to remain faithful to their salt were carried away by the majority. Now the people were perfectly well aware that Government was almost entirely dependent on the sepoy army; when therefore it became known that, that army had revolted, the people also became riotous. They no longer were in awe of the Government.

Why the mutiny did not break out in the Punjab?

Let us now see how these opinions of mine effect the rebellion or 'part rebellion' which took place in the Punjab. The Muhammadans there had been greatly oppressed by the Sikhs, and had received no injury at the hands of the British. When the British first took the country oppression was rife. This was day by day decreasing, whilst the contrary was the case of Hindustan proper.

The whole of the Punjab, when first annexed, was disarmed, and thus the weapons necessary for rebellion were not forthcoming. The Sikhs, too, though not so wealthy as in former days, had still sufficient to live upon, chiefly from monies which they had inherited. The poverty which was rife in Hindustan had not yet had time to become rife in the Punjab.

Besides these, there were other cogent reasons why the Punjab remained tranquil. Firstly, there was a powerful European army on the spot; secondly, the wisdom shown by the officials in atonce disarming the sepoys. Thirdly, the number of the rivers and the shutting up of the ferries on them, which rendered the few who did rebel, powerless. Fourthly, all the Sikhs, Punjabees and Pathans, who might otherwise have tried their hand at rebellion, had already taken service or were being formed into corps and the desire for the plunder of Hindustan [i.e., areas of the U.P.] was strong in them. We thus find that the service which the people of India took in the rebel army under such difficulty and changes was easily obtained in government services in the Punjab. The circumstances of the Punjab were quite different from those of Hindustan proper.

CHAPTER 10

The Story of the War of Independence, 1857-1858

'ALLAMAH FAZL-I HAQ OF KHAIRABAD

Fazl-i Haq (1797-1861) belonged to Khairabad, once a leading centre of learning and scholarship in the Sitapur district of Uttar Pradesh. His father, Maulana Fazl Imam Khairabadi, a gifted scholar, was chief judge during Akbar's time. He served the Delhi government as a *serishtadar*, and held the office of chief judge in Lucknow under the annexation of Awadh. Thereafter, he appears to have joined the revolt against the British in 1857, though his exact movements are still shrouded in mystery. There is, however, some evidence to indicate that he travelled to Jhajjar, Saharanpur, Tonk, Rampur, and parts of Awadh. At the time of the revolt, he was serving in Alwar. He was ultimately captured in Khairabad and was deported to the Andamans. He died on the island. A versatile scholar, Fazlul Haq belonged to the Waliullahi school that later became the chief source of inspiration for the Dar al-ulum at Deoband. According to the judicial commissioner of Awadh, 'he has always been a notable well-known man. Most of the witnesses who had not before seen him have all their lives frequently heard of Maulvi Fazl-i Haq.'

This excerpt is, in all probability, an English translation of an Arabic manuscript at the Raza Library in Rampur. It came to light in 1947 when another copy of the manuscript was published, with an Urdu translation, at Aligarh. The Arabic and its translation have been named variously as *Sauratul Hindiya* (Indian Revolution), *Baghi Hindustan* (Rebel India), and *Nuqaddamat-us Sauratul Hindiya* (Preamble to the Indian Revolution).

*S. Moinul Haq, 'The Story of the War of Independence by Allamah Fadl-i Haqq of Khayrabad', *Journal of the Pakistan Historical Society*, 5, 1957, pp. 23-57.

The Story of the War of Independence[1] by 'Allamah Fadl-i-Haqq is a short but extremely interesting and authentic account of one of the most important problems of our history. Besides being an eye-witness and a participator in some of the events related by him the author belonged to the elite of the Dihli society in the last days of the Mughul Empire. He was widely respected for his learning and scholarship and had attained eminence as a teacher. Sir Syed Ahmad Khan's seemingly fulsome eulogy[2] of the 'Allamah is not devoid of truth. The *Story* and two *Qasidahs* relating to the War of Independence were composed during the imprisonment of the 'Allamah in the Andaman Islands. There were no books to study or refer to and every word had to be written from memory. He had on paper to write upon and had to scribble down his sentences no loose and small chits or torn pieces of cloth. Nevertheless he could manage to send these compositions to his son, Mawlana 'Abd-al-Haqq, through a co-prisoner, Mufti 'Inayat Ahmad of Kakuri, who was fortunate enough to have been released at the recommendation of a European officer.

The style of the 'Allamah is unique and is characterized by a frequent and abundant use of synonyms and antonyms on the one hand and the crowding together in the same sentence of the various derivatives of the samer root.[3] In fact the *Story* like other works of the 'Allamah is an excellent piece of Arabic literature and cannot be easily subjected to a faithful translation in another language. It has not therefore been possible to import into this rendering the beauty and the elegance of the original, but an effort has been made to remain as near the text as was practicable. The reader will not only know the thoughts and ideas of the author but will also be able to appreciate the extent of emphasis which he wants to lay on a particular fact or aspect of the problem. Besides tendencies peculiar to writers primarily interested in literary style the 'Allamah was faced with another consideration. In the post-1857 period no Indian could afford to write on the War of Independence unless it was with the object of presenting the movement as a mutiny against the Government, and much less a 'war-criminal' who had been condemned to transportion for life for signing the *fatwa* for *jihad*. The 'Allamah has therefore resorted to writing his history in almost an enigmatic style, avoiding actual names of places and persons, When mentioning, for instance, Mawlana Ahmad-allah, the great organizer of the movement he refers to him as the person having the same name as the Prophet.

The 'Allamah's account of the War is brief, but it is a masterly survey of the fight for freedom in the Delhi–Lucknow area. An eminent scholar, gifted with penetrating judgement and a keen power of observation his criticism on the actions and behaviour of persons involved in the movement is judicious and convincing. His remarkable analysis of the circumstances which led to the capture of Delhi by the British needs careful examination in the light of the details of facts and events. It is difficult not to agree with him that the hasty, almost sudden, collapse of resistance in the capital was the result of the Emperor's flight to the tomb of Humayun. Many a movement has collapsed as a result of one wrong step taken by the leader: Bahadur Shah and his countrymen had to pay a heavy penalty for his refusal to accept Bakht Khan's advice.[4] 'Equally important is the 'Allamah's reference to the attitude of the Hindus, who began withdrawing from the struggle as soon as they saw that the fortunes of war were changing in favour of the British.

The importance of the *Story* is obvious. It is not only an eyewitness account of the war but is one of the few contemporary documents which present the movement in its true perspective.

The desire—in fact the need—of launching a movement for regaining independence was born of two sets of causes—politico-religious and socio-economic.[5] 'Allamah Fadl-i-Haqq makes a reference to both. His references are undoubtedly brief but for students of history they are useful and interesting. It is a pity he did not have an opportunity of writing the history of the movement in detail.

بسم الله الرحمن الرحيم

In the Name of Allah the Benevolent, the Merciful

All praises are due to Allah from Whom can we have great expectations for deliverance without delay from calamities, frustration and afflictions, and hopes for rewards to those who emerge successful from trial through the bestowal of His blessings and to those who call Him by His most gracious names, particularly the oppressed and the distressed ones while being tested through misfortunes and maladies.

And may peace by upon that excellent person (Holy Prophet), the announcer of good news and the giver of warning, whose prophethood was prophesied by the earlier prophets and whose recommendation is hoped for ending the calamities and epidemics, the removal of the darkness of the tyranny of the enemies and protection against fatal diseases and the curse of bad luck!

May peace by upon his descendants who were noble and generous chiefs and leaders and upon his great companions who were strong (against the infidels) and gentle-hearted towards their own people particularly upon his true caliphs! May the blessings of God be upon him (Prophet) and upon them for as long as the angels remain busy in praising the Almighty in the heavens and the orbits and the ships continue sailing on the waves and the seas!

This book of mine is no doubt the work of a heart-broken and suffering prisoner[6] who is sighing for what has been lost to him, who is afflicated with every kind of injury, who has no power of bearing hardship even for a short time, and who is entertaining hopes of deliverance through (the grace of) his God for Whom it is very easy. He, inspite of his having lived in plenty and ease from the time of his birth, is now in fetters and in preplexity and trapped in a snare, but he expects his God, through prayers which are accepted, to dispel his afflictions. He is in the grip of great misfortunes and bad luck and is in the custody of a frowning tyrant who has deprived him of all that he had of beauty and style in fashion and dress, and has put him to test by forcing him to live in the valleys of sorrows and in the narrow prisons which are places where dark sufferings assemble.

Considering the domineering ways of the Jailor, the harsh and hard-hearted usurper, he is despaired of his deliverance, but he has not lost hope in the grace of his God. He is humble and compliant, sick and dejected, and is in the prison of a mischievous and fiendish (person). He is perplexed, and has become incapable of acting by his own power and miserable on account of the tyranny of a cruel, arrogant, quarrelsome and ill-natured person. He is needy and disappointed and is put to so severe a trial through adversities as is beyond the guess of one who guesses. He has been deceived and cannot ask for what he wants, is in embarrassment due to the severest imprisonment and blood-pouring misery. He is in the detention of a white-faced, black-hearted, blue-eyed, stern-looking, red-haired, inconstant and dissimulating person. This fellow has deprived him (author) of what he had from clothes and has clad him in the coarsest garments and the roughest possible dress. Therefore, he (author) is helpless, uneasy and terrified, and has thrown himself on the mercy of his God. He has been separated completely from his family by imprisonment and is yearning for them. He is a litigant whose case was decided without a prosecutor or accuser. He is ashamed before and helpless for all his friends or servants. His arms have been weakened by the severest blows. He is dejected, lonely and forlorn and subjected to drudgery; he has been exiled from his country and town. He is distressed, afflicted, and in banishment; he has been made to suffer, and separated from his family and children. The tyrant oppresses him and maltreats him and has kept his family and neighbours away from him; he has been isolated from them. He (the tyrant)· has imprisoned him, coerced him and depressed him by putting him to all sorts of hardships because of his staunchness and zeal for his faith *(iman)* and Islam and for his having the reputation of being one of the most learned and famous scholars. By this the tyrant aimed at removing the traces of learning and destroying the banner of knowledge, even from the paper of paper.[7]

This was due to the painful event, which has rendered the cities and towns desolate and made them the targets of the aims of disasters and which has brought lightning and thunderbolts from the clouds of misfortunes on their residents. It was a calamity which turned the nobles into beggars and destitutes, and the kings[8] into prisoners and slaves.

The story of this event is now related.

The early British Christians ftera [after] having seized the territories, the countries and the towns and villages of India, (Hind-Pakistan) had filled their hearts with hidden grudge. They captured her borders and frontiers and encircled her rear and front parts completely; they humiliated thoroughly all her respected chiefs, not leaving even one who could raise his head in defiance. They decided upon converting to Christianity all her people and inhabitants, including her nobles and chiefs, leaders and prominent persons and servants, as well as her noted and common people, thinking that helpless as they had become they would find no friend or helper and would have no way of escape or goal other than submission.[9]

This was being done with one object only; (it was) that all the people should become infidels like them, following the same religion, and there should remain no difference between sections of the population belonging to separate faiths; because on account of their political ideas they thought that the differences between followers of various religious and communities would be the strongest of the causes of disruption of the continuance of their domination and government and that they would become a source of revolution in the countries and states. They left no stone unturned and tried their utmost to bring to an end the various religious [religions] (excepting Christianity) by inventing devices. They established schools in towns and cities in order to teach books of their language and faith to the children and illiterate adults. They wiped out of existence the centres of knowledge and learning and *madrasahs* and institutions which had been established in earlier days.[10]

Having seized power they decided to bring under their hold the various sections of the people by controlling eatables, by taking possession of the ears of corn and grain and giving the peasants and cultivators cash in lieu of their rights of farming. Their object was not to allow the poor men and villagers a free hand in buying and selling grain. By giving preference to their own people they wanted to control the cheapening or raising of the rates so that the people of God might submit to their (Christians') policy of monopolies, and their dependence on them (Christians) for their requirements might force them to meet the purpose of the Christians and their supporters, and the desires and ambitions which they had in their hearts and the mischiefs and evils which they had concealed in their minds, as for instance, forbidding the Muslims to circumcize their boys and remove purdah from among their ladies and wives and the abolition of the observance of the commands of the firm Faith.

They started their machinations by making the Hindu and Muslim sepoys give up their (religious) rites and practices and leading them astray from the path of their religions and faiths, because they were under the impression that if the brave sepoys would agree to denouncing and changing their religion and obeying their orders then the others (civil population) would not dare to recoil (disobey) because of the fear of chastisement and punishment.

(Accordingly) they forced Hindu soldiers, who were in overwhelming majority to taste the fat of the cow and the Muslims who were in a minority to taste the fat of the pig. Thus each of the two peoples (*fariqayn*), in order to safeguard their faith and religion, left the path of obedience. They began to murder, loot and kill their officers (*tarkhan*) and chiefs. Amongst these were those who did evil things and went beyond limits and committed excesses and cruelties. The children and women were also killed. They earned degradation and disgrace by murdering women and disrepute and dishonour by killing children.

The forces who had risen in revolt set out from their cantonments after murdering their commanders and officers. Laxity and chaos found their way into the functioning of the government officers, and disturbance and disorder spread along the roads; law and order broke down; mischief resulting from mutual enmities between the people became rampant, and ruin began to spread over cities and [the] countryside.

Many of these troops reached Dihli, the capital, which was a famous and thickly populated city and had been the home of the majority of Timur's descendants. They made their *amir* (emperor) the person who had been their ruler formerly.[11] He had his own *wazir*[12] and staff; he was advanced in years but was inexperienced; he was very old and was, in reality, governed by his wife and *wazir.* The said *wazir* was a high authority but in fact he was a friend of the Christians and had excessive love for them and was a bitter enemy of their opponents. The same was the case with some of the members of his (emperor's) family; some of these were near to him and his throne and were in his confidence. They did as they liked, and acted according to their own views, making at the same time a show of obedience to him. He was so completely devoid of experience that he knew nothing and did not do but strange things. He issued no orders according to his independent opinion and could not understand (what was) good and (what was) evil. He could not decide anything openly or in secret, and had no power of doing harm or good to any one.[13]

This was the state of affairs when there arose a party of strong and brave Muslims for *jihad* and fighting after having asked for a *fatwa* from the pious *'ulama* and their (*'ulana's*) declaration that *jihad* had become obligatory in accordance with *the fatwas* of the authoritative *imams.*

In the meanwhile this inexperienced *amir* appointed as officers of the army some of his son[14] and grandsons who were stupid, dishonest and coward. They hated honest and wise persons. They had never witnessed a battle nor had they any experience of the blows of swords and lances. They selected men from the gutter for their society and consultation. These inexperienced fellows drowned themselves in the ocean of luxuries and extrvagance and submerged themselves in the flood of debauchery. They were poverty-stricken and (suddenly) they became opulent; when they became opulent they took to a life of dissipation. They obtained enormous sums from the people under the pretext of securing provisions for the army but did not give anything to any one belonging to the army and ate themselves all that they got. The leading-most of the prostitutes made them negligent in the matter of leading the rebel forces and their association with mistresses kept them from marching in the night with the army. The abundance of luxuries and enjoyments rendered them neglectful and made them stay behind the vanguard; their cowardliness and mean anxieties, hidden in their hearts, made them withdraw from taking a firm position in the centre of the army; misfortune kept them away from the right wing, while gambling and luxury kept them from remaining in the right wing, and their vulgar companions prevented them from marching along with the rear guard. Such is always the case of a person who is given the charge of a great campaign in spite of his incapacity and on whom is placed a heavy burden despite his being devoid of strength. They passed their nights in sleeping and their days in intoxication. When they woke up and came to their senses they felt embarrassed and amazed.

(Ultimately) the forces of the Christians attacked them and climbing over a lofty hill[15] they turned their faces towards the city. They surrounded it, dug trenches around it and set up ballistas over it. They threw balls from them towards the city on its wall and its houses and buildings, which fell as if they were meteors and thunderbolts.

The forces of the rebels were in different groups and had adopted different ways. Some of them obeyed no one, while others had no place of refuge; some had their strength reduced because poverty and starvation had kept them from active service in the war; some had been prevented from fighting by their loot; some of them fled because their hearts were full of fear; some of them exceeded all bounds in wickedness and committed adultery, selecting from the prostitutes as they liked; some of them felt ashamed of putting on red woolen uniform to join the ranks of soldiers. Nevertheless there was one section among them which exhibited courage and fought the Christians, met and attacked them.

The Christians becoming enfeebled and humiliated, requested the Hindus of the west for help and begged their assistance in war.[16] They sent large numbers of soldiers and considerable supplies of war in successive batches within the minimum period. So, the Christians assembled in large numbers their own forces and those of their allies on the said hill for a fierce onslaught. Among their forces were their white-faced soldiers and their mercenaries who were drawn from the base and mean Hindus and from those Muslims who had turned apostates on account of their friendship with the Christians inspite of their faith and had sold their *din* for a very low price.

Thousands of the residents of the city also were in sympathy with the Christians. The entire Hindu population was with them. But the Muslims were divided; some of them detested the Christians and some were their supporters, being very firm in their sympathy for them. They tried their utmost to break the revolutionary forces by their tricks and deceptive devices, make ineffective the power of the *mujahidin* and uproot them, and then scatter and disrupt them. No stone was left unturned by them in this respect.

The Christians then started assaulting the city and its gates and attacked their keepers and guards. The *mujahids* who were present there and a section of the forces were stopping them from entering in the city. They encountered the Christian attacks and stood between themselves and their (enemy's) efforts. Both the parties were busy day and night fighting bravely, on horse and on foot. Fighting with varying fortunes continued for four months successively.[17]

The enemy, in spite of his great strength, vast numbers and extensive preparations, could find no way and had no power to enter the city. Whenever the besieging forces attacked they were repulsed and whenever they advanced they were pushed back. The strong and brave *ghazi-mujahids* offered severe resistance and put up a strong fight against them. They kept their feet firm even in hot encounters and met every body who tried to advance forward. Many of them tasted the honey of martyrdom and attained high ranks of good fortune (*Sa 'adat*). 'And for those who do good is good (reward) and more than this'.[18]

Ultimately there remained only a small party of *mujahidin* who passed the nights in hunger, but rushed to fight at dawn, and waged war against the enemy. They together with a company of the forces guarded the wall of the city and stopped the enemy's entry through breaches until one night a party of soliders was appointed to stay in an ambush and watch, in front of the hill. These fellows were born cowards and were timid, accustomed to living in ease and lethargy. They disarmed themselves and fell asleep. The enemy launched a night attack, seized their arms and killed them and made these sleepers sleep in a way that they could never rise.

When the Christians captured this ambush and entered therein they set up ballistas in a large number for pulling down the wall close to it, demolishing the ramparts and opening the gate in its front. They showered continuously heavy balls throughout the day and night. The wall of the city was breached and cracked, and openings became apparent in the wall and the ramparts. The gate was demolished and sources (of defence) were cut short; the curtain rose. None from among the soldiers was able to stand or sit there, nor could anyone peep from or ascend over the wall. Any one who tried to peep from it was shot and fell into the ditch.

After this the Christians deceived the defenders and played a trick. They sent a division of their forces in front of another gate, so that (their opponents) should think that the other gate was being attacked. The *mujahids* and a section of the forces, therefore, busied themselves in fighting and resisting them; they were thus deceived by this trick and the device of the Christians. A party of the Christians and their forces then entered through the gate they had broken and the wall and the rampart which they had demolished. They found there none of the defenders, or fighters nor those who could resist, check, stop or fight them. They entered the houses of those who had already become the supporters of the Christians. They (the supporters) raised walls in their houses for their protection and hurried to entertain them with whatever food they had prepared for them. They fed them to satisfaction with meat and milk and supplied them with all they needed. They opened holes in the walls and shut the doors to enable them to fire guns and guard themselves against those who were likely to attack them. Whenever any citizen or soldier was sighted by them they shot him dead and their opponents found no way to strike at them. They would wait for an opportunity to enter the other houses as well, so that they might utilise them like the houses of their friends for rest during the night and day. But whenever these cursed ones appeared or were found anywhere they were caught and killed. So wherever they feared they would meet any fighter or opponent they did not come out but rarely. Nevertheless, they were receiving continuous help from the ridge, which was coming to them through every Christian-loving Hindu.

Thus there remained no place for protection in the city, nor was there any ruler, because the king along with his sons and family had gone to a tomb situated at a distance of three miles from the city.[19] He was obedient to his wife and his treacherous *'amil* (*wazir*)[20] who had completely deluded him by his falsehoods and calumnies. He used to entice him by saying that the Christians after having gained victory would treat him well and would restore him to power and greatness in the Empire. Thus he was kept under delusion and was happy, with the promises and ambitions that Satan put in his mind.[21] The courtiers and servants of the king also went with him along with their families and children, leaving behind their property and belongings in the mansions and houses which they had evacuated. Many of the citizens became frightened by their departure from the city, and every one of them left his house. When the houses were evacuated by their occupants the Christians and their forces entered them and fell upon whatever they found there from wealth and riches. They butchered all women, children and invalids who had stayed in the houses. Thus none from amongst the brave citizens remained there to fight and resist them.[22]

Of the revolutionary forces some had escaped before the entry of the Christians while some remained firm. There were others who fought with them again and again. The money-changers and other Hindus who were in alliance with the Christians[23] and the late servants of the King who were enemies of the fighters (*mujahidin*) devised a scheme of destroying them and severely restricting their supplies. They concealed all the grain and cereals which were available in the city and stopped all supplies which used to come from the towns and villages until they were forced to pass their days and nights in hunger, thirst, excessive heat and anxiety. Their perplexity was extremely great, and so they fled in a helpless manner. The Christians took possession of the city and its gates, its wall, its fort, its markets and its houses and mansions.

Many of the members of my family and children were in Dihli at the time and I had been invited there. And as there were hopes for betterment and success and victory and prosperity were expected, and as whatever had been destined for us was hidden in the womb of futurity, I set out for Dihli where my place of residence was. Having reached there I unpacked my luggage and met the members of my family. I advised the people according to the dictates of my judgement and understanding, but they did not act on my advice and did not accept my council.[24]

When the Christians took possession of the city and there was left none from among the (defending) forces and the residents, a severe need of the supply of grain and sweet water was felt because these had been stopped by the enemies. I stayed there for five days and nights.[25] Then having no means of carrying my luggage I felt my property comprising my books, money and effects, and placing reliance on the Almighty God I adopted a suitable course for my safety. 'Allah is sufficient as a protector.'[26]

The Christians after having captured the city and its suburbs with the help of a large force of white-faced (soldiers) directed their whole attention to arresting the king, his sons and grandsons. They had not even left their place of staying,[27] and (in reality) Fate and kept them in that place and settled them there. They had placed their confidence in the person who had deceived them and made them happy by his lies. He (king) was in the tomb living under delusion and happiness, surrounded by a crowd and served by many. (The result was that) he was made a prisoner, regretful and heavy at heart and was put in chains. They captured his sons and grandsons who were with him and put them in chains. Then they carried him to the city along with his wife and children. On the way one of their officers who was *tarkhan* or *bitriq* murdered the sons and grandsons of the King with his gun. Then they sent their severed heads in a tray to the King as a present.[28] Their bodies were thrown away and (later) also their heads which had been cut off. They imprisoned him (the king) in a cell which was narrower than the hole of a needle. He was put under the guard of white-faced, black-hearted, red-haired and blue-eyed watchmen. They exiled him from these vast territories to some distant islands with his wife who had been for them and was their friend even when she was a queen. She failed in obtaining what she had coveted and all she had collected was looted. She became disfigured although she was *Zinat* (meaning decoration) and was dishonoured although she had always been kept in protection.

They (Christians) killed, shooting and hanging, every body whom they found from his (king's) people as they did (shoot or hang) many of the other inhabitants besides these. No one was saved from these feeble persons except those who took to flight secretly, leaving in concealment during the night or those who escaped with promptitude, stealthily marching in the day time. But the number of these was small.

Then the Christians killed the great officials and notables living in the vicinity and the suburbs of the city; (they) usurped their lands and property, houses and mansions, chattels and wealth and their arms and goods, horses and elephants and their he-camels and she-camels; (they) annihilated them with all their families and children although they had become their subjects and had submitted to them because of fear and expectations. Then they stationed their forces on every route so that they might seize those who were trying to escape and torture them. They captured many of these fugitives and none could escape but a few. They looted first whatever from gold and silver was found with the captives, and also plundered their covering sheets, clothes, *tah-bands* and trousers. Then they sent them to their officers who sentenced them to death by hanging or beheading. None escaped these killings, neither the young nor the invalids, nor the nobles, nor the low-born. Thus the number of those who were beheaded or hanged reached upto thousands.[29] Most of the persons who suffered these tyrannies of the tyrant were the believers in Islam. As far as the Hindus were concerned they remained safe with the exception of those who were regarded as hostiles. From amongst the Muslims none survived except those who had left their houses as *muhajirs* or those who had supported the Christians and were lax in their faith (*iman*) or those who were their spies and had not pinned their hopes in the mercy of the beneficent and merciful God, as for instance that *'amil'* of the ex-king, who was in friendship with them and in fact had enabled them to seize power and become the rulers. But he suffered grievously because he could not get what he had coveted and had to remain distressed for his losses. His position underwent a change and his power was lost. He had to pass his days in a state of contemptible disrepute. 'He loses this world as well as the hereafter; that is the great straying.'[30]

Then the Christians sent messages to those Hindu chiefs, who were owners of the lands and estates and had submitted to them, to the effect that they should capture all those who entered their lands as fugitives or were found passing through them. They captured large numbers of these poor travellers, made them prisoners and sent them in chains to the officers of the Christians. The latter killed them all, sparing neither a noble man nor the low-born. Then they (Christians) assembled their forces and supporters and scattered them in the various parts of the country; these (forces) tried to capture the people and destroyed those whom they seized.[31]

During this great calamity the noble and chaste women had come out of their houses and were helpless; among them were old women and those who were unable to escape because of fatigue; and among them were those who died of excess of fear and those who committed suicide by drowning themselves in order to protect their honour and position and their chastity and modesty. Many of them were made captive, subjected to tortures and were made victims of hardships; some of them were made concubines by despicable fellows and some were sold for low prices. A large number of them perished on account of hunger and thirst and many of them disappeared and could not return, nor was any trace found of them, nor any news heard. Most of the women were separated from their guardians, husbands, fathers, brothers and sons. Every day of this calamitous period had become 'the day on which a man shall fly from his brothers, and his mother, and his father, and his spouse, and his sons.'[32] Many a woman became widowed in the evening, many a children rose an orphan in the morning; many a mother rendered childless was (seen) weeping and wailing, and many a father bereaved of his children was (found) shedding tears from sorrow and betraying his hidden (grief). The city was changed into a desert and waste land and was turned into a jungle, and its inhabitants were scattered and dispersed.[33]

The Christians then directed their attention towards the east and the villages and cities situated therein. They created horrible conditions there. They committed a general massacre, hanging and shooting the people. Death overtook many men and many purdah-observing ladies, and a large number of people were annihilated. Hundreds and thousands of persons were made the victims of death and destruction.

As to myself, I was now on my way to my beloved home. The route was full of dangers and the traveller suffering afflictions. Between me and my homeland there lay many a region, full of risks and dangers. The Christians and their forces were busy in seeking and searching the travellers. They had issued orders to the Jats, their clansmen and their parties to kill the passengers, frighten them, rob them and plunder them. They (Jats) had left no way for the travellers nor any boat at the ferries. They had seized the boats and made holes in them; in fact they had burnt them, rendered them unserviceable or had sunk them. They had ordered the boat-men not to allow the travellers or swimmers to cross (the rivers) at any time.[34] The Holder of Power (God) saved me and my companions from each calamity and misery and enabled them and me to cross the big and small rivers without resorting to (the use of) bridge or boats. Thus we survived all the hardships of these routes and dangerous places and the accidents and mishaps of the roads and ways. We reached our home and neighbours, and (joined our) family and friends under His (God's) perfect protection, effective help, over-flowing blessings and comfort-giving mercy. He saved us, undoubtedly, from the risks of this journey and graced us by granting us safety from all sorts of calamities. We, therefore, offered profuse praises to our Lord for this.

A number of those who had risen against the Christians and the soldiers and fighting forces who were in our land had after their revolt, made their ruler a woman [35] from amongst the wives of their previous King who had abdicated and her son who had not even attained the age of puberty. The Christians had taken over this country from the said ruler who was a weak man and used to waste his time in worthless amusements and neglected the business of the government. He was neither prudent nor wise; he was an expert in violating his agreements and promises. When the authority of the Christians broke down and their government was overthrown the country passed into her hands; her son was young, conceited, delicate and vain, and was given to playing with boys of his own age, absolutely neglectful of his enemies. He was incapable of managing and administering the affairs of the government and executing its projects, and he could not issue orders or have them acted upon, nor could he lead the forces or secure necessary equipement for them. All the officers of his government and the ministers of the state were worthless, timid and cowardly, and were foolish and dishonest; they were neither wise nor trustworthy. They were all mean fellows and some of them had been slaves. Amongst them were illiterate, ease-loving, impertinent, noise-making, lazy and feeble fellows and flatterers, hangers on, and sycophants. They were mean and of undetermined parentage, low-born and rascals, irresolute and incapable of acting dishonest and tyrannical, cruel, deceitful, treacherous and scheming. Among them were slaves of gold [*sic*] and chiefs who were hypocritical some of them were administrators but they were wretched and their policy led the administration to misfortune, destruction and ruin, providing the discerning people with opportunities for taking lessons; most of them were allies of the Christians and advocates of their friendship. All of them were helpless against the mortal devices of the enemy and they were negligent, slow and careless. The Christians, with their families and children, had been besieged in the palaces in the city,[36] but they were in safety because of the defects in the arrangements and the management of (the affairs of) their opponents. They had fortified these palaces by trenches and ramparts. The rebel forces attacked them again and again but were repulsed. They 'say that which they do not do'.[37] Then, there arrived a force of white-faced soldiers to help the besieged and entered the city. The brave *ghazis* fought against them and many of the white-faced people were killed; those among them who survived managed to join the besieged, broken-hearted and weary. After this, all those who were in the palaces came out but no one offered them resistance because of cowardliness and weakness. The Christians now shut themselves up behind the walls of a garden,[38] situated at a distance of two miles from the city. With courage and bravery they fortified it and continued asking for help, collecting in the meanwhile supplies in large quantities.

The troops who were already present in the city and the forces who after having escaped from Dihli had come to the Queen (Hedrat Mahal) and had received protection and honour from her and on whom she had conferred bounties as well as the mercenaries of the earlier days, who had never witnessed a battle, nor seen fighting or the piercing of the lance, nor had any idea as to what was advantageous, nor had used arms and taken an active part in a battle or faced a danger, gathered in front of this garden and dug trenches and ambushes. Now fighting was on and the flinging of arrows and playing of lances continued for a long time between the two forces. The struggle between them was long-drawn. The Christians asked the chief of the mountainous region to help them. He gave them help according to their desire and hopes, sending regiments of hill-men who numbered more than thirty thousand. Then the Christians, their white forces and their mercenaries and supporters launched severe and successive attacks which uprooted their opponents from their positions and shook them. They fled from their ambushes so badly that they could not stop anywhere even in the city and its neighbourhood. Thus they left the queen and her son alone in her palace. Many of their supporters, officials of the state, servants of their government and the villagers of their territories betrayed them, although they had come to help, aid and support them and to protect and maintain their property and honour. They broke their pledges apd promises and exchanged *kufr* for *iman*. They acted as hypocrites, began to favour the Christians, joined them and helped them to achieve victory.

The Christians and their supporters entered the city. The citizens left their houses and dwellings empty and went away. Ultimately the Christians, their white-faced soldiers and their forces and supporters besieged the palace in which the queen was living. Consequently, accompanied by her son and two female attendants, she came out of the besieged palace, barefooted, from its backdoor and hurriedly went to another part of the city (*mahallah*). She stayed for three days in the city, reassembling and recalling her fugitive forces and appealing to them to help and support her. These soldiers, however, had become terror-stricken and therefore shrank from and shirked their duty of facing the extremely dangerous situation. None of them returned to her and there remained no place of safety for her in the city. Thus, disappointed of all help from her supporters, she took to flight accompanied by her son and a few attendants, and proceeded towards the desolate and deserted plains. At that time parties of terror-stricken horsemen, a large crowd of barefooted persons and groups of citizens, including veiled women, crowded round her. They were all barefooted and almost without clothes, although they had been amongst the leading persons. The women were without veils and were barefooted, although they were purdah-observing ladies of rank and used to live in palatial houses. They had been thrown out of their palaces into the open fields and had to content themselves with patched clothes. They were thrown from one desolate place to another and their veils and *burq'ahs* had been removed (from their bodies). They had been living in comfort and luxury but had now to wander in the jungles and deserts.

These people had to leave their mansions and estates as well as their ranks and positions although they did not want to part with them. Thus the conditions had changed; evil had befallen and confusion had spread. This misfortune was ruinous; it converted the cities into wildenesses, the freemen into slaves, the wealthy into destitutes and the nobles into lowly persons. They had been living in ease and comfort with their families and children but now they were forced to come out; they had been enjoying happiness and prosperity and were satisfied, but now they were reduced to a state of perplexity. Destitution and poverty had dissociated them from the company of their friends and misfortune had forced them to abandon the society of their equals.

Among the weepers were those who had suffered, among the lamentors were those who had been hurt, among the tender-hearted were those who were crying in prayers; the aggrieved ones were reciting *Inna Lillahi-wa-inna ilaihi raji'un* (We belong to Allah and verily we shall return towards Him). The babies were deprived before time of sucking milk from the breasts of their mothers and the old and young had lost all hopes of the fulfilment of their desires and requirments. There was no dwelling-place or abode left for them, nor was there any remedy for their malady; and their hearts were completely depressed. They liked no pleasure and had no desires; for them life and death were equal. They used to live in happiness and in regal styles, and rolled in silks and satins, in fruits and pleasures, in cleanliness and prosperity, ease and comforts, wealth and riches, songs and happiness, and had possessed property, palaces and plentitude; but now thorns were spread under their feet. They had no more army provisions left with them; their clothes were worn out and ragged.[39] They had no share in comfort. May God forgive them in His mercy and take the tyrants into the grip of His severe punishment.

Then the queen, Hadrat-al-'Aliyah, with parties of the former fugitive forces who had come under her protection and many others who had decided to migrate, went across the rivers, large and small, which could not be crossed without boats. She stopped in a village on the bank of a river in the northern parts of the country. From here she posted horsemen and foot soldiers at the ferries so that they might seize the boats and stop the enemy from crossing the rivers. She also sent her *'amils* to the village and the towns to collect revenues and reclaim the people. She now equipped the forces and sent them to take positions in the ambushes, lying near her capital which the Christians had taken, so that they might offer them resistance, fight them and stop them in case they attempted aggression in the country around it. But she entrusted the execution of this entire task and major and minor questions connected with it to a contemptible, negligent *'amil* whose ideas were confused and who was absolutely unfit for it. He did not consult any one except (his) ignorance and considered every simple matter to be difficult and every complicated affair to be easy. He was stupid, a coward and a liar. He chose none for his companionship, consultation, society and conversation except foolish, illiterate and mean fellows. He avoided the company of the noble, the sagacious and the wise leaders on account of his vanity. He did not make friends with, nor consulted, nor gave authority to, nor appointed as officers except those mean and ignorant persons who belonged to his family and his kinsmen. This inexperienced fellow appointed officers for these forces from amongst the mean, coward, wretched, weak-hearted worthless and despicable persons who were greedy and would eat themselves whatever was given to the forces as rations. They committed perfidy because of malice hidden in their hearts; they stole the grain and then solid it for higher price. Every cry that reached them was considered by them to have been raised by the enemy; they always trembled with fear and had no tranquility or peace of mind. On account of extreme fear they took every cry to be their death-knell; every sound was to them the harbinger of death. It appeared as if they were going to meet the mean enemy in a friendly and apologetic manner.[40]

The Christians after capturing the capital stayed there and did not go to the suburbs or the neighbouring places. They began to win over the infidels and the leading persons of the countryside as well as the farmers and the villagers by pardoning their misdeeds and crimes and granting reductions in the revenues and taxes. The Christians advanced them loans and they offered their support to them; they (Christians) helped them and the latter became their hands and arms. The Christians then went out into the suburbs and neighbouring territories in order to establish their control on the villages and towns.

The Christians now repaired to an ambush which lay eighteen miles[41] from the capital towards the north and where were posted horsemen and foot soldiers, commanded by an officer of high rank who, however, belonged to the mean and low classes of people. On hearing the news of the arrival of the Christians this low-born commander took to heels even before seeing any sign of them, along with his companions who also belonged to the same class. But a small party of the fighting Hindus, under a reliable officer, who was one of the gallant heroes, remained firm in their position. They were not more than one hundred in number; but they fought with them, killed them and were killed, until not one of them was left alive, because they hated a shameful flight and because they received no reinforcements from their fugitive leader in spite of the fact that he had a large number of soldiers and plentiful supplies. When the Christians found the village, in which that coward and treacherous leader was posted to keep watch, evacuated and deserted, they took possession of it and made it their great and well-defended stronghold. Then having collected the forces they remained there for a long time. During this period they did not advance (from their positions) even a mile. It seemed as if they were waiting for something which they expected from the commanders of the forces and for the fulfilment of the promises which had been made to them by those perfidious people, and in satisying which they were making delay.

Then they (Christians) turned and marched towards the west of the city and proceeded to those regions where all the farmers and residents had submitted to them and were helping them against their enemies. In this region was posted an officer of the queen (Hadrat Mahal), who was worthless and lacked resolution and was neither experienced nor sagacious. He turned his back towards them, made a retreat and fled away, leaving his men there. He escaped without fighting or combating the enemy, making his way through a subterranean passage, because the number of his horsemen and foot-soldiers was small and the villagers and the infidels had revolted against him, although they had pledged themselves to support him. They betrayed him although they had become his allies, and committed treachery and perfidy and became ungrateful despite the blessings which they had been enjoying and the comfort in which they had been living happily for a long time; thus they added to their disbelief and infidelity by violating their pledges and breaking their agreements, in a most thankless manner.

Now there arose an '*amil*'[42] of another district, who had piled up a treasure of virtues, charitable actions and good deeds. He was a righteous, good-fearing, devoted, pure, brave and gallant person. He was named after the Prophet, the hero of great battles and a messenger of mercies. He attacked the Christians and their forces and put them to rout in his first charge. They made a determined effort and the party shut itself up in the house of a Hindu in the town. This house was well-protected and strongly-guarded. Then they sent a message to the Christian chiefs who were in the city, to help them by sending battalions of troops. The Christian chiefs sent a battalion for their help from their army corps and large numbers of those villagers and hyprocrites who had broken their pledges and had rendered themselves guilty of infidelity by violating their promises. Some from amongst the infidel landlords deceived the said pious and brave *'amil*.[43] He had given him assurance on oaths that he would help him with four thousand brave soldiers at the time when the two armies would meet in battle. However, when the parties came face to face with each other this efficient and honest *'amil* had to attack the Christian forces with a number of youthful followers, deceived as he had been by the promises of help given by this infidel land lord. The Christian forces showered bullets by their guns and canon on their forces and chests from their front and the party of that treacherous and perfidious infidel fired at their backs from the rear. This party was in reality a supporter of the Christians and their allies and the helpers of Satan and his brethren. This perfect and righteous *'amil* sought for and got martyrdom in an action and all those who accompanied him also gained martyrdom in this attack. After this pious and brave person and his good comrades were martyred those wretched ones who had followed them turned their backs and took to flight. They fled in such confusion and anxiety that they did not see what lay behind them, because they had been overwhelmed by failure and defeat and the Christians were pursuing them and slaughtering them. Only a few of them could manage to escape as they had resorted to great haste and speed in their flight. The landlords, the leading persons, the ryots, the villagers and others who lived in these regions—all offered submission and allegiance to the Christian forces except two brave, gallant and warlike persons who were jealous of their honour. They fought against the Christians fiercely and in spite of the inadequacy of equipment and soldiers they killed through their zeal and courage a large number of the horsemen and foot soldiers of the enemy. By dint of sheer dauntlessness they were able to save themselves from them. The Christians did not take steps to pursue them. Thus the territory was cleared of the opponents of the Christians, but this unfortunate incident terrified the people who were opposed to the Christians. This was one of the most calamitous events of the struggle and became the cause of considerable grief. It appeared to be the end of the long series of battles and combats (of the war). After their victory in this region the Christians spread themselves over other territories also. Nevertheless, whenever they thought of entering any place and took steps to capture it their opponents living there decided to offer resistance and make every possible effort for it. But they dispersed before actually meeting them.

In spite of this the queen of the Christians played a trick which considerably added to their strength and power. She had a large number of printed posters distributed and published in towns and villages in every part of the country, through which it became widely known that she had forgiven all the rebel forces and all her subjects who had revolted against her, except those who had been guilty of murdering women, children and the Christians who were forced to seek shelter in the earlier stages (of the war) and had been killed by them out of enmity and hostility, and those who had set up (independent) governments and states, and those who had instigated to people rebellion and hostility.[44]

The rebel forces and other people who had supported and agreed with the queen (Hadrat Mahal) had in fact joined her because they had no means of livelihood. With the shortage of food and stoppage of the payment of their salaries in consequence of her inability to collect revenues which were paid to her, because of the spreading of Christian forces in the various parts of the region and their hold on them, the land (world) in spite of its expanse became narrow for them. Their lives became afflicted with severe distress and long-drawn tortures. Every one of them was empty-handed and devoid of rest and comfort. Being at a distance from their children and families, their thoughts had become confused on account of worries. Therefore many of them turned to the Christians and their followers and offered submission to them, accepting their authority. The Christians seized their horses and arms and gave them *parrwanahs* of security. Then they returned to their families and homes, disappointed and having suffered losses. Now the Christians got full control over the country, as there was no one left to dispute their authority; they were rid of fighting and could now take rest. The queen after these embarrassments and troubles, sought shelter in the hills.[45]

As my travels had extended over a long period and my dejection and anxiety had been long-drawn, my desire to return to my home, family, neighbours and friends had become very intense. When, therefore, I saw the charter (Proclamation of Victoria) which had been strengthened by oaths I returned to my family, home and dwelling-place because I was satisfied with its authenticity, neglecting, however, the truth that the oath of a person having no *iman* (faith) is meaningless, and that the oath of a man who follows no faith and does not fear the Day of Judgement should not be relied upon. After a few days a Christian officer sent for me from my house, put me in prison and subjected me to torture, causing me great pain. Then putting me in chains he sent me to the capital of the Kingdom which had become by then the home of ruin and destruction. He entrusted my case to a cruel officer of dominating personality, who had no sympathy with those who sought justice. Two apostates, who were by nature quarrelsome and had had religious disputations with me in regard to a *Quranic* verse, meaning that one who befriends the Christian is a Christian himself, had supplied information about me. They used to insist on friendship with the Christians and had ultimately turned apostate, exchanging *iman* with *kufr.*

That officer passed an order for my life-long imprisonment, punishment, exile and banishment as well as the confiscation of my entire property, comprising my books, effects and wealth. He forcibly seized the house that belonged to my family and my children.

I was not the only victim of this shameless, breach of faith; a large number of people were generally meted out treatment that was far more hideous than this. They (British Government) violated all the pledges that they had given and massacred a large number of persons by shooting and hanging them; many of them were caught and thrown into imprisonment and sent in exile without delay. They completely broke every promise that they had made and destroyed numerous lives and precious articles. The number of persons whose blood was shed was beyond counting even by hundreds and thousands. Beyond enumeration was also the number of those who were arrested from amongst the nobles and common people, particularly those living in the vast territories between Delhi and our land which had many cities, villages and towns and was the homeland of many respected and noble families.

In the meanwhile a chief professing Islam and the Faith sent parties of those who had sought protection in his state to these people (offering security) and then arrested them and made them helpless, after having promised them safety. To win over the Christians he betrayed them in a way which is condemned by all religions. In his attempt to please them (Christians) he did not even fear the wrath of the Almighty God. The Christians imprisoned these people who were sent to them in chains and fetters and subjected many of the nobles to imprisonment, exile and other tortures. Thus, this chief also shared with the Christians the consequences of inflicting upon the servants of God the most severe tortures. This is the story of the War.

Thus the Christians punished me with imprisonment by fabricating falsehoods and deceptive devices against me; they shifted me from one jail to another and inflicted on me one injury after another. They continuously added to my grief and pain, deprived me of my shoes and dress and clad me in coarse and rough clothes. They snatched from me my good and soft bedding and gave me a coarse and highly uncomfortable one, which looked as if it was a thorn-bush or a burning ember. They left with me neither a pitcher or a bowl nor any other pot and gave me insufficient meals to eat. They made me drink hot water and I was thus given hot drinks instead of the love of bosom friends. In spite of old age and weakness every moment I was subjected to humiliatation and insults.

The excesses of the heard-hearted enemy cast me on the shore of a great saltish sea in a plateau which has a cape (*ras*), also named *ras*. Here the sun always shines straight upon my head. It has difficult mountain passes and hilly roads full of trouble. There are passes in the hills, enveloped by waves of the tumultuous sea whose water is bitter; its breeze is hotter than *simum* and its comforts are more dangerous than poison; its eatables are more bitter than the taste of colocynths and its water was more harmful than snake poison. Its sky is a cloud which rains sorrows and its raining clouds shower afflictions and miseries. The ground is spread over with stones like measles and small pox (on the diseased body). Its air, because of calamities, is full of disasters. Every house in this place, built with grass and weeds, is infested with lasting illness and misery; from its roof always drizzle drops like the tears of my eyes which never stop. Its air is contaminated and therefore a source of disease. Illness is cheap, but medicines are dear. Epidemics are frequent and scabies and ring-worms very common. For the wounded there is no cure, for the healthy no security, and for the sick no treatment. The one who treats the sick brings back the disease, and the one who is treated is sure to meet death; the one who attends the sick ill-treats them and enhances their trouble. The aggrieved is not sympathized with, nor does anyone feel sorry for him. No anxiety in the world could be guessed upon the pains that one has to bear in this place. No disease is found here which is not fatal: fever brings the message of death and even ordinary types of hypochondria and pleurisy are sure causes of death. Besides, many diseases prevail here whose names or symptoms are not to be found in medical works. The physician makes the bowels of the patient burn like a furnace and instead of helping him raises a dome of fire on him. He cannot diagnose the disease but makes the patient take medicines which bring him near death. When any one from amongst the people breathes his last an unclean person from the impure ones, who is a sweeper and is like a devil or a monster, drags the dead body by catching the leg and after removing the clothes buries it in a sand hill without a coffin or funeral bath He does not dig a grave, nor is funeral prayer performed for him. If the dead were not subjected to this abject treatment then dying would have been a thing keenly desired, and a sudden death would have been something longingly hoped for; if suicide had not been unlawful in the eyes of the Faith and people had not feared its punishment on the Day of Judgement no one who was brought here as a prisoner and put in trouble would have remained alive to bear these hardships: deliverance from the afflictions which one has to suffer here would have been easy.

It was in this environment that I became a victim of several diseases and severe illness. These made me lose my patience; my heart became melancholy: my full moon was dimmed and my honour was lost. I do not know how can deliverance and emancipation be effected from this condition which has made me sorrowful, so that I might be compensated for. In addition to the grief caused by these hardships I had a severe attack of scabies and ring-worms. I am made to move about in the morning and evening while my whole body is suffering with wounds. Along with soul-breaking pains, my wounds and injuries are increasing. The time is near when my boils would take me to the verge of destruction and death, after a long life of ease, comfort, enjoyment and happiness. Before this I was healthy and had never had small pox; today I am disabled, wounded and ulcerated. I am undergoing severe hardships and struggling against difficulties and oppression.

We have suffered at the hands of Time what we have no strength to bear. Our forbearance for them is like that of a fractured bone which has to bear the load of bandage.

In spite of all this I praise the Glorious and Almighty God and thank Him for His favour and kindness, for I see other prisoners, besides me, heavily fettered and suffering with diseases, being dragged in chains and fetters. A harsh, stern hard-hearted man drives and drags them along with their iron fetters and imposes upon them every type of hard and laborious work. He exhibits every kind of malice and enmity against them and tries to intensify their hardships. He shows no sympathy with them when they are thirsty or hungry. I thank God, therefore, for remaining safe against these miseries and offer my gratitude for His favours on me and for saving me from these troubles. Looking at the apparent means, I am completely disappointed as to my deliverance and have given up all hopes, because my enemies are endeavouring to harm me and are anxious to bring about my ruin, while my friends have no power to cure my disease, and hostility and malice against me have become as deep-seated in the hearts of my opponents as religious beliefs are in the hearts of the people; their wretched hearts are full of grudge and rancour. Nevertheless I have hopes of mercy from my God, the Strong, the Merciful, the Righteous, the Kind, the Benevolent, Who delivers the weak and the disabled from the clutches of the cruel Pharaohs and heals the wounds of the oppressed and the wounded by the ointment of His healing mercies. He is the repairer of every broken heart and compensator for the needy and sufferers; He is the deliverer of every prisoner who is neglected, and He makes difficult things easy. It was he who saved Noah from being drowned, Abraham from being burnt, Job from what he suffered of the diseases and miseries, Jonah from the belly of the fish and children of Israel from their hardships. He saved Moses and Aaron from Pharaoh, Haman and Korah and saved the Messiah from the evil designs of the crafty and saved his friend, Mustafa (Muhammad) from the machinations of the infidels. If therefore misfortune has specifically fixed its eyes on me, and looks at me fixedly, incidents and calamities have befallen me, hardships have surrounded me and sins have encircled me, I am not disappointed from His favour nor from his mercy. It is my Lord who is the true Curer, the Perfect, the Comforter and the Forgiver. Many a sick person, on the verge of death, recovers when he prays to him; many an apologiser is forgiven when he apologizes to him and begs his forgiveness; many an aggrieved one is relieved of griefs when he prays to him; a traveller receives succour when he approaches him directly with prayer, and on many a prisoner, tied in chains the Creater who creates without limits places his obligation without the mediation of any helper or redeemer by giving him deliverance and emancipation from imprisonment and fetters.

I am an oppressed, injured, anxious, dejected, humble and needy person and I call to him in secret prayer and supplicate before him with great hopes and pray to him, through the mediation of his friend (Muhammad). He verily has promised and would not go back on His words about responding to the prayers of the perplexed ones, removing their miseris and helping the oppressed while they pray and call him, crying bitterly. He will rescue me from what makes me aggrieved, deliver me from what makes me perplexed, respond to my request against what renders me petitioner, cure me from what keeps me uneasy, save me from the person who has taken me in his grip, and from one who oppresses me. He will have mercy upon my weeping and crying. He will remedy my complaint, and will bring to an end my misfortune and misery. Surely he is a listener to prayers, bestower of great bounties, a remover of calamities. It is he from whom I have hopes of relief from the hardships of exile and the end of the best trials about the gifts.

Oh Lord! save me from the condition in which I am. Oh Supporter of those who hope, Protector of the seekers of protection for the sake of the honour of your friend, the most trustworthy and the greatest giver of security and his blessed descendants and his supporting companions, Oh the most Merciful, the most Powerful Ruler, the Avenger of the oppressions of the tyrants! And our last prayer is that all praises are due to Allah, the Sustainer of all the worlds.

I have mentioned some calamities that befell me and some of the misfortunes which struck me in (my) two *qasidahs;* one of them is *hamziyyah*[46] and refers to instigations of Satan, and the other is *daliyyah*[47] which mentions the hardships that this sad and disabled person has suffered. I have ended them both with the eulogy of the leader of the prophets, who was a steadfast and trustworthy messenger (of God). May the purest blessings of those who send their blessings on him be upon him and may the salutations of the Muslims be upon him! Prior to the said poems I had composed a *qasidah* with rhymes of NUN (ن) which was peerless like the concealed pearl. Each of its verses was as stable as a strong mansion or a lofty palace. The number of its verses was three hundred or more. However, it could not be completed. The onslaughts of misfortunes and their accumulation kept me from its completion. Its openning verse is:

There bemoaned no leaves from amonst the leaves of (the tree of) pathos,
which did not excite my sorrows and did not move my tender emotions.

If God Almighty favours me with deliverance and emancipation I shall supplement it with the eulogy of one who has been distinguished by the nobility of his morals and his most perfect share from them. May the choicest of blessings be upon him, and his descendants up to the Day of Judgement!

The Glorious Almighty is the only Lord of the favourable circumstances and their realities.

NOTES

1. The Arabic text with Urdu translation and an account of the author's life was published by Maualana Muhammad Abd-al Shahid Khan Shirwani in 1947, under the title *Baghi Hindustan*. The author has not given any title to his work. It has been referred to as *Risalah-i-Ghadriyah* or *Fitnat-al-Hindiyah* I have cal'ed it *The Story of the war* because the author refers to his account as *qissah*.
2. See *Athar-al-Sanadid*.
3. I am grateful to Mr. Zikriya Mail for his help in the translation of the Arabic text.
4. Bakht Khan had advised the old Emperor to leave the Capital and reassemble his forces and reorganize them in the open country.
5. The Western writers have emphasized the military causes, but in fact they were covered by one or the other of these two groups.
6. This brief account was written by the 'Allamah when he was undergoing imprisonment in the Andamans.
7. The 'Allamah refers to his case only but he is in fact trying to make out the point that the *'ulama* were particularly victimized. To appreciate this point one has to bear in mind that the first half of the nineteenth century was a period of brisk missionary activity. The *'ulama* had to meet the challenge of the Christian missionaries. Some of them played a prominent role in the War of Independence. For the activities of some of the leading Christian missionaries, particularly Pfander, see Sir William Muir, *The Mohammedan Controversy* (Edinburgh, 1897), pp. 13, 20, 32ff. It is obvious that jailor, usurper, tyrant and other terms of a similar nature are used for the Company's Government.
8. Obviously this refers to Bahadur Shah.
9. This view is correct. We have contemporary and recorded evidence to show what the trends of the ideas and expectations of the British officers and other servants of the Company on this question were in the pre-1857 period. Macaulay, for instance, betrays these feelings in a letter: 'if our plans of education are followed up, there will not be a single idolator among the respectable classes in Bengal thirty years hence.'
10. Besides the account given by Sir Sayyid Ahmad Khan in his well-known *Causes of the Indian Revolt* we have a vast amount of contemporary and nearly contemporary evidence in support of the argument of the

'Allamah. Of the activities of the poineer Christian missionaries, Carey, Marshman and Ward the Literary Secretary of the Y.M.C.A. (India and Ceylon) writes: 'They laid great stress on education, and opened numerous schools around them for both boys and girls. . . . They were most eager to send out native missionaries to preach throughout the country. . .'. Again he says, 'In missions these decades (1828-70) are marked chiefly by great activity in education, especially in English education and by a brilliant development of missionary method in many directions.' (Farquhar: *Modern Religious Movements in India*), pp. 14-19.

It is interesting to note that 'certain British officers, indeed, preached the Gospel to their men with the enthusiasm of Cromwell's Ironsides. . . .' (*C.H.I.*, vol. VI, p. 173.)

Sir Sayyid Ahmad has referred to and given in *extenso* the Urdu translation of E. Edmund's circular letter containing an appeal to the people of the subcontinent to accept Christianity. See *Risalah-i-Asbab-i-Baghawat-i-Hind* (edited by Dr. Mahmud Husain, Karachi), pp. 45-49.

11. The revolutionary forces entered Delhi on 11 May 1857. Bahadur Shah was proclaimed Emperor on the same day.
12. This refers to Ahsanullah Khan.
13. The 'Allamah's verdict is to be accepted as incontrovertible because he was closely associated with the emperor and his court.
14. Mirza Mughul was the commander-in-chief of the revolutionary forces, see Kaye and Malleson, *History of the Indian Mutiny* (London, 1899), vol. V, p. 327.
15. The famous Ridge on which the British forces had encamped. For its description and military operations during the War of Independence see Fanshawe: *Delhi—Past and Present*, pp. 77-85.
16. This seems to refer to the Sikh States.
17. The revolutionary forces had entered the capital in May, but the siege and assaults commenced in June. The imperial palace was captured by the British on September 20.
18. *Holy Qur'an*, 10: 26.
19. Humayun's Tomb.
20. 'When at last, on the 19th, the Burn bastion had been captured, the Commander-in-Chief, the old artillery Subahdar, Bakht Khan, represented to the King that his only way of safety lay in flight; he begged him to accompany the sipahi army, which still remained intact, and with it to renew the war in the open country. That was the course which the descendant of Babar, had he been young, would have undoubtedly followed. But . . . the King was persuaded to reject the bold counsels of his general and to accept those of his Queen and courtiers.' G.B.

Malleson, *The Indian Mutiny,* 309. Of course Malleson has suppressed the very important fact that the Queen and the chief courtier, whom the 'Allamah describes as the treacherous '*amil*, were in league with the British and were acting as their agents and spies.

21. 'Of the perfidious acts of Ahsanullah Khan one may be mentioned by way of illustration. 'At three o'clock,' writes Munshi Jeewan Lal under May 20, 'Hakim Ahsanullah represented that the soldiers were looting in the city, and requested that they should be expelled. To get rid of them, orders were this day issued to Mirza Mogul to proceed with a strong force towards Meerut to attack any English force assembled there. . . . It became known that the dispatch of troops to Meerut to fight the English was a device of Hakim Ahsanullah Khan to rid the city of the mutineers and soldiers, who were beyond all discipline.' *Two Native Narratives of the Mutiny* (tr. by C.T. Metcalfe, 1898), p. 99. For the intrigues of Mirza Ilahi Bakhsh see Kaye and Malleson, vol. IV, pp. 50-52.

22. The details of the references made by the 'Allamah to the atrocities committed by the British soldiers can be easily substantiated by the incidents mentioned by the western writers themselves. Giving a resume of the history of the war until the fall of Dihli Charles Ball refers to the condition of the city after the entry of the British soldiers in these words: 'Streams of people and cattle also poured out of the Ajmere Gate; and, a few days later, the city was described as void of inhabitants. Houses, mosques, bazaars were tenantless; and large districts of the capital of Mohammadan India, with its 200,000 inhabitants, were changed to the desolateness of Pompeii.' *(The History of the Indian Mutiny*, vol. I, p. 528).

    The horrible conduct of Hodson in sending the severed heads of the princes to the King has been suppressed by the western historians. But the 'Allamah's statement cannot be ignored because he was in Dihli on 21 September when this took place.

23. Jeewan Lal says under date 14 September:
    'About midday the Mahomedans ceased to oppose the English. They, together with the Sepoys, began to take refuge in the houses of the Hindus whom they upbraided for not cooperating with them.'

24. It is difficult to determine the exact date of the 'Allamah's arrival in Dihli. He is however, reported by Jeewan Lal, to have attended the *durbar* and 'conversed with the King upon the situation' on August 16. Three weeks later (on September 6) he 'reported that the force from Muttra had gone to Agra, and after defeating the English had advanced against the city.'

25. Thus he must have left Dihli on 24 or 25 September, as the city was captured on the 20th.

26. *Holy Qur'an*, 4: 81.
27. Refers to Humayun's Tomb.
28. In a letter written by an Engineer officer who was a participant in the operations we read; 'September 23—we have all moved down to a capital house on the banks of the river in the city; the breeze is delightful, and we are all getting as fat and jolly as if we were at home. We are getting on capitally; we have got the King (the Great Mogul) prisoner, and are only waiting for leave from Calcutta to hang him. His eldest son and heir, Mirza Moghul Beg, a most infernal scoundrel, who set the example of murdering the Europeans, was caught and shot like a dog; and his son, a man about twenty years old; as well as the King's eldest son Mirza's brother. I saw all three bodies exposed in the Khotwalee this morning. I am happy to say we are not so lenient as we were.' (Quoted by Ball, vol. I, p. 516).
29. According to the author of the *Qaysar-al-Tawarikh* the number of persons executed in Dihli was twenty-seven thousand, vol. II, p. 454. The figure is by no means an exaggerated one. Lord Elphinstone refers to the massacre at Dihli. He writes to Sir John Lawrence, 'After the siege was over, the outrages committed by our army are simply heart-rending. A wholesale vengeance is being taken without distinction of friend or foe. As regards the looting, we have indeed surpassed Nadir Shah.' *Life of Lawrence*, vol. II, p. 262.
30. *Holy Qur'an*, 22: 11.
31. 'Before closing the present chapter, it will be proper to refer briefly to the operations of the troops, dispatched in various directions from Delhi, in pursuit of the discomfited and fugitive rebels.' Charles Ball, *The History of Indian Matiny,* vol. II, p. 185.
32. *Holy Qur'an,* 80: 34, 35, 36.
33. Of the devastation wrought by the British in Dihli we have considerable evidence in contemporary records. A few sentences from the work quoted above would give the reader some idea of the terrible fate of the capital. 'The city of the Moguls was now, indeed, but little better than a vast and hideous ruin—its houses and streets deserted; its defences unmanned; and the sentence of utter demolition suspended over its shattered gates and once defiant towers, the carcasses of some thousands of its defenders, who had fallen in their insane struggle ..., had been necessarily gathered by the sweepers and camp followers into deep pits, and were so hidden from mortal sight . . .' (ibid., p. 167).
34. Colvin, the lieutenant-governor of the North-West Provinces, had succeeded in persuading Sindhia and the Jat *rajah* of Bharatpur to give the British 'material assistance. Plundering and highway robbery had long been the favourite pursuits of the Jats; and with active encouragement from the Company authorities they must have ruthlessly indulged in

their 'semi-barbarous activities' referred to here; undoubtedly the 'Allamah is telling us the bare truth about what he actually saw and experienced. The editor of the Arabic text of this short pamphlet says on the authority of the late Sadr Yar Jang Habib-al-Rahman Khan of Bhikanpur that the latter's father and uncle had played the host to the 'Allamah when he was on his way to Lucknow. He is stated to have stayed with his family and companions at Bhikanpur for 18 days and then arrangements were made for their safely crossing the Ganges at the Sankrah ferry.

35. Hadrat Mahal, the wife of Wajid 'Ali Shah, was the regent of her minor son, Birjis Qadr. Even the British writers admit that the queen was a 'woman of much energy of character.'
36. The 'Allamah's reference to palaces (*qusur*) is of course to the various buildings and houses in the Residency, which has been rightly described and 'a small town, rather than a mere single building, occupied by the chief commissioner'. Machhi-bhawan was another fortified building.
37. *Holy Qur'an*, 26: 226.
38. 'Alam-bagh.
39. How the guilty and the innocent alike were butchered by the victor is indicated by recorded evidence. 'At the time of the capture of Lucknow—a season of indiscriminate massacre—such distinction was not made and the unfortunate who fell into the hands of our troops was made short work of—sepoy of Oudh, villager, it mattered not; no questions were said: his skin was black and did not that suffice. A piece of rope and the branch of a tree, or a rifle bullet through his brain, soon terminated the poor devils existence.' (Majendie, *Up among the Pandies*), pp. 1956.
40. For a brief but informative account of the queen's activities see Mirza Ali Azhar's article: 'Hadrat Mahal's Role in the War of Independence', in *JPHS*, vol. I, part III.
41. Eight miles in *Baghi Hindustan,* p. 404. This refers to Nawabganj on the Fyzabad road. It had become a stronghold of the fighters for independence.
42. Mawlana Ahmad-allah Shah who, in fact, was the supreme organizer of the movement. Even his enemies have testified to his greatness as a fighter in the cause of freedom. 'Of this conspiracy,' write Kaye and Malleson, 'the Maulvi was undoubtedly a leader. It had its ramifications all over India. . . .' *History of the Indiany Mutiny,* vol. V, p. 292.
43. This refers to Jagannath Singh, the perfidious *zamindar* of Powain. He invited the Mawlana and had him shot dead when he was entering his house. The British Government rewarded his treachery by a gift of Rupees fifty thousand. 'The Maulvi was a very remarkable person. . . . In person he was tall, lean and muscular, with large deep-set eyes, beatle

brows, a high aquiline nose, and lantern jaws. Sir Thomas Seaton, who enjoyed, during this suppression of the revolt, the best means of judging him, described him as "a man of great abilities of undaunted courage, of stern determination and by far the best soldier among the rebels." ' (Mallesson, *The Indian Mutiny of 1857,* p. 17).

44. The exact words of the relevant paragraph in the Queen's Proclamation are: 'Our clemency will be extended to all offenders, save and except those who have been or shall be convicted of having directly taken part in the murder of British subjects.

    With regard to such, the demands of justice forbid the exercise of mercy.' The Proclamation was issued on November 1, 1858.
45. She was driven by the British forces to the hills of Nepal and lived there till her death in 1879.
46. *Hamziyyah*: The last letter of the rhyme in each verse of the *qasidah hamzah*(*s*). By instigation of Satan (*homazat-al-Shayatin*) the writer means the wild ideas which overwhelm the mind of an aggrieved person.
47. *Daliyyah*: The last letter of the rhyme in each verse is *dal*.

CHAPTER 11

Dastanbuy

MIRZA ASADULLAH KHAN GHALIB

This is an extraordinary document written by Mirza Asadullah Khan Ghalib (1796-1869), the greatest of Urdu poets. Ghalib lived in Delhi for the entire period between the coming of the mutineers from Meerut on 11 May 1857 and the successful British assault upon the city on 14 September. 'The tumult of arrests and killings' reached his lane, renting 'the heart of every man with fear.' He wrote bitterly of the execution of the three nawabs of three small estates in Delhi's neighbourhood. His brother's house, close to his, was plundered. His family went away. This was another sorrow, another calamity that descended on him like an avalanche. 'We live,' the poet added, 'in anxious thought for bread and water, and die in anxious thought for shroud and grave.' Delhi had become a city without a ruler, a slave without a master, a garden without a gardener. Ghalib told his friend: 'I write a letter to Munshi Nabi Bakhsh Sahib and receive his reply, and today I get a letter from you, and your name is still Munshi Hargopal and your takhallus Tafta, and the city I live in is still called Delhi and this muhalla is still named Ballimaron muhalla—yet not one of the friends of that former birth is to be found. By God, you may search for a Muslim in this city and not find one—rich, poor, and artisans alike are gone. Such as here are not Delhi people.' Alas, wrote Mirza Nausha, perhaps in June or July 1858:

Aaj kuch dard mere dil mein siwa hota hain
Rakhio Ghalib ma'af mujhe is talkh nawai mein ma'af.

If Ghalib sings in bitter strain, forgive him;
Today pain stabs more keenly at his heart.

*Mirza Asadullah Khan Ghalib, *Dastanbuy: A Diary of the Indian Revolt of 1857*. Translated from the original Persian with a critical Introduction, Glossary and Notes by Khwaja Ahmad Faruqi, Delhi, 1954, pp. 25-68.

The first edition of five hundred copies of *Dastanbuy* was published in Agra in november 1858, and was sold out within five months. The subsequent two editions appeared in 1865 and 1871. This translation from Persian to English by Khwaja Ahmad Faruqi (b. 1917), based on the first edition, was published in 1954 with an introduction, glossary, notes, chronology, and index. The *Dastanbuy* is, states Faruqi, 'the story of the planned revolt, the ebb and flow of changing fortunes, of alternating hope and gloom as it affected the Delhi citizen—the throbbing of a sensitive soul and the reactions of a poet to an important historical situation—a story untold.'

I am a tear trembling on an eyelash.

I begin this book in the name of the Lord,Who is the Giver of Strength, Who is the Creator of the Moon and the Sun, of the Day and the Night.

He is the Possessor of all Power, the Emperor who has raised nine skies and given light to the seven great stars. He is the Master of Knowledge and has exalted the body by infusing it with the soul. He has endowed man with wisdom and the sense of justice. Without matter or means He has created seven layers of earth and nine skies. Difficult things become easy and ordinary or extraordinary impediments are removed, all by means of the movements and effects of the stars.

The Lord has arranged the skies in such a manner that although the stars possess various qualities producing various effects, and although He has given them the power to remain separate or to assemble and has endowed them with great influence, they cannot do other than obey His commands.

How can you know the secrets of the skies and the stars when you cannot distinguish between black and white, between front and back? Do not bow down before the stars, for they have no ultimate power to wield in the affairs of the world—for the Lord is above all and his light has enveloped all things hidden and secret.

Whereas Venus and Jupiter, being auspicious, assure our good fortune, Saturn and Mars, being inauspicious, are responsible for our losses. Those who know the truth know wherein lies the source of happiness and sorrow, inauspiciousness and grace—for the stars are but servants of the most just Emperor. The soldiers of His court can never step form the circle of His justice; nor can they do other than remain in conjunction with one another. If an inauspicious star provokes pain, or if an auspicious one increases the beauty of the world by gentleness, both are devices for the adornment of life and this contradiction cannot be constructed as wantonness or indifference.

A musician strikes his bow against the strings of his violin. As music issues from within the instrument, so joy emerges from the vibrations of sorrow. It is not in anger that the Washerman beats his clothes against a stone.

The cycle of death leads to the cycle of life. The Lord gives to man sorrow and joy, loftiness and lowliness, and these are the instruments of his well-being and the channels of his happiness. If a rich man gives to a poor man a few pice or thousands of rupees, if he gives bolts of silk or a simple blanket, he does, in fact, sustain the poor man and he performs generously. It would be a lack of wisdom to divide the gifts of the Lord into compartments of good and evil or, when we see inequality, to attribute this to an injustice of the Lord.

It is by the grace of the Lord that this world of illusion, floating upon the waves of death, has been endowed with life. I know that my words are powerless to plumb the depths of these profound ideas, and that the ideas themselves are beyond the comprehension of the uninspired; however, I shall descend from rhetoric and speak in simple and direct style

The rotation of the skies is like the rotation of a hand-mill. You know there must be a person who rotates the mill; why, then, do you not believe there is One who rotates the stars? Into the spinning wheel of the skies a spindle has been inserted which pertains to the auspicious and inauspicious aspects of the stars. The wheel has spun veils which have been placed before the eyes of men; but the inspired ones, who know the divine secrets, can see the Hand of the Lord behind these veils, and can know the reality of the Lord.

How can we think that the effects of the stars are cruel when the skies are turned by the hand of the Lord?

Praise the Lord who has created being and vanquished non-being! Praise the Lord who has put an end to atrocity and has spread the light of justice! By His wisdom He diminished the influence of the powerful; by His grace He increases the strength of the weak. The pebbles that slew the mighty elephant-mounted legions were dropped by a swallow, a mosquito killed the proud Nimrod. Truly there can be no understanding of these things other than as signs of the limitless power of the Lord. These destructions were different from one another and they took place at different times. Tell me what star by its blandishments could have caused such things to happen?

Zahhak seized the throne and the crown from the mighty Jamshid. Young Alexander slaughtered the powerful Darius. A nameless demon stole the ring of Solomon, who was king over the demons and the fairies. All you, who think these things are due to the effect of the skies and the influence of the stars, must learn the divine secrets of recompense and punishment.

The Lord who has brought the world into being from non-being, may also bring the world to the Day of Judgement. The Lord who has created the world by His word 'Let it be!' may also end the world by His word. And who can question the Lord?

During these days the harmony of all music, the principle behind all things has been altered. The soldiers have turned against their captain. Without indulging in ornament we can say simply that the times have changed.

Astronomers have told us that Saturn and Mars were in confluence in the sign of Cancer at the time when the courtly revelries of Yazadjird, last emperor of Iran, were disrupted by the Arab invasion. Today, also, Saturn and Mars are in confluence in Cancer and will so remain until the turmoil in the world has ended. This turmoil—the cruelty, bloodshed and degradation—issues from the inauspicious conjunction of these stars. But those who can read the truth will find the differences between these two periods quite obvious.

The Arab invasion of Iran was the invasion of one country by another; in India, however, the army has revolted against its own leaders. Religion was behind the invasion of Iran. Knowledge and wisdom had withered away and the country had become a desert—but the graces of Islam caused the desert to blossom and freed it of fire worship and slavery. In India, however, the people cannot be expected to offer the security of new laws. Iranians left the worship of fire and came to the worship of one God, but Indians have left the skirt of the just rulers and have been caught in the net of beastly men. Do you not see the similarity between the protecting *daman* (skirt) and the enslaving *dam* (net), and between *dād* (justice) and *dad* (beast)? In truth one cannot perceive of justice under other auspices than those of the British. The whips of the Arabs left scars, but these were soothed by the graces of Islam. Harmony and peace came after the welfare and the affections of Iran were forgotten. If any good can come from this insurrection, then the subtle and discerning man who can see this good must explain it to me and so comfort my fearful heart. How strange it is that officers responsible for peace should rise in rebellion against their rulers, that soldiers should assassinate their leaders, and that neither should feel shame at these outrageous acts. O you who can see what is hidden and you who can distinguish between loss and benefit, know that this is the wrath of the Lord. The invasion of Iran was neither as devastating nor as full of despair as is the rebellion in India.

The music from my harp is discordant and sad because, in my agitation, I strike the strings haphazardly and without skill.

I am not so dull as to call the bright stars lightless, or to believe the high heavens are impoverished, nor am I so ignorant as to consider the effects of the stars as false, or the confluence of inauspicious stars an illusion; for I know the terrible issue of the confluence of Saturn and Mars which took places one thousand years ago

I, who am entangled in the irremedial anxieties of the times, consider that those who have not seen the sign of Cancer, those who are not aware of the effects of Saturn and Mars but only of their names, should not now concern themselves with these things about which they do not know. These people should study the present which has concealed within it the secrets of the past and the future; for the times, which so often undo the works of good men, did not, in fact, permit the British to be harmed by external powers. Rather, it was from within their own territory that the British armies were attacked.

Readers of this book should know that I who, through the strokes of my pen scatter pearls on paper, have eaten the bread and salt of the British and, from my earliest childhood, have been fed from the table of these world conquerors.

Seven or eight years ago the Mughal emperor of Delhi summoned me to his palace and asked me to write a history of the Timurid dynasty, for which he proposed to pay me six hundred rupees annually. I accepted his offer and began the work. Eventually the emperor's master of verse died and I was also appointed as the one responsible for the correction of the royal poems.

I was aged and weak and had become used to my corner of loneliness and quiet. Further, I had developed a deafness which was a source of great inconvenience to my friends and I could only watch the lips of those who spoke. Twice a week I visited the royal palace where, if it was his will, I would remain for a while in the presence of the king. If the did not emerge from his chambers I would sit briefly in the hall of private audience before returning to my home.

During this time I used to take to the emperor whatever writing I had completed or send it by messenger. This was my connection with the court and the nature of my work. Although this small position gave me some restfulness and peace and was free from courtly entanglements, it assured me neither prosperity nor happiness. But even then the revolving skies were conspiring to destroy what little well-being I had.

No man, neither friend nor enemy, can escape the wounds inflicted by the sword of the cruel, indifferent skies.

We have a chronogram for this year, which is expressed in the phrase *rast khezi bija,* which means unwarranted revolt. If you should ask I would tell you that suddenly, at noon on Monday, the sixteenth of Ramazan, 1237 AH, which is the same as the eleventh of May 1857, the walls and ramparts of the Red Fort shook with such force that the vibrations were felt in the four corners of the city. This was not an earthquake. On that infamous day rebellious soldiers from Meerut, faithless to the salt, entered Delhi thirsty for the blood of the British. It would not be surprising if the guards of Delhi's gates, being brothers in profession with the rebels, had entered into conspiracy with them. Ignoring their orders to protect the city, forgetting their loyalty to the salt, the guards welcomed their uninvited, or invited, guests. Swarming through the opened gates of Delhi, the intoxicated horsemen and rough foot soldiers ravished the city like madmen. They did not leave their bloody work until they had killed officers and Englishmen, wherever they found them, and had destroyed their houses.

A few poor, reclusive men, who received their bread and salt by the grace of the British, lived scattered throughout different parts of the city, in lanes and by-lanes, but quite distant from one another. These humble, peaceful people did not know an arrow from an axe; their hands were empty of the sword; and even the sound of thieves in the dark night frightened them. These were not men who could do battle. They could do nothing but sit, helpless and grief-stricken, in their locked houses; for no blade of grass can stop the swift flow of the running water.

I was one of these helpless, stricken men. Shut in my room, I listened to the noise and tumult, and I heard it shouted that the guardian of the Red Fort and the British agent there had been murdered. From all sides one could hear the foot soldiers running and the hoof beats of the horsemen and, looking out, one could see the earth stained by the blood of the rosebodied. Every corner of the garden had become the graveyard of spring.

Oh, pity those great men, who embodied wisdom, who personified justice—those courteous rulers bearing a good name! Oh, pity those fairy-faced, slim-bodied women whose faces shone like the moon and whose bodies glittered like raw sliver! A thousand times pity the children, innocent of the world, who put roses and tulips to shame and whose step was more beautiful than that of the deer and the partridge! All of these were sucked into the whirlpool of death and were drowned in an ocean of blood.

Even Death himself—who strikes sparks of extinction and consumes by fire, who finally clothes all men in black—must wail at the bedside of the slaughtered, and wear mourning in grief for the murdered ones. The skies in their sorrow must fade like smoke, and the earth, like a cyclone, spin from its accustomed place.

> O Spring, be dust and blood like the slaughtered ones! O Times, be dark as the dark night! O Sun, beat your cheeks in grief until they are blue! O Moon, become, in despair, the scar of the heart of the sorrowful times!

Somehow this long and terrible day came to an end and darkness fell. The black-hearted, cruel killers made camp throughout the city; they stabled their horses in the Red Fort and took the royal chambers for their sleeping rooms. Gradually news flowed in from distant towns: the rebel soldiers had broken out. All through the country soldiers and landlords had joined forces and become as one body in a shameful lust that only waves of blood could satisfy. As the straws of a broom are tied up with one string so the multitude of rebels were bound together by a single cord. Such cataclysmic strokes swept India that, if one sought prosperity or peace, no single grass blade would be found. Some of the soldiers, although they had no leaders, prepared themselves for battle by seizing guns, gunpowder and gunshot from the British. All the tactics they had learned they employed against their former teachers.

The heart is not stone or steel but will be moved. The eyes are not lifeless cracks in a wall but will shed tears at the panorama of death and at India's desolation. The city of Delhi was emptied of its rulers and peopled instead with creatures of the Lord who acknowledged no lord—as if it were a garden without a gardener, and full of fruitless trees.

The raiders threw off all restraint and the merchants ceased paying taxes. Houses were abandoned and the apartments were like free tables of booty to be plundered at will. In its shamelessness, the rabble, sword in hand, rallied to one group after another. And if peaceful, good people came into the bazaar they were made to acknowledge their defeat and humility before the lawless multitude. Throughout the day the rebels looted the city and at night they slept in silken beds.

In the noblemen's houses is no oil for the lamps. In total darkness they must await the flash of lightning, and so find the glass and jug with which to quench their thirst.

How can I describe the lack of judgement, the indifference of these times? Those rough labourers who spend their days digging and selling mud, have now found in it pieces of gold. And those other whose assemblies were illuminated by the blaze of flowers are plunged into failure and despair.

With the sole exception of the wife and daughter of the police chief, the ornaments of all the young women of Delhi have been seized by the black-hearted, cowardly robbers. Bereft of their embellishments, these women have been further debauched of their remaining charm and grace by the newly rich sons of beggars, and they have no choice but to satisfy the conceit of this rabble. Those loving and courteous people who sheltered the coquetries of the young women with their respect and affection, can do nothing now but bow beneath the wickedness of these newly rich, vile-natured ones who are so filled with pride that to see them you would say they were not men but whirlwinds puffed up with conceit. These lowly men, engrossed only in their own self-importance, are but small blades of grass floating pompously on the wide water.

Noble men and great scholars have fallen from power; and the lowly ones, who have never known wealth or honour, now have prestige and unlimited riches. One whose father wandered dust-stained through the streets now proclaims himself ruler of the wind. One whose mother borrowed from her neighbour fire with which to light her kitchen declares himself sovereign of fire. These are the men who hope to rule over fire and wind and we unhappy ones have no desires left but for moments of respite and a little justice.

For you this only a sorrowful story, but the pain is so great that to hear it the stars will weep tears of blood.

The postal system is in utter chaos and service has virtually stopped. It is impossible for postmen to come and go: thus letters can neither be sent nor received: However through the telegraph system which operates by vibrations and not wires, messages can be sent out.

Tell me, you who believe in law and justice, is there not cause for weeping and breast-beating in the complete breakdown of administration, the looting of God-given wealth, the chaos of the postal system and the failure of news as to the welfare of our relations and friends? In this anarchy brave men are afraid of their own shadows and soldiers rule over dervish and king alike. Is this not cause for grief? Do these heartbreaking events not merit our tears? None can ridicule our sorrowing, for to lament such wrongs is not unbelief or lack of faith.

How can poetry soothe me when my heart is burned with hot sighs? My heart fails, my limbs weaken and I neither fear punishment nor do I crave reward.

This prisoner of loneliness, this afflicted Ghalib, now resumes his narrative of grief. When these wayward, hostile rebels first entered Delhi, they brought treasure with them. This they deposited with the royal treasury and they bowed their heads on the royal threshold. Rebellious armies from various directions converged on Delhi and assembled here. When the emperor could no longer control this army, the army itself took control into its own hands and the king was rendered helpless.

As the moon is eclipsed, so the army overshadowed the King. An eclipse cannot obscure the crescent moon, but only the full moon of the fourteenth night. The King was a waning moon, yet his light was eclipsed.

Although it is worth mentioning, I have not yet said that these adventurers, before starting towards Delhi, opened the doors of the prisons and set the prisoners free. In their newly found liberty these culprits came to the royal court and knelt in obeisance to the emperor demanding governorships; these faithless slaves who had escaped their masters came to kiss the royal threshold and demand fertile lands for themselves.

No one has told me, and I am at a loss to understand, how all who sought audience were allowed to go before the emperor; how every seeker after shelter was, by the royal authorities, given shelter. This can only be considered as part of the strangeness of the times.

At the moment, inside and outside of Delhi, there is an encampment of approximately fifty thousand cavalry and infantry; and the British, those possessors of knowledge and wisdom, control no ground except for a ridge at the western edge of the city. Here they have skilfully arranged their batteries and so have converted it into a kind of fortress. On all four sides they have fixed their fire-breathing, lightning striking cannons; and, in this manner, through their perseverance they have made a haven of peace in a land of adversity.

The soldiers have seized guns from the armoury, which they have set up on the ramparts of the city, and the rebels are now actually confronted with the courageous British officers. The heavy smoke from the guns and cannons is like dark clouds hanging in the sky and the noise is like the rain of hailstones. Cannon fire is heard all day long, as if stones were falling from the skies.

These are the hot months of May and June and the heat has become intolerable. The sun has entered into the sphere of Gemini, and the heat increases steadily, until it seems that the sun itself is consumed by its own fires. People who lived comfortably in cool and ventilated houses are now scorching under the flaming sun and they spend their nights in restlessness on burning stones.

Had Isfandyar been engaged in this war, he would, in spite of his renowned bravery, have lost his will and confidence. If Rustam had heard this story he would have been overcome by despair.

The soldiers who have assembled from all parts of India leave their encampments when the sun is well above the horizon and go forth to fight the lion-hearted British. They return to their camps just before sunset. That is the situation outside the town.

Now I shall relate an incident which has occurred inside the town.

> Concealed within the strings of my harp are notes, which flare out like sparks. I am fearful that the musician will himself be burned by fire. On my lips is a story, which cuts like a knife relentlessly into my heart.

A servant who was filled with pride and a hunger for power became the secret enemy of his master. He believed that if his master lived, it would become known that he (the servant) had wrongfully accumulated treasure. Wishing harm to the master, who was called Ahsanullah Khan, some rebels sought him in his mansion, but it so happened that the Hakim Sahib was with the emperor. These impetuous people then rushed to the Red Fort and there besieged the Hakim. But out of gracious love for his faithful subject, the emperor threw himself over the Hakim, and so saved him from death. Although his life was saved, the mischief was not finished until his house was completely devastated. That mansion, which in beauty and ornament, was equal to the picture galleries of China, was looted and the roofs were burned. The great beams and the inlaid panels of the ceiling were reduced to ashes. The walls were so completely blackened by smoke it seemed that, in grief, the mansion wore a black mantle.

Do not be misled by fortunes the skies may bestow. The treacherous skies entangle in anguish and torment those whom they formerly laid in the lap of love.

Unless he were a bastard, the meanest slave would not behave in such a manner towards his master. This contemptible man, this wretch untrue to the salt, with cheeks pitted by smallpox and a gaping mouth, whose eyes stare in shamelessness, considers himself a Venus. He walks with swaying hips and believes his gait lovelier than that of the partridge. I have purposely not mentioned his name, as he is the infamous son of a tramp. Now that I have heaped coals of fire upon the head of this man, I shall resume my story.

The rebel armies were assembling from various places in India. Since the name of the emperor was associated with the revolt, many officers from great distances had joined the rebellion. A nobleman of Farrukhabad, Tafazzul Husain Khan, who previously had not explicitly expressed his loyalty to the emperor now paid homage to him from far and signed his message as from an old royal servant.

Khan Bahadur Khan, a misguided nobleman who was thirsty for power, collected around him some soldiers from Bareilly and proclaimed himself leader. He sent to the emperor one hundred gold coins, and horses and elephants caparisoned with silver paraphernalia.

May the effects of the evil eye be warded off! Nawab Yusuf Ali Khan Bahadur, the sun-symbolled ruler of Rampur, the successor to his parents and grandparents, enjoys ties with the British government so strong that, even after a lapse of one thousand years, they would be impossible to sever. This ruler sent only a verbal message to the rebels and so circumvented them.

In Lucknow the army had separated itself from the British and most of them left the city and went over to their relatives in other towns. However some officers, together with their soldiers, made camp in Bailey Guard and bravely barred the gates of the town (against the rebels).

Ignoring the small group of distinguished British, Sharafuddaulah, a wise man of considerable understanding who had been *wazir* during the days of the Nawab of Awadh, installed the ten-year old son of Nawab Wajid Ali Shah as *wazir* of India's emperor and declared himself chamberlain and deputy *wazir*. Surely this renowned man had captured the fabulous *huma* in his net. When these things were done he sent a messenger to Delhi with appropriate gifts. The messenger arrived in the city where he remained for two days before seeking audience with the emperor and presenting him with two wind-swift horses, two elephants as high as mountains, one hundred and twenty-one gold coins, and a golden cup which was ornamented with priceless pearls of many colours. To the queen inside the women's palace, he sent a pair of armlets, studded with diamonds.

All of this grandeur was like a flickering lamp, as if the evil eye was watching the short-lived splendour; for, after the arrival of these rare gifts from the kingdom of Awadh, this fable of pomp and splendour, which equalled that of Alexander and the fabulous mirror, and Jamshid and the wonderful cup, came to an end. No sooner had the din and clamour of the rebel army caused the eyes of fortune to turn towards the emperor than those same eyes turned away from him. I put it in different words when I say that the emperor's auspicious star reached such lofty heights that it went quite out of sight of the world's eyes.

When the path of good fortune's star wavers the crown shall fall. See how the sun in the fear of change trembles in the sky!

On the fourteenth of September, the twenty-fourth day of the lunar month and the very day after the arrival of this inauspicious messenger and his subsequent reception at the palace, the British, who had taken refuge on the outskirts of the ridge, attacked Kashmiri Gate with such violence that the rebels were forced into headlong flight.

In the month of May justice was taken from Delhi; in September the days of atrocity drew to an end and justice again prevailed. After four months and four days the shining sun emerged and Delhi was divested of its madmen and was conquered by the brave and the wise.

The lapse of time from the eleventh of May to the fourteenth of September is actually four months and four days. However, since the town fell on a Monday, and was also re-captured on a Monday, it is as if the city were lost and retaken on the same day. The victors killed all whom they found on the streets. Those of noble birth and position, in order to protect their honour, which was all that remained to them, stayed inside their locked houses.

Some of the black-hearted (rebel) army attempted to escape but others, out of pride, were determined to fight and confronted the lion-hearted conquerors. In their own view they were attacking the enemy but in actual fact they were destroying the honour and prestige of Delhi.

For two or three days all the roads from Kashmiri Gate to Chandni Chauk became battle-grounds. Delhi Gate, Turkman Gate, and Ajmeri Gate were under the control of the Indian army. The house of sorrow in which I dwell, down-hearted and dejected, is situated exactly between Kashmiri Gate and Delhi Gate. Although we had locked the gate of our lane, at certain times we were able to open it and bring in food.

I have told you that when the angry lions entered the town, they killed the helpless and the weak and they burned their houses. It may be that such atrocities always occur after conquest.

Seeing the anger and fury, the townspeople turned pale. Hordes of men and women, commoners and noblemen, poured out of Delhi from the three gates and took shelter in small communities and tombs outside the city. There they remained, hoping, at a later time, either to return to Delhi or to move on to another town.

In my heart I felt no dread nor did my legs tremble in fear. I said to myself that I am not a wrong-doer and I deserve no punishment, for the English do not kill the innocent. The atmosphere of Delhi was not unfavourable to me and I believed I should entertain no thought of escape. Now, in desolation, I sit in a corner of my house with my pen as my sole companion. My eyes weep tears and from my pen issue words of anguish.

I am destitute and utterly impoverished! O lord, how long will this idle fancy give me comfort—that my verses are jewels and these jewels are treasures from my own mine?

All has been written in eternity and nothing can be changed. Our fates are decreed in an eternity that has no beginning and no end; and each of us has received according to his written destiny. Sorrow and joy issue from this eternal order. So I should leave my cowardly state of listlessness and, in my old age, watch like a child, with ready excitement, all the astonishing things, which are occurring.

At noon on Friday, the twenty-sixth of Muharram, which is the eighteenth of September, an eclipse occurred when the sun, which sheds joy and light upon the world, entered into a new constellation. The darkness so frightened the people that inside and outside of the city the misguided rebels fled like swine, and the victors captured the city and the Fort. The horror of mass arrests, assassinations, and slaughter now reached our lane and the people shook with fear.

In this lane there are ten or twelve homes and only one entrance. There is no well inside the lane. Most of the people have left—the women clutching their infants to their breasts and the men with their belongings on their shoulders—and only a few of us have remained behind. We shut the door of the lane from the inside and piled stones against the entrance, so closing it completely. Our little lane which was shadowed is now shuttered.

Sooner than my body's weakening, my spirit faints; for my heart is trapped as if imprisoned in a narrow cell.

During all this turmoil something occurred which was of considerable help to us. The ruler of Patiala, Raja Narendra Singh, magnificent as Mars, exalted as the skies, supports the conquerors in this battle; his army has been assisting the British from the very beginning. Some of the raja's highest officials live in this lane: Hakim Mahmud Khan, Hakim Murtaza Khan, Hakim Ghulamullah Khan—all of them progeny of Hakim Sharif Khan, who dwells now in paradise—and themselves very honourable and famous men. The double row of their extensive homes stretches for some distance and for the past ten years I have been the neighbour of one of these rich men, Hakim Mahmud Khan who, with his family and relations, lives a very respectable life according to the traditions of his ancestors. The remaining two stay in comfort and honour with the raja in Patiala.

When the British recapture of Delhi was imminent, the raja, out of his great kindness, had arranged with the powerful and warlike British that as soon as Delhi was reconquered, guards from Patiala would be posted at the gate of the lane to prevent the British white militia from damaging the houses or molesting their inhabitants.

Occasionally during the course of this narrative I have had to speak of other things (than the actual rebellion); however, after this digression, I shall return to the main topic.

Since the fourteenth of September every door in the entire city of Delhi has been closed. There is neither merchant nor buyer; there is no seller of wheat from whom we can buy flour, nor is there a washerman to whom we can give our soiled garments; there is no barber to trim hair, or sweeper to clean our floors. However, as I have written earlier, during these five days it was possible for us to leave the lane for water and occasionally to get flour. But later even this became impossible. The door of the lane was blocked with stones and the mirror of our hearts was clouded with sorrow.

All our endeavours have been chilled and sorrow now burns in our blood like fire.

Gradually, whatever provisions we had in our houses were consumed. Although we had used the water with great care, not a single drop remained in cup or jar. The people have lost all their power to endure and the illusion that passing our days courageously would bring an end to our hunger now faded completely and we were hungry and thirsty throughout the days and nights.

Oh, pity our wailing, beggary and dishonour! A hundred times pity our helplessness, affliction and poverty!

As I have said earlier, on the third day the soldiers of the army of the Maharaja of Patiala arrived and began patrolling. In this way the inhabitants of the lane were relieved of their fear of looters. After saying 'Come what may!' they asked permission of the soldiers to leave the lane. As the patrolling was done out of friendship and not out of enmity, the people were allowed to go as far as the bazaar of the Chauk. Beyond the Chauk mass slaughter was rampant and the streets were filled with horror.

These tormented and helpless people opened the gate of the lane, but it was impossible to find a water-carrier or waterskin. Therefore they selected one man from every house and, together with two of my servants, managed to procure some brackish water. They filled their jars and pots with this salty water since the sweet water was at some distance and it was not possible to travel so far. In such a way they quenched their fire with brackish water. The other name for this fire is thirst.

Those who went out for water told us that in the lane beyond which we are not allowed to go, the soldiers had broken into several houses. In these houses there are now neither sacks of flour nor pots of oil. I told them that the Lord's creatures do not speak of pots, sacks, flour and oil. Our bread is with the Bread-Giver who will not forsake us. It is the work of Satan to be ungrateful for the gifts of the Lord.

In these days we think of ourselves as prisoners and we are, in truth, passing our days like prisoners. Nobody comes to visit us and we receive no news. We cannot leave the lane so we are unable to see what is happening with our own eyes. In fact, it is as if our ears were deaf and could not hear, and our eyes were blind and could not see. In addition to this trouble we have neither bread to act nor water to drink.

One day clouds suddenly appeared and it rained. We tied up a sheet in our courtyard and placed our jars beneath it and in this way we collected water. It is said that the clouds take up water from the river and so spread rain over the earth. But this time the cloud was like *huma* and gathered water from the very fountain of life. It was as if this treasure, for which Alexander had searched during the days of his sovereignty, was found by one in anguish during the days of destruction.

O Ghalib, our Heavenly Friend does not fail us but rather supports us in ways that are beyond our understanding!

At this point I would like to write a bit about my life and my activites. I will try to do this in such a way that it will not be divorced from the main story.

I grieve myself by telling of my afflictions but it is like a healing ointment on the wounds of my hearts. By means of this lancet I remove the arrows which have pierced into my heart.

This is the sixty-second year of my life. For many years I have been straining the dust of this world through a sieve; and for the last fifty years I have been opening the depths of my heart through poetry. I was five years old when my father Abdullah Beg Khan Bahadur died—may the Lord shower His innumerable graces on his spirit! My uncle Nasrullah Beg Khan Bahadur adopted me as his son and raised me with considerable indulgence. When I was nine years old this uncle, who was also my patron, slipped into the sleep of death and with this death my fortune also slept.

My uncle, an estimable man of position and prestige was the captain of four hundred horsemen and a loyal associate of General

Lord Lake Bahadur. Through the kindness of this victorious and generous leader he was appointed overlord of two *parganas* near Agra. After his death these *parganas* reverted to the British Government and in place of his *jagir* my brother and I were awarded a pension, which became the source of my comfort and livelihood. I received the pension from the treasury of the Delhi Collectorate until the end of April 1857, when the treasury was closed. Now I am confronted by misfortune and my heart is the house of anxiety.

Earlier I had only my wife—no son or daughter. Nearly five years ago I adopted two orphan children who had belonged to my wife's family. I am extremely fond of these sweet-tongued children who, in the extremity of my misfortune, are the flowers of my life.

At the age of thirty, my brother, who is two years younger than I, went mad. For the past thirty years he has been living quietly and inoffensively in a house which is situated approximately two thousand paces from my home. His wife and daughters, together with their children and maid-servants, have departed and have left the crazy master of the house and all his belongings in the care of an aged *darban* and a maid-servant.

Even if I had magic powers I could not possibly, during such times, have brought these three persons or their possessions to my home. Because of this I am suffering grievously and my heart is troubled.

The two children whom I have raised with such indulgence ask me to give them fruits, milk and sweets but I cannot satisfy their wishes. Alas, how can I explain that as long as I live I shall struggle for bread and water, and for a shroud after my death? Day in and day out I think only of whether my brother has eaten, how he sleeps at night. My lack of information is so complete that I do not know if he is living or if he has died under his afflictions.

On my lips are wailings and sighs; and on my lips, O Lord, is my final breath!

These incidents which I have narrated are painful but the incidents I have not told of are heart-breaking. However, I expect those in authority will listen with compassion to my sorrowful story and, after hearing it, will see that justice is done.

In this old age I am like the flickering morning lamp or like the sun which will soon go down. I do not mean as the full lamplight or the spreading rays of the mid day sun but as the last drops of oil in the lamp at morning make a dim light or as the light of the sun grows weak at evening—this is my situation.

Two years ago I sent a panegyric in praise of the just, exalted Queen Victoria, splendid as the stars. This was sent to London from Delhi by way of Bombay through the courtesy of Lord Ellenborough, a renowned administrator who valued talent and who, through his generosity, was my patron during the time he was governor.

Although my fortune did not lead me into the presence of the World-Conquering Queen, yet I have found ways to hold conversation with her.

This verse concerns the panegyric and the entire poem is written in the same metrical pattern.

Who could have thought that the way out of my difficulties would have been made so easy, and in such a direct manner! Suddenly, after three months, an auspicious courier arrived bearing a courteous letter from Lord Ellenborough, that cyprus of the garden of sovereignty. This letter was written in English, affectionately, and reported that the panegyric had been received and had been entrusted for presentation at the court of the queen.

Hardly thirty days had passed since the arrival of this auspicious and welcome reply when I received a letter from the gracious official, Mr. Resington, saying that 'with regard to the panegyric sent to us through Lord Ellenborough, it is pointed out that the petitioner, in respect to the norms of administrative procedure, should channel his petition through the administrator in India.'

Therefore, in obedience to this request, a petition was sent to the queen of England through that administrator who is magnificent as Alexander, splendid as Faridun—Lord Canning Nawab Governor-General Bahadur. In this petition it was requested that, as the kings of Rum, Iran and other countries had rewarded their poets and well-wishers by filling their mouths with pearls, weighing them in gold and granting them villages and recompense, the exalted queen should bestow upon Ghalib, the petitioner, the title of *Mihr-Khwan*, and present him with the robe of honour and a few crumbs from her bounteous table—that is, in English, a 'pensions'.

The exalted Nawab Governor-General Bahadur was pleased to lighten my grief-stricken heart with the happy tidings that my petition had been sent to England. At this fortunate news I was extravagantly happy, so much so that I could scarcely contain my joy.

Four months later a reply to my petition came in the form of a friendly letter from the pen of the respected Mr. Russel Clerk Bahadur. So was the period of my expectations and unfulfilled desires prolonged.

I have no doubt that had the administration of India not been disturbed during the recent revolt and had the course of justice not been diverted at the hands of ungrateful soldiers, who did not fear the Lord, a royal decree would have been issued from England satisfying all my desires, and my eyes and my heart would have rejoiced in mutual merriment.

Now I have nothing but these letters of good omen, which are a talisman on the arm of wisdom and remind me of my deep longings. I hold my heart in my hands and I weep tears of blood as a token of my great agony.

No sword or arrow wounds me. No tiger or lion does me harm. But in the abandonment of my grief I bite my lips and I dip my tongue in blood. I drink the blood of my heart and I am sick of my life.

On Wednesday, the thirty September, seventeen days after victory and the closing of the door of our lane, news was brought that looters had raided the house of my brother and the other houses in that street. However the lives of my mad brother, Mirza Yusuf Khan, and of the two aged servants were spared. During the tumult two Hindus asked for shelter in his house; and through the help of these Hindus the old *darban* and maid servant did everything possible to procure food and drinking water.

It may be worth mentioning that during this storm and turmoil the nature of calamity is different in every lane and bazaar. The manner of killing and looting by the soldiers is not uniform but varies, and whether a soldier shows kindness or unkindness depends on his individual nature.

Orders have been given to spare the lives of those who do not resist these assaults, but whosoever does resist them will lose his life along with his possessions. It is believed that those who were killed were ones who did not show obedience (to the British) and it is widely known that although looting was common, killing was generally abjured. Even in the few incidents, in two or three lanes, where the soldiers killed first and then looted, the lives of old men and women and children have been spared.

Now the steed of my pen halts. Let me cry out that the steed may again go forth! O you who commend justice and you lovers of truth who condemn injustice, if your tongue and your heart are one in this, for the sake of the Lord, think of what we have done! Although everyone knows that disloyalty is a sin, without reason for enmity or cause for envy we raised our swords against our masters and we killed helpless women, and infants playing in their cradles. The British rose up in revenge against such atrocity and, in order to punish the transgressors, deployed their armies with care. Their anger at the citizens of Delhi was so great that, after capturing the city, one would think they would leave not even a dog or a cat alive. However, although their hearts were full of the fire of fury, they restrained themselves. Women and children were not molested. No general guarantee was offered for the protection of life or property because they were determined to distinguish between the guilty and the innocent and only those called for questioning were allowed to approach the authorities.

Most of the citizens had fled the city but some, caught between hope and despair, are still living inside the walls. So far no information has been received concerning those hiding in lonely places outside of Delhi. Those outside and those still living inside are both in great distress and there is no cure for their misery. If only each could know the fate of the other, whether they were alive or dead, much of their grief and anxiety would be allayed. This lack of knowledge is such that wherever one, is, one is in despair. The hearts of the helpless inhabitants of the city, and those of the grief-stricken people outside, are filled with sorrow, and they are afraid of mass slaughter.

Monday, the fifth of October, was a day of calamity. Suddenly, at noon, white soldiers scaled the wall near the closed entrance of our lane, climbed over the rooftops, and from there jumped down into the street. The guards of Raja Narendra Singh tried to intercept them but were unsuccessful. Ignoring the small houses nearby, the soldiers entered directly into my house. They did not, in their consideration, touch my possessions but took me, my two children, two or three servants and a few good neighbours to the wise and experienced Colonel Brown* who was staying in the merchant Qutbuddin's mansion, situated on this side of the Chauk at a distance of some furlongs. Colonel Brown talked with me gently and

*This should be Burn. Colonel H.P. Burn. He was military governor of Delhi.

humanely, asking of me my name only, but of the others their profession, and so dismissed me politely. I thanked the Lord, praised the courteous Colonel Brown and returned home.

During the evening of October seventh I heard a salute of twenty-one guns, of which, although I was pleased to hear it, I failed to understand the meaning. I remembered that on the arrival of the Lieutenant-Governor Bahadur there is a salute of seventeen guns; when the Nawab Governor-General Bahadur arives nineteen shots are fired; but I was at a loss to know the reason for the twenty-one gun salute. The following day, although on this point neither was my knowledge increased nor my ignorance decreased, I came to the conclusion that the British, those levellers of the high and the low, had somewhere won a victory over the rebels.

In Bareilly, Farrukhabad and Lucknow there are still bands of rebels engaged in extending the rebellion and the futile struggle. May the Lord cause the blood to run from their hearts, and may He wither their hands, for their hearts and hands are openly engaged in this warfare.

In the areas of Sonh and Nuh the Mewatis have run amuck as if crazy men had thrown off their shackles and rampaged. Under the devil's guidance, the rebel Tularam, who was fighting in Rewari, joined forces with the Mewatis, and this group has been fighting the British savagely in the plains and on the mountains. The warfare is so bitter that it seems as if the entire land of India is engulfed in whirling storms and flaming fires.

In these painful circumstance, the beginning of which I do not remember and the end of which I cannot know, if I have seen anything except tears, then may the holes of my eyes be filled with dust! Since my eyes have seen only the black day of misfortune I have seen nothing, for it is impossible to see in darkness.

Except for the day I was taken out by the white soldiers, I have not been out of my house, put my foot on the threshold, walked into the lane or bazaar, or seen the Chauk even from a distance. It is as if the wise poet Nizami Ganjwai had said it for me and with my lips:

I know nothing of what is happening in the world—I know neither what there is that is good nor what there is that is evil.

Because of wounds which resist all healing and griefs which defy all cure, I have been like a dead man. I was raised up for judgement and now, for the punishment of my transgressions, I am suspended in the pit of hell. I can do nothing but exist in this prison of helplessness and despair.

How shall I endure if what happens to me today falls again to my lot tomorrow?

In this book I have, from the beginning to the end, told only of those events which have actually occurred to me or of which I have personally heard. One should not think that the events I have learned of through hearsay are lies, or that I have diminished their intensity in the writing. I seek the shelter of the Lord from these unwarranted arrests and I seek my salvation in the truth. My eyes cannot see, my heart is a prisoner of grief, my lips are silent, and my ears receive alms from the tongues of the people. How degrading is this helpless beggary!

Perhaps I should have begun my story of the capture of Delhi by relating the fate of the emperor and his sons, about which I have not yet written. The reason I have not is that the treasure of my writing is derived from what I hear, and there are many things yet to be heard. Certainly when I am freed from this confinement I shall gather information about what I have still not heard and shall write it as confidences from an informed person. Out of deference to me I hope that my readers will be patient with the disarrangement of sequence.

Monday, the nineteenth of October, should be erased from the calendar. Like a fire-breathing dragon that day engulfed the world when in the morning the unfortunate *darban* brought the relieving news of my brother's death. He told me that this traveller speeding on the path of death (Yusuf Mirza) had been afflicted with a high fever for five days and, close to midnight, had departed from this world.

Oh, do not speak to me, I beg you, of water or of the kerchief to clean the face, of the man who bathes the dead body or digs the grave, or of bricks or mortar! Please tell me how I can go out (of this lane), where to take this dead body, and in what graveyard to bury it? In the bazaar it is impossible to get cloth, either good or bad. It is as if labourers and earth-diggers had never existed in the city. The Hindus can carry their dead to the shores of the river and burn them, but the Muslims dare not go abroad, even in groups of two or three, so how can their dead be borne from the city?

The neighbours took pity on my plight and offered to perform this task. With one Patiala soldier leading them, they took two servants and set out. They bathed the dead body and wrapped it in two or three white sheets, which they had taken from my house. They dug a grave in the mosque adjoining my house and put the dead body in the pit before returning.

O pity this man who lived for sixty years and thirty years were happy but thirty years were sad! In his grave not even a pillow of stone, and dust is his destiny. O Lord, pity this dead one who found no comfort in his life! Send an angel for the solace of his heart and deliver his soul to paradise!

The kindly but unfortunate man spent sixty years of his life in happiness and sorrow; for thirty years he was sane and for thirty years he was mad. During the days of his sanity he restrained his anger and during the days of his madness he gave pain to no one. This was his custom. He died on the 29th of Safar, 1274 AH.

Someone asked me, the afflicted, the date of the death of Mirza Yusuf, who lived his life a stranger to his own self. I answered this question by sighing, and said '*diregh diwana*'.

It should be known that from the letters of *diregh diwana* we get 1290. If sixteen, which is the number equivalent to the word '*āh*' (sigh), is subtracted from this, it gives us the correct date 1274 AH.

I address myself to the Lord in whose presence we should do penance. Wheresoever you bow your head, there shall you touch his threshold.

During the week in which the British captured the city, those wise and esteemed men, Aminuddin Khan Bahadur and Muhammad Ziyauddin Khan Bahadur, in order to uphold their dignity and in the hope of bettering their positions, decided to leave the city. In addition to their wives and children they had with them three elephants and forty horses and they set out for the *pargana* of Loharu, which is their ancestral estate. First they went to Mehrauli, where they stayed in the luminous and sanctified burial ground. During this time the plundering soldiers besieged their encampment and did not leave until they had taken from them everything they owned except for the clothes they wore. Only the three elephants, which their faithful and kindly companions had taken away before the looting began, remained, like three great burnt-out silos, as symbols of disaster.

These people, after suffering this calamitous looting, set out for Dujanà, stripped of all their possessions. The illustrious and warm-hearted ruler of Dujana, Hasan Ali Khan Bahadur, welcoming them with affection and generosity, took them to Dujana, and told them to consider his house as their home.

In brief, this good natured leader (Hasan Ali Khan) showed the same courteous manner towards his guests as was shown by the king of Iran towards the fugitive Humayun. When the Commissioner Bahadur heard of heard of this story he summoned these men to him and they returned to Delhi. At first the commissioner spoke to them sarcastically but when he received only polite answers he desisted and allowed them to stay near the chamberlain's palace in the Fort.

Because of the sequence of the story I have not been able to tell of all the outrage and looting which fell to the lot of this family. I can only say that they were robbed in Mehrauli and also in Delhi. While the masters were away their homes were pillaged and all that they had carried with them was seized by looters in Mehrauli. Only the people themselves reached Dujana unharmed. Their palaces were plundered and only the bricks and stones were left behind. Neither their silver and gold was spared, nor a single thread of their clothes or bedding. May the Lord pity these guiltless ones and may their inauspicious beginning come to an auspicious end! May they find comfort after calamity!

It was Saturday, the seventeenth of October, when these distinguished men returned to the city and, as I have said earlier, they stayed at the Fort. Two or three days after this incident the army was ordered to apprehend Abdur Rahman, the ruler of Jhajjar, and they brought him in like a culprit. He was put in a small corner of the Diwan-i-Am of the Fort and all his *jagir* was confiscated by the British.

On Friday, the thirty-first of October, the army seized Ahmad Ali Khan, the ruler of Farrukhnagar, and brought him, in the same manner as they had brought Abdur Rahman Khan, to a secluded place in the Delhi Fort. Farrukhnagar then became a target for the swift-handed looters, and the possessions of the inhabitants of this town also were plundered.

Bahadur Jung Khan, the ruler of Dadri and Bahadurgarh, was captured on Monday, November second, and arrangements were made to put him in the Fort. On Saturday, November seventh, Raja Nahar Singh, ruler of Ballabhgarh, was added to this company. In this way all the noblemen who lived at a distance were brought to the Fort.

I should say that the *jagirs* under the Delhi agency are equal in number to the days of the week. They are Jhajjar, Bahadurgarh, Ballabhgarh, Loharu, Farrukhnagar, Dujana and Pataudi. As I have said earlier, five of these *jagirdars* are in the Fort, and the remaining two, the *jagirdars* of Pataudi and Dujana, are pierced by the arrows of fear. Let us see what their all-seeing eyes behold and what befalls them.

It is no secret that Muzaffaruddaulah Saifuddin Haidar Khan and Zulfaqarrudin Haidar Khan, who carry the title of Husain Mirza, like many other respectable men during these stormy days, fled the city with their wives and children. They went into the wilderness and left behind them their homes, filled with precious possessions. The adjacent houses, palaces and mansions of these *jagirdars* were so vast that on surveying them they would be found to be, if not equal to the area of a town, surely equal to that of a village. These great palaces, being completely uninhabited, were ransacked by the looters.

In the night following the morning on which Raja Nahar Singh was captured some heavy and less precious things such as curtains, canopies, tents, and rich coverings and carpets, which had been left behind in the palaces, accidentally caught fire. The flames leapt up and all of the wood, walls and stones were burned. These buildings are so near to my house on the western side that, from my roof, I could see the glare of the roaring fire; the hot smoke reached my face and my eyes and a strong west wind blew ashes over my body. Music comes freely like a gift from the home of a neighbour: why then should not fire from a nearby house shower ashes upon me?

The speed of my pen is like the speed of a half-dead ant, and it is difficult to put all of this on paper for the benefit of my readers.

Nothing more can be said of the fate of the Mughal princes than that some were shot and devoured by the dragon of death; and some were hung by their necks with ropes and, in their twisting, their spirits left them. A few unfortunates are imprisoned, others have fled, wretched and disordered, into the wilderness; and the aged and fragile Mughal emperor is under trail by the court.

The *jagirdars* of Jhajjar, Ballabhgarh, and Farrukhnagar were executed separately on different days. Their lives were ended in such a manner that none could say blood had been spilled.

In January 1858, the Hindus were given a proclamation of freedom by which they were allowed to live again in the city, and these people have begun to return from the places where they had found refuge. But the houses of the dispossessed Muslims had long remained empty and were so covered with vegetation that the walls seemed to be made of grass—and every blade of grass tells that the house of the Muslim is still empty.

Probably because of the spying of devilish informants, the city administrator learned that the home of Raja Narendra Singh Bahadur's physicians had become the rendezvous and refuge of the Muslims. It would be no surprise if some of these troublesome, evil-tongued informers are here also. Because of them, on Tuesday, February second, the city administrator entered that house and took away with him sixty innocent refugees along with the masters of the house. Although these people were held in confinement for several days and nights the dignity of their position was respected.

On Friday, February fifth, Hakim Mahmud Khan, Hakim Murtaza Khan and his nephew Abdul Hakim Khan, who went by the name of Hakim Kale, were released. On Friday, February twelfth, a few more people were released and on Saturday, February thirteenth, others were permitted to leave; but more than half were ordered to remain in the prison. Because of this terrible calamity which has befallen my neighbourhood, and the storm which has swept through my lane, the heart of this grief-stricken, suffering dervish is distracted. In spite of everything, during all these arrests and seizures, I was not challenged. But even now I am uneasy all the time and at night I sleep restlessly.

During the magnificent month that extends from February until the month of *Farwardin*, when the sun takes one month to enter into the sign of Aries, and which is really the first month of spring, when the light of the sun becomes warm, news went round that the benevolent ruler, glorious as the sun and exalted as the stars, the Chief Commissioner Sir John Lawrence, was about to arrive.

Since it has been my practice to send a panegyric to whoever comes as ruler of India, and particularly of Delhi, I composed a *qasida* of congratulations and welcome in praise of his lordship. This was posted on Friday, February nineteenth.

In the evening of February twentieth we heard, like the roar of a dragon, the terrifying sound of a twenty-one gun salute. And on Sunday morning we received news of the capture of Lucknow, along with the information that the bright star of the skies of sovereignty, I mean the illustrious commander-in-chief, had attacked the rebel warriors with such skill that Mars, the commander of the heavens, blessed him, prayed for the safety of his hands and arms, and commended him at such length that his tongue wearied and his lips blistered.

This was welcome news for the homeless, a propitious message of liberation, for the goal of the free and good-natured British was achieved and the rule of the vicious rebels was overthrown. I learned then that the gun salute and the music of the *shah-nays* had been in celebration of the seizure of power by the British. During this battle the generals of the victorious army were concerned with fearlessly slaughtering opponents, rather than with occupying the town. After killing and wounding as many of the enemy as possible they returned to their encampment.

At a propitious time in the mid-morning of Wednesday, February twenty-fourth, the sole cyprus of the garden of justice, the bright moon of the glorious sky, the blessed, gracious and exalted one—I mean the Chief Commissioner Bahadur—with the hooves of his horses marked the ground of Delhi like the starry sky and, by means of a thirteen-gun salute, assured to the suffering the balm of love and charity.

> At this coming a new soul has entered into the dead body of the city. A wave of happiness has swept through the city as if the Emperor Shahjahan himself had returned.

Saturday, February twenty-seventh, came to an end and darkness fell over Delhi. When most of the night had passed such sighs from the hearts of the oppressed had risen into the skies that they obscured the face of the moon and people cried out saying that the moon was eclipsed. On that same Saturday, the orders of *durbash* came to an end an those who sought justice, or audience, or refuge were given these things.

There is a prison outside the city and a house of detention inside. In both of these places so many people have been crowded together that it seems as if they must even be one inside the other. The angel of death alone knows how many people have been hanged by the neck in these two prisons.

In the entire city of Delhi it is impossible to find more than one thousand Muslims; and I am one of these. Some have gone so far from the city it seems as if they were never residents of Delhi. Many very important men are living outside the city at a distance of two to four *kos,* on ridges and thatched roofs, in ditches and mud huts, as if their fortunes were sleeping with blindfolded eyes. Among the people living in the wilderness are those who are anxious to return to Delhi, relatives of the imprisoned and those living on alms, that is, on pensions. The ones who have sent petitions ask only for release from prison, permission to live in Delhi, and renewal of their pensions. The courts have received two or three thousand petitions from the supplicants. These seekers after justice keep eyes and ears open so that they may see and hear what the future holds for them.

I, too, am eagerly awaiting a reply to the letter of respect and praise which I had sent by post. Because of my acute distress it was impossible for me to visit the administrator of Delhi at his residence. In short, there are hardships encompassing me on all sides as if I am surrounded by thorns. If one goes abroad one will find them spread on the path, if one remains inside, thorns stick to one's clothes. Until now forebearance had restrained impatience and on Monday, the eighth of March, the letter was returned to me with a note. The face of the letter was illumined with the prudent administrator's decree that it be returned to the sender to be channelled properly through the district authorities. Everyone said, and I also thought it myself, that this answer was a promising sign and not devoid of advantage and that it would be likely that my representations would be accepted. I sent the letter which contained these orders, with a suitable additional note, to the just, charitable and prudent Charles Saunders, Chief Commissioner Bahadur, along with an accompanying memorandum to the afore-mentioned acclaimed lord relating to my old desire for the renewal of my pension.

On Wednesday, March seventeenth, a communication arrived stating that my first letter (the panegyric), which contained nothing but congratulations, should not have been sent. I said to myself that during these turbulent days there was no place for love and affection, happiness and felicity. I am merely a slave to my belly and seek only bread. Let us see what is the outcome regarding my second wish.

On the evening of Friday, March eighteenth, the soul-shattering sound of gunfire again rang through the blue skies, heralding the victory at Lucknow and the spread of the vengeful British armies throughout the town. There is no fort in the town, no city wall, no gate, and undoubtedly it was the compact wall of the rebel army that was obstructing the advance of the courageous British. Surely when this soild wall was breached by the whirlwind onslaught of the brave British soldiers it must have given way and the length of the thoroughfare must have been buried in dust because of the passage of these horsemen and foot soldiers.

When the Lord confers sovereignty he confers dignity also and the talent for victory. Because of these thing, whosoever opposes the will of the ruler merits punishment, for to oppose the king is to do harm to oneself. It is fitting for the people of the world to obey those whom the Lord has blessed with good fortune and, in obeying them, they should consider it obedience to the Lord himself. When one understands that fortune, power and sovereignty are the gifts of the Lord there should then be no occasion for disaffection or for disobedience. How skilfully this idea has been put into verse by that gifted ornament of music, Sa'di, of Shiraz:

The slave must bow his head before the master.
The ball has no choice but to follow the swing of the mallet.

Since the twenty-second of March the heart of this demented one has been stricken because throughout the world it is the month of *Farwardin*; and Nau-roz—the day that lights up the earth—falls within these two or three days. This year, since the city has become the abode of the dead, we hear no shouts of pleasure at the arrival of spring. Nobody can tell me when, according to the Turkish calendar, this year began and nobody can tell me which is the day of the equinox. If all of the astronomers have died, and no longer write daily of matters pertaining to the travels of the solar king, then it can be presumed that we have fewer liars, and that we have listened to fewer lies. But the sun has not forgotten to remain in Aries and so the vegetation still grows, the flowers still bloom and the principles of birth do not change; for it is not possible for the skies to alter their fixed laws of rotation.

I do not shed tears for the garden. I shed tears for myself. I do not complain about the spring, I complain of my own misfortunes.

The world is filled with tulips, and the scent of roses; but I am locked in a small place, helpless, having nothing. It is the flowering season of spring, but, I, who am wholly without means or possessions, have shut the door of my house because of my impoverishment.

I weep and I think that the times are completely uncaring. If I, who am closed in my corner of grief, cannot look at the green and the flowers or, by smelling the sweet flowers, fill my mind with perfume—the beauty of spring will not be diminished, and no one will punish the breeze.

During the month of April, of which two thirds is comprised of *Farwardin* and one third of *Urdi*, those who still remained in prison with Hakim Mahmud Khan were released and went on their various ways. The serene, high-born Hakim Mahmud Khan, with his wife, children, relatives and retainers set out for Patiala. They say he is now in Karnal and his future plans are not known.

Early in May I was happy to hear the news that the intrepid British soldiers had conquered Muradabad which was on the route held by the depraved rebels. The city was then presented to that fountain of knowledge and wisdom, the noble Nawab Yusuf Ali Bahadur, and so received the crown of justice. He who is capable of conquering and ruling the world, now, under orders of the British, rules over this province and I hope will continue to do so.

Further, it is reported that the mountain-shattering, dragon-killing army invaded Bareilly and the rebels were thrown out like flotsam tossed up by powerful waves. Judging from the events so far, one can hope that the regime of the stubborn rebels who still remain to torment the occupants of towns and villages and to harass those who walk on the streets, will soon come to an end and the whole area pass under the banner of the righteous rulers.

During the evening of Sunday, June thirteenth, the city administrator summoned Bahadur Jung Khan, who had been imprisoned in the Fort. This man answered the summons with high hopes and there he was given the welcome news that he had been pardoned, and had been granted a pension of one thousand rupees a month. However, he was also ordered to leave Bareilly for Lahore; and although he would then be a free man, he could live nowhere but in Lahore. Certainly it would be prudent of him to shake off his grief over the loss of wealth and position, and to be cheerful and contented with his freedom.

The Kind of Day, that is the Sun, whose head rotates on a spear, had risen up from the east more than the length of a spear when, fierce as lightning, twenty-one gun salutes rang out. The number of these salutes was equal to the lapsed days of this month of June and they filled the hearts of the faithful with joy and spread ashes hotter than the fires of grief over the heads and faces of the enemy. By the capture of the city of Gwalior and its rocky fort—which is truly the heart of the world and the darling of the mountains—the death decree of the rebels was issued from the court of the Lord, and the British rulers and their allies rejoiced at this good news which lit the lamp of their ambition.

This is the story: When the rebels captured Gwalior, Maharaja Jayaji Rao, the monarch of Gwalior, fled his city and his realm and went to Agra to seek the help of the British. With their support he re-took the city. The rebels had converged on Gwalior from many different directions but there they suffered a severe defeat. So now they will be scattered and, in weakness and disarray, they will rove and plunder until, finally, they will be disgracefully defeated everywhere and their forest-running horses will die in plains that are without water and without grass. From that time on the land will be rid of thorns and thistles and the gardens will bloom and every path will glitter again like the bazaar.

Sixty-three years of the life of this writer have gone by. Because of the sorrows that consume my soul I cannot hope to live much longer. Therefore let me recite some verses of the magic poet of Shiraz (Sa'di), God bless his soul, and as one sufferer to another I repeat these verses, if not to bring joy to my heart, at least to find relief from the pangs of sorrow and despair.

> Alas, when we have gone from the world, innumerable springs will still refresh the land and flowers will bloom in profusion. The months of spring—*Tir*, *Day*, and *Urdi*—Bihisth—will return to the earth again and again while we in our graves turn to dust.

To conceal the truth is not, in fact, the practice of honourable men. I am only half Muslim, and quite free from the rigidities of religion; and I am unconcerned with slander and infamy. It has always been my habit at night to drink a foreign wine and if I cannot have it I cannot sleep. During these days the price of English wine has become prohibitive and I have no money at all. If it had not been for one who knows and loves the Lord, the generous Mahesh Das, bounteous as the river, I would have died of my consuming thirst. This man sent me Indian wine made of sugar, with a bouquet even superior to that of imported wine, with which to cool the fire of my heart.

My heart has craved the satisfaction of its thirst—and the thirst is for two cups of neat wine. The wise Mahesh Das has offered me the elixir of life for which Alexander searched.

I cannot resist letting it be known that this kindly man left no stone unturned in his effort to bring back the Muslms to the city but, as it was not the will of the Lord, he did not succeed. Everyone knows that it is because of the gracious administrator that the Hindus now live freely in the city. However, that lover of righteousness and virtue, Mahesh Das, has had a hand in these affairs. In brief, he is a much-blessed man, considerate of others, and lives in comfort and felicity. Although we have not known each other long and meet to talk only occasionally, now and then he favours me by sending a gift.

Among my pupils and associates is Hira Singh, a well-known youth, conscious of his duties, who comes to me very often and dispels my sorrow. There is another discerning young man in this half-inhabited, half-empty city, who is as dear to me as a son—I mean the excellent Shivji Ram Brahman. He seldom leaves this sorrowing dervish alone and in every way tries to assist me to obey my wishes. His son Bal Mukund , a courteous and reverent youth, always does what I ask of him and is always ready to share my sadness.

Among the friends who live at a distance is Hargopal 'Tafta', the full moon of the sky of love, the sweet-tongued poet and my dearest friend and intimate. Since he considers me his master, his poetry, endowed with all God-given excellence, is my proud treasure. In short, he is a fine man, full of affection and sincerity. He is renowned for his verse and because of him the poetry readings are full of warmth. In my great love I think of him as part of my own soul and I have given him the title of Mirza Tafta. He has sent me a *hundi* and regularly sends letters and ghazals from Meerut.

These things, which are not actually necessary to record, I have written down in order to thank these people for their generosity and love. Also, when this account reaches the hands of my friends, I want them to know that the city is empty of Muslims—their houses are not lit at night and during the day their chimneys give forth no smoke. And Ghalib, who had thousands of friends in the city and acquaintances in every house, now in his loneliness, has none to talk with except his pen and no companion but his shadow.

No brightness colours my cheeks until my face is washed a thousand times in tears of blood. Within my body grief and affliction have become my heart and soul; and my bed is woven of thorns.

If is had not been for these four people there would have been no witness to my helplessness.

Blessed by the rotation of the skies, my house was spared the onslaughts of the raiders although during these days of plundering even the mud was looted from the houses of the city. However, I swear that nothing in my house has been saved except bedding and the few clothes which I am wearing. The solution to this perplexing enigma, the explanation of this paradox, is as follows: when the rebels captured Delhi my wife, without telling me, gathered together all of our jewellery and precious things and sent them to the house of Kale Sahib, the son of a saint. There they where secured in a cellar and the entrance to the cellar was plastered over with mud. My wife revealed this secret to me when the British had conquered Delhi and their soldiers had been given orders to plunder the city; but by then it was too late to go to retrieve our possessions. I composed myself and consoled my heart with the knowledge that these things were destined to vanish;and I was glad that it was not from my house that they were taken.

It is now July, the fifteenth month since the start of the rebellion, and there seems to be no way for me to get back the old pension which I used to receive from the British government. I live by selling my clothes and my bedding. While others eat bread, I eat clothes. I am afraid that when I have sold all my clothes I shall die, naked, of starvation.

During these anxious days, two or three of my old servants have stayed with me and I must care for them. It is true that men cannot live without each other, and it is very difficult to live without a servant. In addition to these servants there are other needy people who have always looked to me for help, and even during these difficult times they call to me in a voice that eats away my soul. This soul-demolishing voice is as painful to me as the untimely crowing of a cock.

Now that the weight of physical suffering and spiritual agony has broken both my body and my soul, I suddenly wonder how long I can continue embellishing this plaything with words. Surely the end of this struggle will be death, or beggary. In the first case there will be no alternative to the story remaining unfinished, and my readers disappointed. In the second case there will be no ending to the story except that Ghalib will be publicly turned out of a lane here and given some crumbs at a door there. How long can such things be told and how long can one be put to such shame! Even if I now receive the balance of my pension the film of sorrow caused by my debts will not be wiped from the mirror of my heart. However, if I do not receive the arrears of my pension my heart will be broken in pieces as a mirror by a stone. Ruin is certain, and moreover, since the climate of Delhi is not congenial to this suffering one, I will have to leave the city and live in some other place.

I have written herein an account of the events from May of last year to July 1858. On August first I have laid down my pen. I long for orders from the auspicious sovereign concerning the three petitions about which I have written in this book—that is, for title, for robe of honour, and for pension. My eyes and my heart look forward to this order from the Empress whose crown is the moon, whose throne is the sky; who is as renowned as Jamshid, as splendid as Faridun, as majestic as Kaus, as noble as Sanjar, as exalted as Alexander; to whom the Emperor of Rum is in debt for the preservation of his throne and the honour of his crown; the Empress for fear of whose conquering armies the heart of Russia's czar is broken. Why does the sun tremble if not in terror of the Queen's displeasure at his burning heat? Why does the moon wax and wane if not to seek forgiveness for lighting the world as if he were equal to the Queen?

She is the Commander of the Sword, of Jewels, of Banners. She is the Giver of Kingdoms and the Maker of Kings. She is wise and her face reveals fortune and her nature is gracious. She is more exalted in the realms of justice than Noshirwan; and Jamshid kept safe the marvellous bright banner that it might be passed to this great Queen. The seven treasures and the golden leaf of Khusrau have been given to her as her due, and invisible angel has brought her Solomon's throne, borne on the wind. Surely the hearts of the stones of the mountains open to reveal her diverse jewels; and the sun does not concern himself with pearls but for those in her crown. Should the Queen scatter her pearls the fingers of those who count them would be worn away with their counting. Her armies destroy mountains and rivers, strike terror among demons and dragons. So Great is her splendour and glory that mighty kings are but beggars at her door. The sun is bright because of the abundance of her light; and because of her bounty the clouds have the bounty of rain. Her generosity and munificence glorify the sages and scholars, and the people are made wise by her wisdom. Her liberality and her judgement fill us with wonder. Her name is Victoria, Queen of the World. May God Protect her and may she long remain in the assembly to the living.

If through the generosity of the Queen of the World I obtain some benefit I will not have left this life a failure.

Now that I have come to this point I shall fall silent, for I have no desire to repeat my story.

After completing this book, which is entitled *Dastanbuy,* it was sent to various people so that the souls of these persons of insight and knowledge might derive satisfaction from it and the stylists might admire its style. It is hoped that in the hands of the righteous this nosegay of wisdom will remain an everfresh bouquet but in the hands of the evil-minded it will be a hot ball. Amen.

Always my powers inspire and move me for I am the fountain of divine secrets. So is this book a part of the sacred *Dasatir*; and, in my understanding of the holy secrets, I am equal to *Sasan the Sixth.*

CHAPTER 12

Wajid Ali Shah in Matiya Burj—the Mutiny

ABDUL HALIM SHARAR

This excerpt is from *Lucknow*: *The Last Phase of an Oriental Culture*, originally written as a series of articles which appeared under the title of *Hindustan men Mashriqi Tamaddun ka Akhri Namuna*. Its author was Abdul Halim Sharar (1860-1926). Educated at the feet of Maulvi Abdul Hai, the scholar at Lucknow's famous Firangi Mahall seminary, Sharar joined the staff of *Awadh Akhbar* and made his mark as a journalist. In 1882, he launched his own magazine *Mahshar* (Day of Judgement). After a brief stay in Hyderabad, he began publishing his monthly magazine *Dil Gudaz* (Quickener of the Heart), from Lucknow. Sharar was a fine novelist as well. His novels are listed and their contents briefly analysed in *Lucknow*: *The Last Phase of an Oriental Culture*, translated and edited by E.S. Harcourt and Fakir Hussain (London, 1975), from which this excerpt is drawn. According to the translators, 'the work has long been recognized by Indo-Muslim scholars as a primary source of great value, a unique document, both alive and authentic in every detail, of an important Indian culture at its zenith. And in many a Muslim household in the Indian subcontinent today this work may be found, read and studied by the older and the younger generations, as a reminder of and an introduction to their post.'

Wajid Ali Shah was extremely fortunate in that immediately after losing his crown and throne he was able to leave Lucknow for Calcutta to put forward his case in an orthodox manner. If he failed with the council of the Governor-General of India, it was his

*Abdul Halim Sharar, *Lucknow: The Last Phase of an Oriental Culture*, translated and edited by E.S. Harcourt and Fakir Hussain (London, 1975).

intention to go to London and plead his case before Parliament and the British Queen. Accordingly, when he had no success in Calcutta he decided to go to London, but his doctors thought the sea journey would be harmful to his health and his advisers stopped him from going. The result was that he stayed in Calcutta but sent his heir, his mother and his brother to England. On this journey my grandfather, the late Munshi Qamar ud Din, was in the retinue of the ruined family. The King refused to accept the allowance allocated by the British Government and insisted on claiming his crown and throne which had been taken from him unjustly.

The King was in Calcutta, his family in London and his case under consideration when suddenly in 1857 the strife about cartridges and the Government's opposition led to the Mutiny. From Meerut to Bengal there was a general conflagration which destroyed the houses of friend and foe. So great was the trouble which arose that it appeared as if the very foundations of the British government were tottering. In the same way as the insurgents from Meerut and many other places had concentrated in Delhi and made Zafar Shah Emperor of India, so in May 1857 the mutineers from Allahabad and Faizabad went to Lucknow. As soon as the mutineers arrived many idle residents joined them. They could not find any other member of the royal family in Awadh, so they placed the ten-year-old son of Wajid Ali Shah, Mirza Birjis Qadar, on the throne, and his mother Nawab Hazrat Mahal became regent of the monarchy. The British troops quartered in Lucknow, and all the European officials of the administration who had managed to escape from the mutineers, fortified themselves in the Baillie Guard. Wajid Ali Shah had left Lucknow, otherwise he would have been proclaimed King and his lamentations would have been more bitter than those of Zafar Shah. The temporary refuge of the Matiya Burj court, which allowed him and his entourage to survive for a while, would never have been the fate of the unfortunate people of Awadh.

In addition to the mutinous soldiers of the British Indian army, most of the landowners and taluqdars of Awadh and the dismissed soldiers of imperial days had collected in Lucknow in great numbers. They had been joined by a mass of bad characters and every class of person in the town was engaged in despicable activities. It appeared as though the encircled small numbers of British had to face the attack of the whole mass of people. But in fact the besiegers consisted of the disreputable elements of the town and unprincipled and headstrong combatants. There was not a single man of valour among them who knew anything of the principles of war or who could combine the disunited forces and make them into an organized striking force. The British, on the other hand, who were fighting for their lives, stood their ground. Facing the gravest danger they repelled their assailants and proved themselves skilled in the latest arts of war.

At that time Birjis Qadar, with the royal consort, Hazrat Mahal, had become effective ruler in Lucknow. The authority of Birjis Qadar was acknowledged, coins were issued in his name, officials were appointed to the State, taxes began to be collected and the siege itself was continued only as a sort of pastime. People praised the efficiency and good intentions of the Queen, who had great regard for the soldiery and would reward them highly for their work and prowess. But to what avail? It was impossible for her to discard her purdah and become commander-in-chief of the army. Her advisers were bad and her soldiers useless. Everyone was a slave to his own desires and no one agreed with what anyone else said. The mutineers of the British Indian army were so arrogant that they thought that everything happened by their grace and considered themselves the true rulers and the only 'king-makers'.

A religious mendicant, Ahmad Ullah, popularly known as Shah Sahib, who had come from Faizabad with the insurgents and who had fought in several engagements, wished to establish his authority by force and even to establish his rule. He set up a separate court in Lucknow in opposition to that of Birjis Qadar. In addition to political differences between the two courts there arose quarrels and prejudices in connection with the Shia and Sunni sects of Islam and the rivalry between King and Shah increased. Eventually, in November of that year, when Birjis Qadar had been on the throne for six or seven months, a British army unit advanced on Lucknow. With the British army were Sikhs from the Panjab and hillmen from Bhutan who were reputed to have committed many atrocities. After two or three days' bombardment the new kingdom disintegrated like a spider's web. The royal consort and Birjis Qadar fled to Nepal with thousands of other fugitives. The Shah Sahib fought on for two or three days and, although this prepared the way for Birjis Qadar's safe escape, he was unable to save his own life. Defeated, he fled through Bari and Muhammdi, arriving at Puwain (Pilibhit District, U.P.) where he was shot dead. The Raja of Puwain cut off his head and sent it to the British, who in gratitude gave him a reward and a grant of land.

In order to clear the town of insurgents, the British put up a massive bombardment and all the inhabitants were terrified. Men and women left their houses and fled and such confusion and distress ensued that people who saw it tremble even today at its memory. Women who had lived all their lives in purdah, whose faces had never been touched by the sun, now stirred up the dust of the countryside with their bare feet and in their forlorn state clung to each other. Whoever they met proved an enemy and the hemistich of Sa'di, 'At the time of famine . . . our friends have forgotten love', was fully substantiated. Whilst these conditions prevailed, the victorious army looted the city.

After much hardship and with immense difficulty the people got permission to return to their homes and the peace that ensued after this time of panic exists to this day by the grace of the Almighty. But those connected with the old government and the royal favourites, who were unemployed after the revolution and who could not derive any benefit from the new government, were gradually effaced from the scene. That is to say that for a period great, rich and honoured families, one after another, continued to disintegrate and then were finally destroyed. One section of the town after another fell into decay, family after family disappeared and most people thought that Lucknow would remain only as a memory. But in the end the methods of the British Government, similar to those used in establishing new colonies throughout the world, prevailed and Lucknow escaped from the calamitous disaster of that era. Those who were to be ruined were ruined and those who remained became capable of taking themselves in hand. If Lucknow continues to receive the services of Governors like the present Mr. Butler I am convinced that there will be much improvement in the future.

It appears to be necessary that I give my readers an account of the remainder of Wajid Ali Shah's life and of his sojourn in Calcutta, without which this history would be incomplete. I spent my childhood in Calcutta under the King's protective shadow. I have described events until now through having heard of them from others or having read about them in the pages of history. I will from now on describe events mostly as I saw them for myself.

About three or four miles south of Calcutta on the banks of the Bhagarthi river, popularly known as Houghly, there is a quiet quarter known as Garden Beach, and because there is a raised plateau there, ordinary folk called it Matiya Burj, the Earthen Dome. There were also some very fine houses, the grounds of which stretched for two to two and a half miles along the river bank. When Wajid Ali Shah came to Calcutta the British Government of India gave him these houses; two for the King himself, one for his chief consort and one as a residence for Ali Naqi Khan. Around them a large expanse of land, stretching on one side for a mile or a mile and a half from the river bank and with a perimeter of not less than six or seven miles, was given over to the King for his personal use and that of his retinue. The municipal road traversed the area from one end to the other.

Of the two house which had been given to the King, he called one Sultan Khana, King's House, and the other Asad Manzil. When he took possession of the house of his chief consort, he called it Murassa Manzil. Ali Naqi Khan's house remained in his ownership to the last and then was passed on to his family, more particularly to Nawab Akhtar Mahal, who was Ali Naqi Khan's daughter and the King's honoured wife and mother of his second heir, Mirza Khush Bakht Bahadur.

During the Mutiny, the rebel Indian officers of the British Indian army decided that if Wajid Ali Shah would become their leader they would start a rebellion in Calcutta. But the King, on losing his crown and throne, had not adopted this course towards the British Government of India and did not wish to do so now. On the contrary, he informed the Governor-General of these people's plans and received his thanks for the information. However after a few days it was thought advisable that the King should be domiciled in Fort William so that the rebels could not contact him again. His case, which was proceeding in London, was suspended on the grounds that the country to which the claim referred was not in British hands. Further consideration would be given to it when the British Government had regained possession of the region.

The King was still in detention when the rebellion in Lucknow subsided and his plenipotentiary in London, Masih ud Din Khan, resubmitted the claim. On the face of it he had every hope that he would succeed and that the monarchy would be restored, but unfortunately the King's advisers and companions in Fort William, either because of outside interests or on their own initiative, hatched a plot. They thought that if Masih ud Din Khan won the case and thus became the honoured one, they would become of no account. Therefore they started to make suggestions to the King on the following lines:

> *Jahan Panah,* Your Majesty, has anyone ever heard of a country which has been taken over being restored? Masih ud Din Khan has misled you, obviously nothing will result and Your Majesty is merely being put to unnecessary inconvenience. No allowance has been received for nearly two years. There is scarcity of everything and we, your servants, are destitute. It would be appropriate if you agreed to the proposals of the British Government, took the allowance sanctioned by the British Government.

The King was short of money and those around him were in a much more distressed condition than he was, so when his companions continued to make these suggestions, he wrote to the Viceroy: 'I am willing to accept the monthly allowances sanctioned by the British Government. Therefore the allowances due up to date should be credited to me and the case which is proceeding in London should be annulled.' He received the reply: 'In the first place, you will not receive credit for the period which has elapsed, the monthly allowances will only start from now onwards. Secondly, only twelve lakhs a year will be paid. It is no longer considered necessary to pay the annual allowance of three lakhs which was proposed for your retinue.'

It is not difficult to imagine that the King by himself would not have agreed to this, but his companions made him accept it. The British Government of India informed England that Wajid Ali Shah had accepted their proposals and that his case therefore should be annulled. I heard of these events myself from my grandfather, Munshi Qamar ud Din, who was chief clerk in the Queen Mother's secretariat, deputy to Maulvi Masih ud Din Khan and responsible for all matters of procedure. When news that the King had accepted the monthly allowance reached London, Masih ud Din Khan nearly went off his head. The King's mother, his brother and his heir were in a state of consternation over the calamity which had overtaken them. All that had been accomplished so far was ruined. At last Masih ud Din Khan, after much thought, devised a plan and put the following legal point before Parliament: 'The King is now under the close supervision of the British Government of India and under these circumstances nothing which he puts on paper can be trusted.'

The point was reasonable and it was accepted. The British Government of India was then informed of the plea put forward by the King's plenipotentiary and at the same time Masih ud Din Khan and all the important people connected with the royal family wrote to the King, 'what are you starting? We fully expect to have the country of Awadh restored to us.'

The Mutiny was at an end. The Government released the King who was very pleased to leave Fort William and return to Matiya Burj. No sooner had he gained his freedom than his companions said, 'Huzur [Sir], Masih ud Din Khan is saying in London that Your Majesty only accepts the allowance because you are a prisoner.' On hearing this the King flared up and wrote, 'I was free and from my own desire and volition I accepted the Government's proposals. It is quite wrong for Masih ud Din to say that I accepted them owing to force or coercion. Therefore from now on I revoke his power of attorney.'

What was to happen now? All transactions had come to an end, the King had started on a life of revelry and orgies, money was flowing like water in the houses of his companions and the unfortunate members of the royal family in England were practically ruined and were deserted by most of those who had been with them. Janab-e-Alia, Her Highness the King's mother, became ill from the shock and whilst still unwell she left England intending to pass through France, make a pilgrimage to the holy places of Mecca and Kerbala and then return to Calcutta. But death did not permit her to do this and she died in France. She was buried in the Muslim cemetery adjacent to the mosque of the Osmani Legation in Paris. The death of his mother was such a blow to Mirza Sikander Hashmat that he fell ill and two weeks later he too died, and was placed near his mother to await the Day of Judgement. The only one to return to calcutta and rejoin his parents was the heir apparent.

They say that when the King first came to live in Matiya Burj he displayed much sagacity and his outlook on life became serious. On seeing this, his entourage collected various musical instruments. Immediately the king was reminded of his old fancies and love for song and dance and as a result troupes of artists started to congregate at his court. The best singers in India were enlisted into the King's service and there was a larger concourse of musicians in Matiya Burj than could be found anywhere else in India.

There was the same desire for collecting together good-looking women and concentrating on beauty and love in Matiya Burj as one hears there had been in Lucknow. In Matiya Burj, however, when embarking on these desires, due regard was given to religious considerations. The King belonged to the Shia sect of Islam, and according to Shia law, *muta,* temporary marriage, is legal. Taking advantage of this religious freedom the King pursued his inclinations to his heart's content. He made it his rule not to look at a woman who was not temporarily married to him, and carried his religious caution to such lengths that he even entered into a temporary marriage with a young female water-carrier who would pass him when she was taking water to the women's quarters; he gave her the title of Nawab ab Rasan Begam, Her Highness the Lady Water-Provider. There was also a young sweeping-woman who used to come into his presence. She too joined the ranks of the temporarily married and was honoured with the title of Nawab Musafa Begam, the Lady Purifier. In the same way, the enjoyment of music was also confined to those women who belonged to him. It was very seldom that a courtesan danced before the King. These temporarily married women were formed into various groups and taught diverse forms of dancing and singing. The following are the names of some of these groups: Radha Manzil, Sardha Manzil, Jhumar (Earring), Latkan (Dwindling), Nath (Nose-ring), Ghunghat (Veil), Rahas (Dance), and Naqal (Mimic). There were scores of similar groups who had been given the best instruction in the dancing and singing in which the King delighted. He had entered into temporary wedlock with all of them and they were called Begams. In some of the groups, there were a few young girls who had not reached the age of puberty. They were not in a state of temporary wedlock and they would be admited to that state immediately on reaching puberty. Most lived near the King in Sultan Khana but some of them lived in separate women's apartments in other houses. Those temporarily married women who bore children were given the title of Mahal. They were given separate women's apartments as their residence, received enhanced allowances and were greatly honoured.

From what has been written above it is clearly evident that, except for music, the King was in every way extremely devout, abstinent and a strick observer of Muslim religious law. He never missed offering up his prayers. He observed the fast for the whole of the thirty days in the month of Ramadan. He was a life-long abstainer from opium, wine and other intoxicants and he performed the mourning ceremonies at the time of Muharram with sincere devotion.

His other interest was building. Scores of women's apartments were constructed on all four sides of Sultan Khana and many new houses with their own female quarters were built. The King had received only Sultan Khana, Asad Manzil and Murassa Manzil from the British Government of India, but in a very short time he built several more houses which were surrounded by beautiful gardens and pleasing lawns. When I saw them, the King possessed the following fine houses which, taken from south to north were: Sultan Khana, Qasr ul Baiza, Gosha-e-Sultani, Shahinshah Manzil, Murassa Manzil, Asad Manzil, Shah Manzil, Nur Manzil, Tafrih Baksh, Badami, Asmani, Tahaniyat Manzil, Had-e-Sultani, Sad-e-Sultani, Adalat Manzil. In addition to these, there were several other houses, the names of which I have forgotten.

There were also many single rooms, bungalows and small kiosks on the banks of the pools inside the parks. In all of these were spotless, ornate carpets covering the floors and silver bedsteads with bedding and pillows. They were further decorated with pictures and a variety of fine furniture. In order to help support the people, more housekeepers than were in fact necessary had been appointed to look after the house. These people used to sweep them every day and ensure that they were kept clean and in good order. In short, all these houses, in their separate settings, were so decorative and trim that no one could help admiring them. Surrounding them were gardens and lawns set out in geometrical designs with such engineering skill that those who beheld them marvelled at the King's talent and sense of proportion.

In Lucknow the King had constructed only the Qaisar Bagh, a few houses in the neighbourhood, an Imam Bara and a tomb for his deceased father, but in Matiya Burj he had established a beautiful town of fine houses. On the other side of the river, exactly opposite Matiya Burj, are Calcutta's famed Botanical Gardens. But they were as nothing compared to the earthly paradise of Matiya Burj and the entrancing wonders it contained. There was a high-walled enclosure surrounding all these houses, lawns and markets.

For about a mile along the municipal high road there were some fine shops. Lower-class employees, whose duties necessitated them being there, were allowed to live in them. One could enter the enclosure only through the main gates on which guards were mounted; there was no means of entry through any of the shops. Near the gate to Sultan Khana there was a very imposing guard-house in which *naubat* [drums] were beaten and the hours of the day and night were announced by gongs according to the old fashion.

Many kings have been interested in architecture but scarcely any other monarch can have built so many houses or established so many parks as did Wajid Ali Shah during his unfortunate life and the short period of his so called reign. Second to Shahjahan in this respect, if one can mention anybody's name then it must be the name of this afflicted king of Awadh. Some of Shahjahan's buildings have remained standing for hundreds of years while hundreds of buildings constructed by others have soon been demolished by fate.

Apart from architecture, the King took an interest in animals and he developed this interest to an extraordinary and unsurpassed extent. I do not suppose that any other individual has ever made half the efforts in this direction that he did.

In front of Nur Mahal there was a large open space, enclosed by a neat iron fence, into which hundreds of spotted deer, buck and other wild quadrupeds had been turned loose. In its centre was a well-built marble pool which was always filled to the brim with water. This was the habitat of partridges, ostriches, turkeys, sarus cranes, geese, herons, demoiselle cranes, ducks, peacocks, flamingoes and hundreds of other birds, and tortoises. Such care was given to cleanliness that droppings or shed feathers of a bird were never to be seen. On one side of the pool there was a cage containing tigers and near the meadow there was a row of large wooden cages into which scores of different species of monkey had been collected from far-flung places. These monkeys performed comic antics which people could not help lingering to watch.

In various places there were pools filled with fish which would gather at a signal and if anyone threw in some food it was wonderful to see them leaping from the water.

The most amazing thing of all was a large, long and deep tank in front of Shahinshah Manzil. All four sides of the tank had been made very slippery and in the middle was an artificial hill, sloping downwards at the front and into which hundreds of pipes had been run, some of which were open at the top to act as fountains. Thousands of large snakes, six to nine feet long, had been released on this hill and would crawl about it. They would go to the top and then come down to the bottom and catch the frogs which had been put there. Round the hill there was a sort of moat where the snakes would swim and chase the frogs. It was quite safe for people to stand by the tank and watch what was happening.

Below this hill were two cages in which there were two large leopards. Normally they lay quiet but if a fowl was given to them they would spring on it and gobble it up whole.

It is unlikely that arrangements for keeping snakes in captivity had ever been made anywhere before and Wajid Ali Shah was the first person to think of it. European travellers were amazed at the sight and would take pictures and write down details.

Apart from these animals, there were thousands of shining brass bird-cages in Sultan Khana itself. There were also scores of large aviaries enclosed by wire netting, which were called *kunj*. A large number of birds of various kinds were let loose in these and all possible arrangements were made for their upkeep and breeding

The King's desire was to collect as many kinds of animals as possible. It is unlikely that there has ever been such a perfect example of a living museum in all the world as the one he possessed. Money was spent without restraint in acquiring these animals and if anyone brought in a new species he was given exactly what he asked for it. It is said that the King paid twenty-four thousand rupees for a pair of silk-winged pigeons and eleven thousand rupees for a pair of white peacocks. There was also a pair of giraffes, very large and strange animals from Africa. The two-humped camel of Baghdad is never seen in India, but the King possessed one in his zoo. There were even a couple of donkeys let loose in a meadow, so intent was the King that all sorts of animals should be included. Beasts of prey such as lions, Indian tigers, cheetahs, leopards, bears, lynxes, and wolves were all kept in cages and carefully tended.

Arrangements for the pigeons were different from those for the other birds. In his various pigeonries, the King had, in all, twenty-four or twenty-five thousand birds which the pigeon fanciers showed great skill in flying.

It is possible to form an idea of the amount spent on the animals from the fact that there were over eight hundred attendants and about three hundred pigeon fanciers; about the same number looked after the fish and there were thirty or forty employed for the snakes. These attendants received from six to ten rupees a month as pay. Officers received a monthly salary of twenty to thirty rupees. Apart from the pigeons, snakes and fish, a little less than nine thousand rupees a month was spent on food for the other animals. The building arrangements for the zoo had mostly been entrusted to Munis ud Daula and Raihan ud Daula who received twenty-five thousand rupees a month for this purpose.

Besides the staff at the zoo there were about one thousand watchmen whose pay was normally six rupees a month although some received up to eight or ten rupees. The same pay was received by the housekeepers who numbered over five hundred. There were some eighty clerks who received monthly salary of ten to thirty rupees. The number of favoured companions and high officials was probably not less than forty or fifty and each received eighty-eight rupees a month. There were also more than one hundred palanquin-bearers.

In addition there were scores of minor departments dealing with the kitchens, vegetables, *abdar khana* [water-cooling], *khas khana* [house cooling] and so on. Then again there were the relations and male members of the family of the temporary wives, all of whom received salaries in proportion to their standing.

All these people had built houses for themselves outside the area of the original houses. These new houses were for the most part on the land which had been given to the King but many were on other land near by. So a town had grown up with a population of more than forty thousand souls, all of whose livelihood derived from the King's monthly allowance of one lakh of rupees. No one could understand how such a large population could live on such a small sum and it was commonly thought in Bengal that the King possessed the philosopher's stone, and that whenever necessary he rubbed iron or brass and turned it into gold.

From the time of the King's arrival in Calcutta, a second Lucknow had arisen in its neighbourhood. The real Lucknow had ended and was replaced by Matiya Burj. There was the same bustle and activity, the same language, the same style of poetry, conversation and wit, the same learned and pious men, the same aristocrats, nobles and common people. No one thought he was in Bengal: there was the same kite-flying, cock-fighting, quail-fighting, the same opium addicts reciting the same tales, the same observance of Muharram, the same lamentations at the recital of *marsiya* and *nauha* the same Imam Baras and the same Kerbala as in former Lucknow. But the ceremony, pomp and circumstance with which the King's Muharram procession was invested probably could never have been equalled in Lucknow even in the days of his rule. After the Mutiny, a Muharram procession of *tazias* could never have been carried out in Lucknow with the former glory, but in Calcutta thousands of people, even the British, came to Matiya Burj as pilgrims.

Although the King was a Shia he was without religious prejudice of any sort. He could say: 'Of my two eyes, one is Shia and the other is Sunni.' On one occasion two people came to blows over some religious difference. The King gave orders that both be dismissed and refused to have them readmitted to his service, saying, 'I cannot have such people near me.' Later on, some unpalatable words had been printed in one of the King's books which caused an uproar among the Sunnis of Calcutta, but no one knew that these words were not actually of the King's authorship but that they had been taken by him from another source. When the King heard about the matter he was ready to apologize without any prompting from others.

What greater proof of this lack of prejudice could there be than the fact that the whole administration was in the hands of Sunnis? The Vazir, Munsarim ud Daula Bahadur, was a Sunni. The Chief Secretary, Munshi ul Sultan, who at one time had been the person nearest to the King and was the senior officer in-charge of the zoological gardens, the secretariat and various other departments, was a Sunni. The Paymaster, Bakhshi Amanat ud Daula, at whose hands all the retainers and even the royal ladies and princes received their salaries and allowances, was a Sunni. Attar ud Daula and the Superintendent, Motabar Ali Khan, who were in fact the highest of officials and in-charge of all organization, were both Sunnis. How could one imagine any greater proof of impartiality than that the management of the Sibtainabad Imam Bara and the royal Imam Bara, called the Baitul Buka, the House of Lamentation, as well as the arrangements for *majlis* and other religious ceremonies were all in the hands of Sunnis? No one even noticed who was a Sunni and who a Shia.

Even the shopkeepers and moneylenders in Matiya Burj were from Lucknow and there was not a single product of Lucknow which was not there in its very best form. Wherever one went one saw great magnificence and activity. All were so charmed and fascinated by their pleasurable existence that they gave no thought to the future. The people of Lucknow, all the royal servants and even other residents of Matiya Burj, had free access to the palaces and meadows. You could not find a more pleasant place to walk in than the parks. If you stood on the bank of the river you obtained a most wonderful view. Ships going to and from Calcutta passed in front of you and as they did, dipped their standards in salute to Fort William; people, however, thought they were being dipped in salutation to the King. If you stood at the threshold of the palaces or at the doors of the female apartments you were filled with a pleasurable emotion. Sometimes you might catch a glimpse of a lovely face and sometimes you heard eloquent, attractive speech and sometimes such delectable talk that it remained in the memory for a very long time afterwards, if not for ever.

How could this beautiful and entrancing scene ever be destroyed! But alas, fate destroyed it and destroyed it so completely that it might never have existed. In 1887 the King suddenly closed his eyes for ever and it seemed as though 'all one had seen was a dream and all one had heard was a story'. Everything was fantasy and illusion, a myth, the origin of which had all at once become effaced. That beautiful spot which European kings and Indian rulers had longed to visit was now reduced to an uncouth void and a place of ill-omen. Whoever had seen its previous state and now witnessed the wilderness it had become, could only heave a deep sigh of grief and sorrow and exclaim, 'Only God is eternal!'

Index